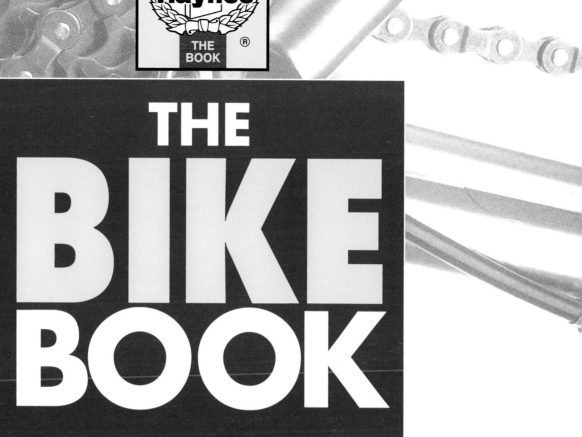

Haynes

THE
BOOK ®

THE BIKE BOOK

The book that brings your bike to life

A Haynes Practical Book

Written by	John Stevenson
Photography	Steve Behr
Project manager	Kevin Hudson
Editor	Matthew Minter
Technical consultant	David Notley
Design	Dave Hermelin
	Rhian Walters
	David Notley
	Sharon Cooper
Production manager	Kevin Perrett
Marketing	David Keel
Sales and enthusiasm	Paul Wells

First published in Great Britain in 1994
A Haynes publication

© John Stevenson 1994

British Library Cataloguing in Publication Data:
A catalogue record of this book is available from the British Library.
ISBN 1 85010 977 X

Printed in France by imprimerie pollina s.a., Luçon
While every effort is taken to ensure the accuracy of the information given in this book, no liability can be accepted by the author or publisher for any loss, damage or injury caused by errors in, or omissions from, the information given.

Haynes Publishing
Sparkford, Nr Yeovil, Somerset BA22 7JJ

Contents

Bicycles and

cycling

Cycling?

*Er...what's that then?
Well, it's a heap of things...*

- It's quiet English country lanes on a June Sunday.
- It's arriving mud-spattered and breathless at an 18th century coaching inn after a morning on dirt roads and trails.
- It's Miguel Indurain being relentlessly pursued by his rivals in the Tour de France.
- It's mum, dad and the kids pootling along the canal towpath.
- It's exploring the Alps with all your needs in four pannier bags.
- It's a toddler racing her trike to the garden gate.
- It's a lycra-and-grime-clad messenger carving through grid-locked city traffic to deliver a package.
- It's a city gent in a suit commuting to the office.
- It's 27,000 people (and a gorilla) on a fun ride.
- It's Chris Boardman pumping round a track on thousands of pounds worth of wind-tunnel developed technology.
- It's grandma riding to the shops on her trusty three-speed.

In fact, there isn't another single word that wraps up as many different ideas and activities the way 'cycling' does.

5

But through all of this, one thing remains more or less the same...

...the bicycle.

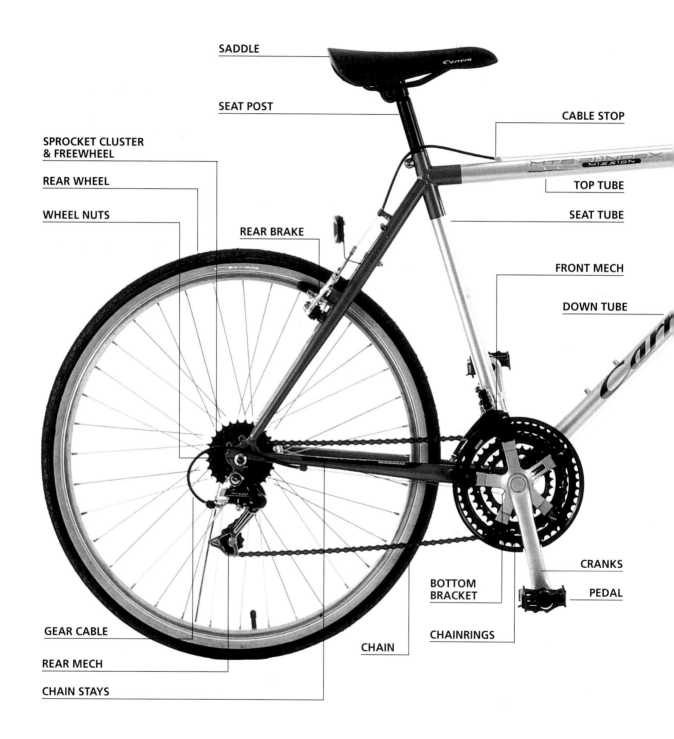

SADDLE

SEAT POST

CABLE STOP

SPROCKET CLUSTER
& FREEWHEEL

REAR WHEEL

WHEEL NUTS

REAR BRAKE

TOP TUBE

SEAT TUBE

FRONT MECH

DOWN TUBE

CRANKS

PEDAL

BOTTOM
BRACKET

GEAR CABLE

CHAINRINGS

REAR MECH

CHAIN

CHAIN STAYS

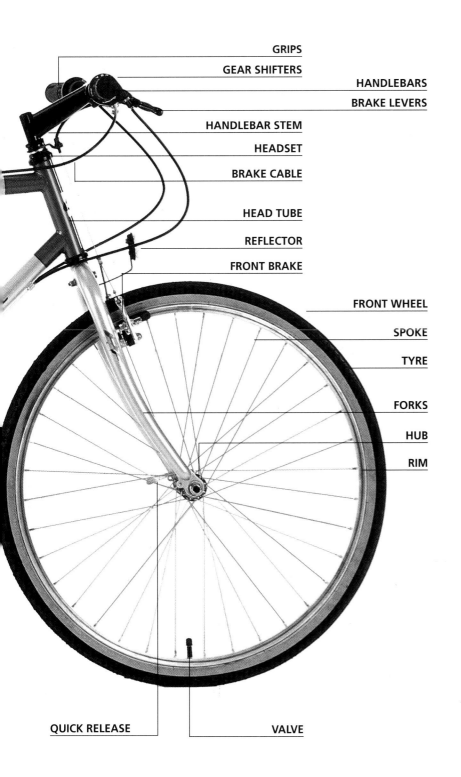

GRIPS

GEAR SHIFTERS

HANDLEBARS

BRAKE LEVERS

HANDLEBAR STEM

HEADSET

BRAKE CABLE

HEAD TUBE

REFLECTOR

FRONT BRAKE

FRONT WHEEL

SPOKE

TYRE

FORKS

HUB

RIM

QUICK RELEASE

VALVE

Contents

Cycling today

Cycling is at once a sport, a pastime, a recreation, a means of transport and a lifestyle. Fundamentally unchanged since its invention and refinement at the end of the last century, the bike is one of the great inventions of the modern era. It is a form of transport so efficient that it can go 1600 miles on the energy equivalent of a gallon of petrol, and a reasonably healthy person can ride over 50 miles in a day, as thousands of participants in annual mass-rides like the 56 miles of London to Brighton prove.

In the last few years bikes seem to have undergone a great revolution in technology. Glossy magazines, both the specialist monthlies and the Sunday supplements, fashion and style mags, are full of lightweight, exotic machines costing many thousands of pounds: mountain bikes that look like motorbikes that have had an enginectomy, and high-zoot road racing bikes. When the finest racing cyclist Britain has produced in two decades won an Olympic gold, media attention focused on the sleek, black, carbon-fibre and titanium machine that Chris Boardman rode, not on the fact that he was an athlete at the top of his form producing the performance of his life. You'd be forgiven for thinking that today's bikes did the riding for you, but were way beyond the wallet of most people

Not so. The technical revolution in bike equipment has changed everything, but, somehow, everything is the same. Modern bikes have gear systems that work better than ever before, brakes that stop you quicker and with less effort, tyres that grip deep mud, or hum smoothly along urban asphalt, bearings that are sealed against muck and water and even electronics that tell you your speed, how far you've gone and how long until you should next chomp a Mars bar. But you are still the engine and the control centre. The bike is still an extension of your body that turns your effort into motion; it still has

wheels, handlebars, a saddle. Even if the details have changed, it's still one of the most familiar machines there is.

Cycling activities

I don't know anyone who just goes in for one type of cycling. I commute to work by bike, spend weekends riding bridleways and byways on my mountain bike or exploring back lanes by tandem, dabble in racing mountain bikes and have raced bikes on the road in the little-publicised but friendly sport of time trialling. My cycling friends and colleagues cover the spread from casual commuters to hard-core road and mountain bike racers and expeditionists who think nothing of a six-month trek across Africa by bike. Nevertheless, the cycling cake is cut into a variety of slices.

Commuting

As the roads of our major cities become increasingly clogged with traffic, so more and more people are realising that it is as quick, if not quicker, to get from A to B by bike. On a bike you are not constrained by the slow-starting bulk of a car and can nip through gaps that even motorbikes can't use. In London especially the time and expense involved in travelling by car or public transport has produced a huge increase in bike commuting and enlightened employers are providing safe bike parking and showers for two-wheeled employees. Some companies even have staff bike schemes.

Commuting has obvious fitness and health benefits; for many of us it's the

easiest way to add some exercise to a busy day, and my own 7 mile ride to the office is often the only exercise I have time for during the week. I arrive at work fresher and more awake than if I have been sitting in a car or bus and the evening ride home is a great stress-reliever.

Leisure cycling

The cycling that most people do falls into this class: A few miles in the country lanes on a Sunday, or a gentle ride with the kids along the towpath or cycle track. Leisure cycling is one of the few forms of exercise that the whole family can do together. Children who quickly get hot and tired on foot can happily ride at a moderate pace with adults. I know one ten year old who has been doing afternoon-long rides with his dad since he was six!

Although traffic levels have made riding on the road less pleasant than it used to be, there are increasing amounts of off-highway places where families can ride: cyclepaths, towpaths and forest roads are all there to be ridden, and the network of country lanes that covers most of the country is still very quiet.

Racing

There are lots of types of bike racing, but the best-known is long-distance stage racing, epitomised by the Tour de France, the world's biggest annual sporting event. Two hundred riders set out to ride a more-or-less circular route round France each summer. The race is split into daily stages and the winner is the rider who has the lowest cumulative time at the end of three weeks of racing. This is undeniably the hardest branch of cycling and the Tour is probably the hardest sporting event in the world. Even run-of-the mill bike racers are supremely fit by normal standards – an average time trialler, who specialises in riding fixed distances against the clock, can cover 25 miles in just less than an hour. The top riders can do the same in less than 45 minutes.

To race you simply need guts, determination and lots of spare time to put in the training needed to get and stay that fit.

Mountain biking

In the late seventies a group of Californian bike junkies began playing with a new form of cycling. Riding modified American beach cruiser bikes with fat tyres they raced down the dirt roads in Marin County, just outside San Francisco. To get back up, they loaded the bikes in a truck and drove, until someone had the inspired idea of adding gears to these 50lb behemoths and riding back up. Soon, custom-built 'clunker' bikes followed and this fledgling branch of cycling was dubbed 'mountain biking'.

What none of those pioneers realised was that the bikes they were developing were uniquely user-friendly. The wide bars needed for control on rough tracks, the powerful brakes and easy-to-hand gear levers on the bars, along with fat tyres and tough frames and wheels, made for a bike that was simple and fun to ride and made getting off the roads into the hills easy and accessible. Almost twenty years later mountain biking is the biggest branch of cycling and mountain bikes account for the majority of bikes sold. Their appeal is simple: Here is a bike you can ride on the road, where its tough wheels and fat tyres are protection against potholed city streets, but which lets you get back to being a kid at weekends, playing in the mud.

Touring

Traditional bike touring is kinda spartan. You carry everything you need with you: tent, cooking gear, tools, clothes, all stripped to essentials and crammed in panniers. You are completely self-contained and free, but crawling up an Alpine pass with 50lb of gear is not everyone's idea of fun. Modern bike tours will let you take it a bit easier. There are lots of companies that will transport your luggage from point to point, allowing you to get on with enjoying the riding and the scenery, knowing that a warm hotel bed and good food are waiting for you at the end of the day. In between these two extremes are camping-based supported tours, or going it alone with plastic and a change of clothing.

Expeditions

Expedition cyclists are a breed apart. Resourceful, brave and intrepid they are a group of riders who have ridden across deserts, up high mountains and to some of the Earth's most remote places. In 1986 Richard and Nick Crane rode specially built bikes to a point deep in Asia that was, they reckoned, the furthest point from the sea anywhere on the planet. They travelled superlight and superfast, relying on the generosity of strangers for food and safe places to sleep. Miraculously, they made it. Less insane, but equally hardy long-distance cyclists have made it across the Sahara, to Everest base camp and across the almost impenetrable jungles of South America's Darien Gap.

Bikes Today

The most common bikes around today are mountain bikes, hybrids, road racing bikes and 3-speeds. Mountain bikes actually split into two categories: the cheaper bikes that are generally used as tough, bashing round town, everyday bikes and the more expensive 'real' mountain bikes which can be and are used off road. Obviously there is some overlap; people pose round town on expensive MTBs and ride off-road on inexpensive bikes because that's what they can afford, but there are significant differences between a £250 mountain bike and a 'real' MTB that costs more like £500.

As it happens hybrids have exactly the same components as mountain bikes, with the exception of larger wheels and narrower tyres; mechanically they are identical, and so their requirements are covered in this book by reference to mountain bikes. Let's take a look at the four main types of bike.

An 'everyday' bike

The inexpensive £180-£300 mountain bike has become the two wheeled equivalent of the Model T Ford. Inexpensive, easily available and easy to use, it is the most common bike on Britain's streets. These bikes have tough frames made from high-tensile steel tubing, which while a bit heavy is plenty strong enough; wide rims with fat tyres, usually designed for mixed on and off road use; flat handlebars which give an upright riding position; gear controls on the handlebars and cantilever brakes which give good stopping power. These bikes usually have 15 or 18 speed gear systems. Most of these bikes will not have toe clips and straps on the pedals.

An everyday bike: This particular bike costs about £250 new, has 18 speeds, steel tubing, and cantilever brakes. It is suitable for general use and modest off road riding. We have also added lights, a lock and semi-slick tyres to make it more suitable for riding around town.

A quality mountain bike: This particular bike costs £500 new, has 21 gears, chromoloy steel tubing, alloy wheels, rapid-fire shifters, a micro adjusting seat post, bar ends, pedal clips, and generally better components all over. It can be taken anywhere.

'Real' mountain bike

High-quality mountain bikes differ from basic mountain bikes in a range of important details. The wheels always have alloy rims, which give better braking and are much lighter and therefore easier to get moving; the reach from saddle to handlebar is longer so that the rider is in a more efficient, forward-leaning position that gives better control off-road; the tyres are 'knobblies' designed to grip in dirt and the gear system has 21 gears to provide a very wide range for climbing and descending step hills. Because the rider has to move around on the bike a lot, the saddle is narrower and less padded. All the components are designed to be both strong and light and at the higher end of the price range exotic aerospace materials like titanium and carbon fibre are used for some parts. Clips and straps on the pedals are a must, and some of these bikes have click-in pedal systems which require special shoes.

Road bike

The narrow tyres, drop handlebars and narrow-range gear systems of road racing bikes make them the best bike for riding on tarmac and country lanes. These bikes typically have 12 or 14 speed gear systems; gear levers on the down tube; compact side pull brakes that provide excellent braking when set up correctly; drop handlebars that give several hand positions and allow a deep aerodynamic tuck and narrow tyres that run at high pressures for low rolling resistance.

3-speeds

The classic English 3-speed is so well-ingrained in our national consciousness that it will probably never completely disappear, and for good reason. In flat town and villages 3-speeds are uniquely practical. These bikes have simple internal 3-speed hub gears which require little or no maintenance; flat handlebar with a comfortable, upright riding position, rubber pedals and, usually, 26in wheels.

A road racing bike: This particular bike costs £300 new, has 12 gears in a narrow range, a thin frame and very thin tyres, drop-handlebars and side-pull brakes. Very skinny, very suitable for heavy road use.

A 3-speed: This particular bike costs £170 new, has a Sturmey Archer 3-speed gear, side-pull brakes, mudguards and a cover for the chain. Very stable and very practical, excellent with a basket on the front or child seat mounted on the rear. Unlikely to be stolen, but a bit tricky with hills.

11

About this book

This book is intended to inspire and inform those millions of people who have come to cycling in the last few years, as the cycling boom of the late eighties has continued into the nineties.

We have assumed little or no prior knowledge of cycling in any of its forms; the aim is to provide the basic information about cycling and looking after bikes which everyone needs to help them get the most out of this excellent way of getting around and having fun, and provide the confidence to allow you to grow and develop as informed bike riders.

What's in the book?

In the Bike Book there are three main parts:

You and your bike

This part deals with the essential information you need to know about cycling; the types of bikes, buying and setting one up, how and where to ride it, what additional equipment there is, how to stop it getting nicked and so on.

Caring for your bike

The second part covers everything you can do to keep your bike in a proper working condition; from the safety checks you should do before going out riding, to the cleaning, oiling and general inspection you should do when you come back. If you follow the advice in this section, then with luck you can reduce the amount of times that you have to refer to the next part of the book.

Working on your bike

In the third and final part we deal with all the maintenance tasks you might want to do on your bike; from repairing a puncture to truing wheels and stripping down your bearings. We start with general maintenance advice and tips and also talk about the tools you might need. We then devote the next nine chapters to each of the major components on a bike: Tyres and tubes, brakes, gears, chainset, saddle, handlebars, headset, wheels and frame.

Lastly in this section, we show how you can maintain your accessories and keep them too in good working order.

Appendices

At the very end of the book are some appendices. Here we have included **roadside repairs** (bodges you can do to get you home), a **fault finding guide** for general 'non-component specific' problems (there are also specific fault finding guides in each repair chapter), and a comprehensive **jargon glossary**.

The Haynes approach

Just as when Haynes make a car manual, they take a car, strip it apart, put it back together, take photographs and write a book about it, so too have we done for bikes. We have adjusted, repaired and dismantled all the appropriate parts of our four main types of bikes in clear, step-by-step sequences. Even very simple tasks are explained in enough detail that a complete novice can perform them, and we have structured the repair chapters so that they lead from diagnosing the problem with fault-finding charts, to identifying the cause to fixing the fault and making the necessary adjustments. Before everything though, each repair chapter deals with routine care you can do to prevent problems happening in the first place.

Tools, time, spares and difficulty

Each repair procedure is graded for difficulty, and has a guide to how long it should take and what tools and spares are needed for it. Where special tools are required we have explained their use and the need for them, and offered alternatives where possible.

Tips!

To round off our explanations we have offered tips and ideas which make working on your bike easier.

Variants

Since bikes are not all exactly the same, we have also indicated the variants in componentry that you are likely to come across, such as all the different gear shifters found on mountain bikes.

Jargon

We have tried to keep everything as clear and as simple as possible, but cycling, like any activity, has its own jargon, so we have explained it all in a full jargon-glossary at the end of this book. Also check the labelled pictures throughout this book if reference to a particular part seems unclear.

However, if jargon is your thing and you want to dine out on some very heavy stuff, then turn to Chapter 8 on Bike-speak, where we have quarantined off an awful lot of the stuff.

Parts of the Bike

Let's face it, there is enough jargon just relating to the basic parts of the bike, even before we delve any deeper. If you (like us at Haynes and the majority of normal bike riding people) ever get confused about the names of parts of the bike – gears and brakes, they are OK, but what is the bottom bracket and the stem – then go back and look again at the big labelled picture we had at the beginning.

Part One

You and your bike

Buying a bike

Contents

Deciding on your bike

Whatever type of riding you're going to do, you need a bike. Because there are literally dozens of different types of cycling, so there are lots of different types of bike. A good bike shop will contain everything from kids' BMX bikes to ultra-light Tour de France racers, alongside the ubiquitous mountain bikes and hybrids that are what everyone who wants to get from A to B round town seems to ride. What sort of bike you need is mainly determined by what you're going to use it for.

Bike types
Mountain bikes

Mountain bikes have fat tyres, wide handlebars, lots of gears (with the controls on the handlebars), cantilever brakes and an upright or semi-upright riding position. The basic design was developed for haring down Californian mountain dirt roads, but has turned out to be dead useful for bashing round pot-holed city streets. Although purists will tell you, rightly, that their road bikes are faster and more efficient, they are missing the point that mountain bikes are uniquely user-friendly. Their control set-up lets you brake, steer and change gear all at the same time and the riding position and powerful brakes make coping with city traffic and road conditions a doddle.

But it's out in the country where mountain bikes really come into their own. Run the fat, knobbly tyres at low pressure (around 40psi) and they will grip almost any surface. The dirt roads and bridleways of the Dales, Lake District, the Welsh mountains, the Scottish Highlands, the New Forest and the North and South Downs have all become the regular haunts of mountain bikers enjoying the combination of being able to get deep into the wilderness, away from roads, towns and people, with the unique sporting challenge of riding a bike up and down the steepest hills.

Fat tyre bikes start from around £120, but these are machines that are really look-alikes and are usually of very poor quality. Spend another fifty quid or so and you start to get machines that are fine for bashing round town, and light use on the canal towpath. Look for 18 speeds and indexed gears, preferably by Shimano. Proper mountain bikes (machines that are rugged and reliable enough to cope with being used out in the back-country) really start at £300-£350, and go up to – well, how deep is your wallet? I recently spoke to a Bristol millionaire who was in the process of spending five grand on the latest super-light titanium-framed suspension bike. He reckoned his friends thought nothing of spending that on a set of golf clubs and green fees for a year, but they thought he was odd spending it on a bike!

Good all-round mountain bikes, suitable for recreational riding, touring and even off road racing, start at around £500.

Road racing bikes

Serious road racing bikes were never very common in the displays of general bike shops, but the mountain bike boom has marginalised them even more. Some shops dropped road bikes completely in the late eighties, while others just carry one or two models, and the once ubiquitous cheap ten speed 'racer' has now almost disappeared.

Real road racing bikes are characterised by very lightweight frames and components, high, narrow-range gears, very skinny tyres and drop

handlebars. A bike that is good enough to line up at the start of a road race will set you back at least £600, while reasonably good, budget road bikes start at around £300.

These are bikes built primarily for speed, not for comfort, and their element is the open road. Unencumbered by excess fat they are the right vehicle for fast, athletic sport riding. If you want to add cycling to a fitness programme alongside, say, running, you are already fairly fit and you know you only want to ride on the road, choose a road bike.

Touring bikes

The touring bike is the road racing bike's practical older brother. Equipped with a wider, lower gear range, racks for carrying panniers, and mudguards to stop you getting quite so soggy when it

rains, a touring bike is designed for all-day comfort. The few manufacturers

who still specialise in touring bikes (companies like Orbit and Dawes) say that sales are steady, but many bike manufacturers have stopped making tourers because the kind of rider who used to use a mid-price tourer to bash round town now uses a mid-price mountain bike.

Hybrids

At first glance a hybrid looks a little like a mountain bike: flat bars, cantilever brakes, lots of gears, gear shifters on the handlebar. However, where a mountain

bike has fat 26in tyres the hybrid usually has narrower, 700c tyres, road bike size. This makes for a combination of mountain bike convenience and road bike nippiness, and the treaded 35mm tyres used on hybrids can be used on good dirt roads and canal towpaths

giving limited but useful off-road capability. A mountain bike with a spare set of slick or semi-slick tyres is more versatile, but if you don't want to do any serious off road work, a hybrid is perfect for commuting or just pootling round the country lanes at the weekend.

Roadsters (3-Speeds)

The traditional 3 speed sit-up-and-beg bike, favoured by vicars, postmen and district nurses since time immemorial, roadsters seem to belong to a lost England of long hot summers, cricket on the village green and fresh-faced young people riding to the town dance on Friday nights. Actually, for inexpensive, basic road transport in flat areas there's still not much to beat a roadster bike, which is why Oxford, Cambridge and York are completely infested with them. If all you need is a bike to ride half a mile to the shops, a sub-£150 roadster is a better bet than a similarly priced 'mountain bike'.

BMX

Fuelled by skateboards and street culture, there is a BMX revival happening out there, and it might just be that BMX bikes supplant electric plumbers and hedgehogs on kids' Christmas lists this year. BMX bikes are perfect for kids who are more interested in a tough bike that they can do tricks on, than in travelling long distances or sport. They

Shimano

Not a type of bike, but a component manufacturer, Shimano is a name you will come across again and again when looking at modern bikes. A technologically innovative Japanese company, Shimano now makes the components for around 85 per cent of the bikes sold in Europe and North America. Quite simply, Shimano's gear systems are the best there is, at almost every level, and their brakes and other components are generally extremely good. Trying to navigate the complexities of their component range will quickly give you a headache (it does me and keeping up with this stuff is my job!) so don't worry about it, just look for the name on, at

have strong 20in wheels, wide handle-bars, a single gear and very strong, compact steel frames. Brands to look out for include GT, Haro and Mongoose.

the very least, the gears of any bike you're considering buying.

Value for money

To many people bikes today seem expensive. They're not. If you last bought a bike ten or fifteen years ago, then, yes, a bike today will cost more money. But so does a car, or anything else. In terms of their cost as a proportion of the average salary, or compared to the cost of a medium-sized family car, bikes are cheaper now than they have ever been.

£100 (or less)

At the very bottom of the price range are very basic, sub-£100 bikes. These are invariably billed as mountain bikes, though they are not suitable for off-road use as they are very heavy and have utterly inadequate brakes and gears for any sort of serious use. For this much money you would be better off looking second hand or going for a basic roadster. It simply isn't possible to build a multi-geared bike, except for a 3-speed, to sell for this little and have it work reliably.

£150–£200

Bikes rapidly get better as we approach £150. You're still not going to get a particularly light bike for this money, but you should be able to find Shimano gears at the very least.

In the £150-£200 price bracket we start to get to viable bikes for commuting and leisure cycling. Beware of gimmicks like 'suspension forks' at this level. You need the manufacturer to have spent the money on a decent frame, components and wheels, and you should find bikes at the high end of this range with aluminium alloy wheel rims. Alloy rims are really the watershed that separates look-alikes from real bikes, because they are lighter, easier to maintain and (most importantly) provide much better braking in the wet. There are some very nice 'hybrid' type bikes in this price range.

£200–£300

From £200-£300 we get into quality hybrids, basic touring and road racing type bikes and the beginnings of truly off-road capable mountain bikes. Look for mostly Shimano-equipped bikes in this price bracket. Frames should have some 'chromoly' steel in them at the high end of this range. Indicated by a

sticker on the seat tube, this is a group of types of steel that are stronger than the high-tensile used for cheaper bike frames. Because it's stronger, less is needed and so the frame is lighter (see Chapter 8.)

£300–£400

£300-£400 gets you into real, good quality bike. It's not snobbish to say that if you are going to take your cycling at all seriously this is the minimum you should be looking to spend, especially for a mountain bike. Bikes in this price range are usually completely Shimano-equipped, have mostly chromoly frames and good components that are strong, light and work well together. The proof is the difference in the way such bikes feel to ride compared to a bike for half the price. A £400 bike will glide along, especially off road, where a £200 bike feels like much harder work.

£500 and beyond

From £500 and up you are into enthusiasts' bikes of one sort or another. While the bikes continue getting lighter and more reliable, there is less difference between, say, a bike for £600 and one for £1,000 than there is between a £200 bike and a £400 machine.

Answers to some common bike buying questions

Q **An everyday bike?** I just want a bike for everyday use. I will probably just use it to ride around town and on roads. I want it to last but I don't want to spend too much. Everyone else has mountain bikes. Is that what I should be getting too? What price limit should I be setting myself in this respect?

A Everyone uses mountain bikes for around town because they are robust, reliable and the upright riding position is very user-friendly. Nevertheless, a mountain bike is overkill for everyday use. Instead you would be much better off with a hybrid, because of the easier-rolling, higher-pressure tyres. Alternatively, for speed around town in the hands of a reasonably skilled rider (which it won't take you long to become), there is nothing to beat a road (racing) bike with a rack and fatter (32mm) tyres to handle the lousy surfaces of most city streets.

Look to spend £170 – £200 on a basic MTB or Hybrid. There are now so few road bikes sold at this end of the market that they are not very good value for money compared to an equivalent mountain bike. One good solution is a mountain bike with lightly treaded, high pressure tyres. See if the shop will swap them when you buy the bike.

Q **Off-road riding** I want a proper mountain bike to ride both on and off the road and really be able to take it anywhere. What are the essential features and components that I should be looking for? What's the minimum that I should be prepared to pay?

A If you are going to get into mountain biking properly then you should make sure you buy from a shop that specialises in mountain bikes and let them advise you. The absolute minimum you should spend is £300, and you'll get a bike that is much more than 30% better for £400.

The bike should have good quality, name brand components throughout. At this level, that means Shimano gears, brakes, chainset and hubs, a micro-adjusting seat post, 22-23in wide bars and a saddle which is fairly narrow so that you can slide off the back of it downhill. Look for bike brands like Dawes, Diamond Back, Dyna-Tech, Gary Fisher, GT, Kona, Marin, Raleigh, Ridgeback, Saracen Scott, Specialised and Trek.

Q **Bike weight** Why do they say lighter bikes are better? Does the weight of a bike matter to me if I'm not a serious cyclist?

A The obvious answer is that a light bike is easier to get moving because it requires less energy to accelerate. However, when you think that you and the bike weigh perhaps 200lbs, and a light bike might knock 4lb off that, it is hard to see why people get so excited about a difference of just 2 per cent.

The answer lies in the way light and heavy bikes absorb and dissipate bumps from the road and trail. A bike with a light frame and wheels feels better to ride because the thinner tubes used in the frame and the other light components are able to flex very slightly and so absorb some of the bumps from the road before they get to the rider. In numerical terms this effect is not very big, but it does seem to result in a very noticeable difference between bikes which are only, say, 4lb apart in weight. Try it for yourself. Talk a bike shop into letting you test ride a couple of bikes

that are significantly different weights. On a more practical front, a lightweight mountain bike is easier to lift over gates if this becomes necessary.

Q **Suspension** Is suspension a gimmick or is it useful? When should I need it? Are there different types? How much should I be prepared to pay for a bike with suspension?

A Suspension is very nice to have for off-road riding. By absorbing shocks from the trail, a suspension fork improves traction and therefore makes the bike handle better. This means you can go faster or you can go at the same speed with less discomfort. There are two main ways in which a suspension fork works. Some use air springs and hydraulic (oil-based) damping systems. Others have elastomer rubber springs which also provide the damping. (Damping is the motion control necessary to stop the fork just rebounding off its spring and bouncing you around). Elastomer forks work almost as well as the air/oil type and are much easier to look after. However the more complicated air/oil system ultimately does a better job of suspending the bike. Cheap suspension forks – like those found on some bikes under £300 – really don't work very well. You are much better off at this budget level with a rigid frame. Expect to pay £500 and up for a bike that has a suspension fork that is actually worth having.

Bikes for kids

The problem with kids is that they grow, usually faster than their parents' pockets can keep up with. Since a bike needs to fit to work properly, many parents are tempted to buy the cheapest bikes they can find for their kids, since they will grow out of them pretty soon.

This is a false economy. Very cheap kids' bikes tend to be unbelievably heavy (I've seen bikes for 8 year olds that weigh more than only slightly more expensive adult bikes) and to have very low quality parts. Spending just a bit more will get your child a bike that will be much more fun to ride, easier to look

after and hold more of its value when you come to re-sell it. And of course a decent bike can be bought for your eldest and passed down.

Kids' bike sizing – wheel sizes

Kids' bikes are sized according to the size of their wheels. 12in bikes fit the very youngest cyclists, 2-3 year old toddlers. Small BMX bikes with 16in wheels fit 4-6 year olds and 7-11 year olds can run 20in bikes, though pukka BMXs will fit riders much older than this. From about 11 you should be able to find a mountain bike with full-size 26in wheels that will fit.

Teenager bike sizing – frame sizes

Once you get into small bikes with full-size wheels another problem rears its head. It's very common to see 13 year olds riding bikes that are, quite simply, much too big for them. Parents want a rapidly growing teenager to get as much use as possible out of a bike, and are often adamant that their kid should get a bike he or she will be able to 'grow

into', despite the advice of the dealer. The end result of this is that a teenager who would fit perfectly on a mountain bike with a 16in frame and would be happy enough on an 18in frame ends up riding a 20in frame with the seat right down and no crotch clearance whatsoever.

In a perfect world everyone would be able to afford to replace a bike for a growing teenager as it is outgrown, but in practice it is sensible to allow some room for growth. The good news is that mountain bikes (which is what we are almost invariably talking about when we discuss kids bikes) have long seat posts which can allow as much as 6in of leg growth. A 16in bike will fit riders in the 5ft 3in to 5ft 8in range, and an 18in bike will accommodate a rider up to almost 6ft. The chances of your offspring ever managing to grow into a 20in bike are negligible. By the way, I am 5ft 11in and ride mountain bikes with frame sizes of 17.5in and 18in. On a 20in bike, especially off road, I fear for my genitals. *For more on sizing, see the section on 'Sizing a Bike' later in this chapter.*

Buying the bike

Where to buy

Bikes are sold in all sorts of places: garages, department stores, car accessory shops and specialist bike shops. A specialist bike shop is by far the best place to buy a bike from. Most bikes come from the factory in either a semi-assembled form, or hastily slapped together on a production line. A good bike shop will assemble the bike properly, often putting right things that are done wrong at the factory and will make sure that crucial bearing adjustments are right. Plus, a bike shop will make sure that the bike fits you correctly, and will help you buy a bike that is right for your needs.

Finding a good bike shop might not be easy, however. Ask any of your friends who are keen cyclists where they shop, and trawl the yellow pages. Look in the ads in the specialist bike magazines, especially Mountain Biking UK and Cycling Weekly, which carry lots of ads from dealers. Visit a few shops and get a feel for the general level of helpfulness and friendliness of the staff.

If you're looking for a particular type of bike, you may even be able to find a shop that specialises in that type of bike. To be honest this luxury is only available in the biggest cities, but you may be able to find a shop that specialises in road bikes, and there are plenty of very knowledgeable mountain bike specialists around. There are even still a few shops that specialise in touring bikes, and plenty of small shops that are the centre of the local time-trialling scene.

Flat-packs – beware!

Unless you are an experienced and competent mechanic, you should walk out of the shop with a fully-assembled roadworthy bike. The flat-packed bikes sold by department stores and some less scrupulous dealers require a level of assembly that is beyond the average person who is not familiar with all the parts of a bike and how they go together. I once watched two researchers from the BBC's Watchdog programme spend two hours attempting to assemble a flat-pack bike, following the instructions provided. They eventually

gave up, leaving a partially assembled bike with a couple of potentially dangerous bits of incorrect assembly which they had not noticed and did not know how to fix.

Bike shop staff from hell

One of the problems with specialist bike shops is that they tend to be staffed by enthusiast cyclists, who may know lots about bikes, but are sometimes a bit hopeless at getting it across. Comedian Alexei Sayle credits 'the fascism of people in bike shops' with getting him into cycling in the first place. "You go into a shop and ask for a hub. They say 'Five or six speed?' and you say, 'Six,' so they say 'counter-bored or off-flanged?' and they've got you!" Bike shop staff are fond of showing off their hard-accumulated specialist knowledge and

sometimes forget than many of their customers are normal, well-adjusted people who cannot recite Shimano part codes. *(And before any bike shop staff write to Haynes complaining, reciting Shimano part codes used to be one of my party-pieces when I worked in a shop!)*

The trick to dealing with these people is to state clearly and simply what you're going to use the bike for and how much you want to spend. Don't expect salesman-type leading questions from bike shops; most bike shop staff wouldn't know a structured selling technique if it bit them on the leg. This lack of sophistication can be an advantage, though; you're unlikely to get a hard sell and more likely to actually be helped by someone who is genuinely into bikes, and who wants to spread that enthusiasm.

Sizing a bike

The most common mistake people make when buying a new bike is to get one that is the wrong size. Like a set of clothes, a bike has to fit properly. Fit is made up of a number of factors, but the most important one is frame size. Frame size is measured from the centre of the bottom bracket (the bearing that the cranks spin on) to the top of the seat tube, where the saddle and seat post fit into the frame. The way to find the right size of bike for you is to stand over the frame with your feet flat on the floor.

Road bike sizing

For a road bike, you should have 1-2cm of clearance between your crotch and the top tube. Typically, this puts an average 177cm/5ft 10in man on about a 58cm/23in frame, and a bike that size will be designed so that the handlebars are in about the right place for that size of bloke. Similarly, smaller and larger bikes are proportionally designed so that the bars are nearer or further away to accommodate the rider's reach.

Mountain bike sizing

Mountain bikes need to be smaller, for a number of reasons. The simplest one is that you are more likely to need to get off the saddle of a mountain bike in a hurry and the top tube needs to be well out of the way to prevent this being a painful experience. The smaller frame also makes a mountain bike more manoeuvrable off-road, and makes the frame stiffer and, to a certain extent, stronger. You should have at least 2-3in/5-8cm of clearance between the top tube and your crotch. More is obviously better, but since mountain bikes are also designed proportionally to their size, you may find a small bike is too short, and the handlebars are too low.

Bike Sizing for Women

A woman's bike should be sized the same way as a man's. If you are buying an open (women's) frame bike of some sort, then determine size by trying diamond-framed (men's) bikes, then switch to an open frame. However, it has to be said that open frames should be avoided. They are more flexible and less strong than diamond frames, and usually have some sort of horrible bodge of a cable routing to the rear brake that stops it from working properly.

The big issue for women is getting the reach right. Women tend to have shorter reaches than men and slightly longer legs, so a bike that fits a 5ft 4in man will be slightly too small "in the legs" for a 5ft 4in women, and slightly too long "in the arms". Try several different models until you get one where the reach to the handlebars feels about right and get the shop to change the handlebar stem if necessary.

Women's saddles

Don't forget to get a woman's saddle. 'Normal' bike saddles are designed for the male anatomy and women usually find them somewhere between very uncomfortable and excruciating. According to all women cyclists I know, the Georgina Terry range of saddles are superbly comfortable.

Test rides

Any shop worth its salt will let you take a bike you are considering buying for a short test ride, though, with bikes being desirable items in the eyes of thieves, you should expect to leave cast-iron security with the shop. If you want to take a test-ride, have with you a credit card and other proof of identity, or, best of all, the value of the bike in cash or equivalent.

Take the bike for a ten-minute ride in some quiet streets where you can concentrate on how the bike feels rather than on dodging traffic. Check if the bike fits, and that the reach to the handlebars feels comfortable. If it feels slightly long or short, ask the shop if they'll change the handlebar stem. Is the saddle comfy, and if not will the shop swap it for a different model, or are you likely to get used to it? (Note, there are different saddles designed for men and women – find out if you're sitting on the right one). Are the handlebar grips too fat or too thin? Most importantly and least tangible, does the bike feel good? Does it respond to your input at the pedals and handlebar, or does it feel dead and sluggish? You can't expect a basic bike to feel like a World Championship racer's bike, but you can at least expect it to go where you point it easily and pleasantly.

New bike delivery checks

From wherever you buy your bike, big shop or small, a proper bike mechanic in the store should give the bike a thorough check over before you walk out with it. If they won't or don't, then take your money elsewhere. Also, if you're unsure about setting the bike up correctly (*see the next chapter*), then ask them to do these necessary adjustments for you at the same time.

In my days of working in a bike shop, the most nerve-wracking jobs were always bike build-ups from scratch for discerning customers. You should be a discerning buyer, too. Don't blindly rely on the shop to have done everything. When you collect the bike, check that everything has been tightened and adjusted correctly. If you're embarrassed about doing this in the shop (you might feel that it implies you think that they don't know what they're doing) then do it when you get home, but do it. Check the following things ▶

Road bikes:

Grab the bottom of the handlebar and try to rotate it in the stem.

1 Hold the front wheel between your knees and make sure that you can't turn the handlebar stem in the frame.

2 Spin each wheel and check that the rim doesn't catch the brake blocks, that the wheel is straight and round, and that the rim doesn't wobble from side to side or up and down.

3 Grab each brake and make sure that the brake hits the rim after the lever has moved 1-2cm and that levers cannot be squeezed all the way to the handlebar without extreme force.

4 Lock the front brake and rock the bike backwards and forwards. A knocking or clicking sound may indicate a loose headset; get the shop to check.

5 Grab the brake levers and try to rotate them round the bar. If they move, is it the levers that are loose or the handlebar in the stem?

6 Lift the rear wheel and turn the pedals while shifting through all the gears *(this will require you either to mutate into something with three hands that will probably have difficulty riding a bike, or to get a friend to hold the bike for you)*. Make sure that the bike will shift into all the gears and doesn't over-shift off the sprockets or chainrings.

7 Loosen the seat quick release (or nut) and make sure the seat post moves smoothly in and out of the frame and has been greased.

Buying second hand

There are plenty of second hand bikes around, either through bike shops and second hand shops that deal in used bikes, or through private sales; you'll find ads in all the bike magazines as well as in places like the local papers. A second hand bike can be an amazing bargain. It's not unusual to find bikes in pretty good condition going for a half to two thirds their new price because the owner is a keenie and has decided to upgrade to the latest machine. However, there are a few pitfalls you need to be aware of.

Where to buy a second hand bike

If you can find a bike shop that sells second hand bikes, then this is obviously the best place to buy one. Just as a used car is more expensive from a dealer than from an ad in the paper, so a used bike will be more expensive from a shop, but you should get some sort of guarantee – six months is common – and the Sale of Goods Act applies so you have some redress if it turns out to be an absolute dog.

A bike shop will also have done a full service on a used bike, replacing any worn-out parts, and that can easily be worth the difference between a shop's price and a private sale.

Second hand stores are a bad bet, in my opinion. I have seen lots of bikes from second hand shops that were in atrocious condition and needed a lot of money spending on them to get them safely roadworthy, and plenty of bikes sold through these places turn out to be stolen.

Buying a bike from another member of the public puts you up against a whole range of possibilities, from picking up a well-loved bike owned by an enthusiast to acquiring a bike that has been gently rusting in a garden shed for a few years. You need to check over any bike that you're buying this way very carefully.

Second hand check over

First, talk to the seller and see what you can find out about the history of the bike. How often has it been serviced and by whom? How often was it ridden? What was it used for? If it's a mountain bike, has it been used off road and if so,

When you go to look at the bike, check the following:

Frame checks

● Inspect the frame for dings and dents. Some paintwork damage is acceptable, but major scratches, rust and dents are going to need work and may indicate abuse or neglect.

● Check the area around the front of the frame for collision damage. A crashed frame usually has tell-tale ripples in the top tube and down tube, two to four inches back from the head tube. Sometimes the only visible sign of a crash is cracked paint in this area. Do not buy a bike that has been crashed.

● Push the bike along by the saddle. A bike that is straight, that is, that has the wheels and frame correctly aligned, can be pushed along from the seat and won't pull to one side.

Bearing checks

● Lift the front of the bike and turn the handlebars. They should turn smoothly with no play and no click-stops or roughness. Problems here will require a new headset.

● Drop the wheels out of the frame and turn the hub axles. Again, they should turn smoothly with no play. Damaged wheel bearings are a big problem because they will almost certainly require replacement hubs, which involves expensive wheel re-building.

● Push the chain off the chainrings on to the frame and spin the cranks. If they don't turn smoothly and without play, the bottom bracket will probably need work.

● Do the pedals turn smoothly on the cranks?

Wear and tear checks

● Inspect the tyres for damage to the sidewalls and general wear.

● Pull the brakes and make sure the cables move smoothly through the housings.

● Shift through all the gears.

● Check the brake pads for wear.

● Try to lift the chain off the chainring teeth. A chain that will lift clear of the teeth is badly worn and will need replacing. It's likely that the sprockets will also need replacing in this case.

● Spin the wheels and check that the wheels are reasonably straight and round.

● Squeeze the spokes; they should feel tight. If any spokes are loose, then the wheel is going to need attention.

how was it cleaned? Avoid bikes that have been frequently jet-washed as this tends to drive water deep into the bearings.

How much should I offer?

For the most part, these checks will allow you to get some idea of how much the bike is worth. A second hand bike in very good condition, with some very minor wear and tear but no need for replacement parts beyond perhaps the brake blocks, is worth about two thirds of its new price. Any other problems reduce the price accordingly. A respray will set you back from £60, for example, while a replacement front hub in a good mountain bike might set you back the same amount by the time you've paid for a new wheel to be built. Bargain accordingly, and if you've got a friend who is knowledgeable about bikes, see if you can persuade them to come along to help check the bike over.

Avoiding stolen bikes

Frame numbers are embossed on the frame under the bottom bracket.

A stolen bike is something you really don't want to get lumbered with. Even if you buy stolen goods in good faith you are technically committing an offence, and, while it's extremely unlikely you will get into trouble, the potential hassle is immense.

There are a number of tell-tale signs that a bike is stolen:

● No frame number. File marks under the bottom bracket where the frame number should be are a sure sign of a stolen bike. There is no other reason to file off the frame number than to disguise a nicked bike.

● Ridiculous bargains. If a bike is in a second hand store with a £50 price tag but is selling for £500 in a bike shop, then it almost certainly stolen.

● Know-nothing sellers. If a private seller can't tell you where the bike was originally bought, doesn't have the original receipt or owner's manual, or just doesn't seem to know very much about the bike, then steer clear.

● Lousy paint jobs. A hand-bodged paint job on what seems to be otherwise a good quality bike should set alarm bells ringing. People just don't put a couple of coats of Dulux on £500 mountain bikes.

Setting up

Contents

Adjusting the bike for you

A properly set up bike is a joy; a badly set up one can be a pain, quite literally. Over the years a number of rules of thumb for comfortable, efficient set-up have been evolved. Some people try to justify them on the grounds of spurious scientific reasoning, but for the most part basic comfortable bike set-up is something that has developed as the result of millions of cyclists trying different fine adjustments to their bikes and gradually finding out what works and what doesn't. What follows, then, is a basis from which to work. If part of the accepted wisdom doesn't seem to

work for you, then make gradual adjustments to one thing at a time until you are comfortable.

The saddle

The saddle can be moved up and down by loosening the seat post clamp bolt or quick release mechanism. The angle and position of the saddle can also be adjusted by loosening the saddle clamp bolt at the top of the seat post *(For the mechanics of how to do this, see Chapter 17.)*

Seat height

The saddle should be high enough that you can comfortably pedal quickly without having to move your hips to reach the pedals. In practise this means that with the ball of your foot on the pedal you will have a slight bend in your leg when the pedal is at the bottom of its rotation. Experiment around this setting

to find out what saddle height feels most comfortable for you. Make sure however that you do not raise the seat post so far that the maximum extension mark is out of the frame.

Saddle position

It's possible to move the saddle backward and forward on the saddle rails and this has a small but noticeable effect on comfort. The classical way to set this fore-aft adjustment is to use a plumbline to position the top of the tibia, just under the knee, directly above the pedal axle. No-one knows why this works, but it's a good starting point.

Saddle angle

Most people like their saddles to have the nose and rear at the same height, though you sometimes see racers with the nose very slightly above the rear, and many women like to set the nose slightly down.

The handlebars

To adjust the handlebar stem, loosen (but don't undo) the stem bolt. Sometimes you may have to tap it with a hammer. *(For more on this, see Chapter 18.)*

Handlebar height

This is entirely down to personal preference. Some people like their handlebar as much as 3in below the saddle, some like it above. Set it to whatever feels comfortable to you, but make sure that you don't raise the handlebar stem so that the max height mark is out of the frame.

Handlebar reach

Again this is largely determined by personal preference, but a good basis is to use a handlebar stem that puts your back at about 45 degrees in your natural riding position. Changing handlebar stems is something that should be done when you buy the bike. A good shop will usually swap in the stem for you when you buy the bike, but you will be charged later.

Fault Diagnosis
'Riding is uncomfortable'

SYMPTOM	CAUSE	REMEDY
Saddle soreness	Saddle angle wrong	Adjust saddle angle
	Uncomfortable saddle	Change saddle
	Not using cycling shorts	Get some
Back pain/neck pain	Riding position too stretched	Adjust handlebar position or change stem
	Riding position too upright	Adjust handlebar position or change stem
Sore hands	No gloves	Get some
	Handlebar tape/ grips worn or thin	Replace with better tape or grips
Knee pain	Saddle too low	Raise saddle
Sore feet	Wearing flexible shoes	Use stiff-soled shoes
`Burning' feet	Wearing nylon socks	Use cotton socks

What else do I need?

Helmet

Helmets offer a limited but significant amount of protection against damage to your skull and brain if you fall off and hit your head on the ground. For mountain biking they are pretty much essential, since you are far more likely to fall off your bike off road, and for nervous beginning cyclists they can be a great confidence booster. However, most serious and fatal injuries to cyclists (over half of which are head injuries) are the result of accidents involving a motor vehicle, and no helmet currently available is designed to protect you against a collision with a tonne of steel doing 60 mph. A helmet will afford you some head protection, then. However, it is not a substitute for good road sense and a helmet will not make you invulnerable. *(For more on helmets, see the end of this chapter.)*

Pump (and a puncture repair kit)

Punctures are a fact of life, I'm afraid.

The pretty well essential

Helmet

Puncture Repair Kit

Pump

Lock

Carry a good pump, tyre levers and a spare tube so that you can sort out a flat if one happens. Zefal's pumps are widely available and their Mt Zefal Plus mountain bike pump is still the best there is for ease of use and durability.

Lock

See Chapter 7 for much more on bike security. In short, if you are going to leave your bike anywhere for any length of time, lock it to something solid with a good lock.

More useful accessories

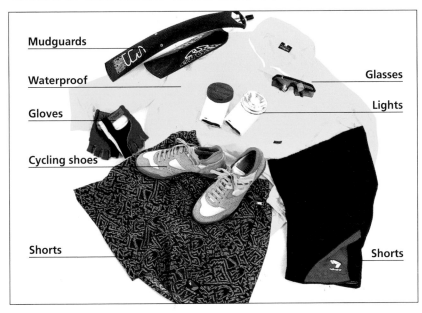

Mudguards

Waterproof

Gloves

Cycling shoes

Shorts

Glasses

Lights

Shorts

Mudguards

It's far more likely that you will have to ride after it has rained rather than while it's actually raining. Mudguards will stop you from getting as wet. Unfortunately mudguards have never been trendy, especially among mountain bikers, and almost every design out there has tended to clog with mud if used off road. However, there are now splash guards such as Sensible Products' Crud Catcher that clip to the down tube to keep mud off your face. The matching Crudguard rear mudguard keeps your bum dry and sits far enough off the tyre that it doesn't clog up.

Cycling shorts

If you are going to ride more than a few miles regularly, get a pair of padded cycling shorts and wear them against your skin, with something warmer over the top if it's cold. The lining in cycling shorts helps cushion you and reduces chafing and saddle soreness. Wash them after every ride. If you don't want the skin-tight Lycra look (which, let's face it is a bit impractical for riding to the shops or over to grandma's), check out a pair of bike and hike shorts or bike briefs (which can be worn under anything); both have the all important padding.

Cycling shoes

You can ride in trainers or tennis shoes, but stiff-soled cycling shoes are much more comfortable because they stop your feet from flexing over the pedals which simultaneously stops you from wasting energy compressing a squishy running shoe sole and stops your feet getting sore.

Gloves

A mountain biking essential, gloves will stop you from shredding your hands if you come off, as well as providing shock-absorbing padding.

Glasses

Flying dust and insects in your eyes can be very unpleasant, and it's hard to concentrate on where you are going if you're having to squint against bright sunshine. Specialist cycling glasses can run to silly prices, but pretty much any shatterproof sports sunglasses that completely absorb ultraviolet light and fit close enough to your face to block airborne hazards will do the job. Make sure they also fit tightly or clip behind the ears, otherwise they're likely to fall off as you ride.

Lighting and visibility

Lights are a legal requirement if you are going to ride at night, and an obvious safety necessity. All the basic battery-powered lights you will find in the shops conform to the relevant British Standard and are more than adequate for occasional round-town use, where the requirement is that you be seen rather than you can see where you are going.

If you are going to ride completely unlit roads at night, then a more powerful front light system is useful, and there are several available which use rechargeable batteries, usually built into water bottles or, as here, clipped to the top tube. These systems are expensive to buy, but pay for themselves eventually in savings on replacement batteries.

LED lights

In the last couple of years rear lights have appeared which use electronic light emitting diodes (LEDs) instead of bulbs. These lights are very cheap to run because LEDs are extremely efficient compared to bulbs. Only about six per cent of the power going into a bulb gets out of the bulb and red filter as red light; the figure for an LED is more like 80 per cent. This means that an LED will run for hundreds of hours on a couple of AA batteries. Even with three or five LEDs to provide a wide angle of visibility (LEDs are quite directional) an LED rear lamp is much cheaper to run than a conventional set-up, and the flashing

versions of these lights are very eye-catching.

Unfortunately it is illegal to use one of these lights on its own, as they do not conform to the Vehicle Lighting Regulations, which call for incandescent lights, and the same regulations forbid the use of flashing red lights. **An LED light should therefore be used as an backup light alongside a conventional lamp, in steady mode.**

Waterproofs

Riding in the rain can be made much more pleasant by a good waterproof jacket. Cycling-specific ones cost anything from £20 to £200 depending on the material and quality of manufacture. Expensive Gore-Tex jackets will allow some of your sweat to `breathe' out through the fabric, helping to reduce the `soaked anyway' syndrome that cycling in waterproofs often causes. The best bargain in cycling jacket fabrics is a material called Pertex, a very lightweight micro-fibre nylon used for parachutes, among other things, that while not actually waterproof has such a tight weave that it is pretty much showerproof. Because a Pertex jacket does not need to have the seams taped, it will usually be a very reasonable price, from about £35.

Unless it's really scything down and very cold, waterproof over-trousers are probably overkill, though if you feel the need, then go for them.

Cold weather gear

When it's cold I wear a couple of layers of warm cycling jumpers or thermal underwear under a waterproof or windproof top, and pile layers of cycling tights on my legs until there is enough insulation there to keep in the heat that the legs generate of their own accord. My colleagues think I'm a bit mad to carry on riding right though the winter, but if you have the right cold-weather kit a 30 minute commute can still be comfortable even if it's snowing.

More on helmets

Replace helmets after falls

The most important thing to know about a helmet is that if you have crashed and hit the helmet it should be replaced, even if there is no visible damage to it. For very active riders this makes helmets like Specialized's and Giro's, great bargains, since they carry a very cheap replacement policy – around a tenner will get you a new lid should you trash one.

A helmet absorbs impact like this: When your bare head hits a solid object it is slowed down very suddenly. This produces very high forces at the impact point, on the order of many hundreds of g's, which can damage the skull. Unfortunately your brain, being a rather messy, jelly-like sort of object, continues moving, and bashes itself against the inside of the now stationary skull. This is not a pleasant thing to happen to a brain, and the resulting damage can produce anything from mild concussion to death.

Add an inch of nice, crushable expanded polystyrene and it's a different story. Because the expanded polystyrene crushes on impact it transfers the forces that are trying to slow down the skull and brain rather more slowly, and the brain gets a chance to slow down too, rather than washing up on the inside of your skull.

Most helmets are designed to absorb forces that would damage your brain and reduce them to a level that they won't. However, there is a level of impact that they won't absorb. Their efficacy against a Volvo doing 60 mph is probably negligible.

Helmet standards

Any helmet you buy should conform to one or more of the following standards: Snell B90, ANSI Z90.4, BSI, AS or TUV. Of these the Snell standard is commonly accepted as the definitive one, at least in the UK and North America.

Types of helmet

Generally helmets now come in two types: hardshell and microshell. A hardshell helmet has a thick polycarbonate shell over a layer of expanded polystyrene, while a microshell has a thinner outer shell and is therefore substantially lighter. In both cases it is the expanded polystyrene inner shell which does most of the shock absorbing. The outer layer is just there to protect the helmet itself from everyday dings and dents, and a microshell, with its thinner protective layer, needs more careful handling than a hardshell.

Microshells are very popular with racers, for whom the reduced weight is worth the extra care needed carrying the lid around. Riders who don't want to have to worry quite so much about the care and feeding of their helmets go for hardshells, although high-quality ones are becoming hard to find.

Fitting a helmet

If a helmet is to do you any good at all it must be fitted properly. Firstly, the shell should be of a size that it fits your head snugly and moves with your scalp if you wiggle your eyebrows.

1 Choose the smallest size that you can get on far enough for the top of the helmet to touch the top of your head, then use the pads that are supplied with the helmet to pad it out so it grips your head snugly.

2 Set the straps up so that the strap grips are just underneath your ears and the helmet sits level on the top of your head. The strap should be tight enough that the helmet doesn't move when you shake your head.

29

Children

Contents

Kids love bikes. To children bikes are as liberating as cars are to adults, allowing them a range of travel and experience impossible on foot. With a bike your child can get much-needed exercise, learn road sense and have fun. From about the age of six, children can ride along with their parents, but before that they will need some sort of help to ride any distance, which is where trailers, child seats and 'trailer bikes' come in.

Child seats, trailers and 'trailer bikes'

Trailers are good for very young children, or if there is more than one.

Child seats are suitable from about 10 months. Get one with head supports, footrests, safety restraints and a grab bar.

An alternative system for older children is a small saddle bolted to the top tube. The child is surrounded by your body and arms.

Even before they are old enough to ride themselves, kids can come with you on a child seat that fits on the bike, or, for very young children, a trailer. Burley and Cannondale both make trailers that allow even a baby to be taken on bike rides. As soon as the child is old enough to sit up and comfortably support his or her head (about 10 months old), it's time for a child seat. The most common types fit on a rear rack and sits the child behind the rider, facing forward. One minimal system which seems to work well for slightly older children is a small saddle which bolts to the top tube of the bike and has footrests on the down tube. The child grabs the middle of the handlebar and is surrounded by your body and arms. Once a child gets to about 40lbs a child seat becomes inadequate; it's time for a small bike.

Trailer bikes

If you want to ride with a child who's too old for a child seat, but don't want to have to keep down to the relatively slow pace a youngster is capable of, ask in bike shops about 'trailer bikes'. These go under various names, but are

basically single-wheeled attachments which fit to the back of your bike and provide your kid with a saddle, handlebar, gears and wheel. These work very well for kids in the 4-8 age range.

Child-carrying essentials

Seat

The seat should have a head support, footrests with barriers to stop the child's feet getting in your rear wheel, some sort of safety restraint system and a grab bar. **Never leave your child alone in a child seat; it's fairly easy for an active child to topple a parked bike.**

Helmet

Helmets intended for use with a child seat are very thick to protect a child's softer skull, and often cover the ears. Some children don't like wearing helmets, so set an example!

Warm, weatherproof clothes

You are doing work and generating heat. Your child isn't, and so needs to be wrapped up as warm and dry as possible. Trailers are good if the weather is bad because they come with covers that keep out the elements.

Child-carrying bikes

The best sort of bike to attach a child seat or trailer is without doubt a mountain bike. The strong, stiff frame, heavy-duty wheels, good brakes and low gears of a mountain bike all make it ideal for the job of carrying around the extra weight of a child. Get a bike shop to fit the lowest possible bottom gear. (Something like 24/30 or 22/28 should be low enough – the exact detail of what can be fitted will depend on the particular chainset your bike has.) You may also want to get the dealer to change the bar or stem so that you have a more upright riding position for coping with traffic.

Teaching a child to ride

General considerations

Where to learn: Teach your child to ride well away from traffic. That means really a park or your own garden. Also in these places, if your child topples over then falling on grass is a far better experience than falling on tarmac.

What to learn on: Don't try to teach your child on a bike that is too big or too small for them. If it's too small, then pedalling and steering is difficult. If it's too big then stopping and starting is dangerous.

Learning to stay upright

There are four very basic skills that a child needs to master to ride a bike, namely; balance, steering, pedalling and stopping. There are certainly many different ways to learn to ride – handed down by each generation – and that we can all ride bikes is testament to the fact that all methods more or less work.

The classic way of teaching a child to ride is to run behind them, pushing them along until they get the idea of pedalling and steering, then let go. However this approach does seem a bit equivalent to carrying someone in the deep end of a swimming pool and hoping they will figure out how to swim after you have held them up for a few seconds. Panic usually wins; the child topples over and is put off cycling. We would like to think that there are better ways of a parent teaching their son or daughter to ride than by giving them a big push off and shouting "pedal, pedal, pedal!"

In this chapter we suggest two alternative methods which teach the child the four basic bike-riding skills, but in a manner that they learn them for themselves, gradually.

Stabiliser method

Stabilisers are useful. They allow the child to learn pedalling, steering and stopping but without all the worry over balancing. The crunch time always arrives when the stabilisers have to come off. An alternative method to straight removal is to raise (or bend) the stabilisers so that on normal upright riding they are off the ground, and will touch only if the bike tips one way or the other. Start with them on slightly off the ground and raise them further as the child gets more confident. Take them completely off when you see that the child is hardly using them at all. This way a child is gradually introduced to balancing on two wheels.

Stabilisers can become a crutch however, and their removal can be traumatic to a child (which won't help them learning to ride without them). Bear in mind that if you're using stabilisers, you should take them off the bike before the child comes to depend on them.

Hobby horse technique

Another technique is to simulate the way people learned to ride bikes in the first place. The very earliest two-wheeled machines were hobby-horses, which riders propelled by pushing along the ground with their feet. Then, when it was realised that a vehicle with two wheels in a line would keep going even without additional stabilisation, someone added a way of driving the wheels and the bike was born.

To teach a child to ride, then, turn the bike into a hobby-horse by removing the pedals and lowering the saddle to the point where both feet can easily reach the floor. In a safe place, well away from traffic (preferably your garden or a park), your kid can then scoot along and coast feet-up for increasing periods of time. With the danger of toppling removed, learning how to steer, balance and use the brakes is easy and after a while you can replace the pedals, then gradually raise the seat to a sensible height.

Developing cycle control

It is not enough for your child to learn to ride, they must also learn some cycle control. Teach them good habits to start off with, namely:
▶ Hands on the grips near the brake levers.
▶ Pedalling with the balls of the foot.
▶ Always sitting on the saddle.

Teaching through play

You can actively teach your child some cycle control by devising games for them. Why not try the following:
▶ **Cycling in a straight line:** Lay out tramlines with two lengths of string – can they cycle between the strings? Make it more difficult by narrowing the gap between the strings.

▶ **Looking behind whilst cycling in a straight line.** (A very important skill): When they've mastered the same course, can they look behind and count the number of fingers you hold up, and **still** stay between the lines?
▶ **Controlled turning:** Try the good old bicycle slalom around some small plastic flower pots (or other harmless objects).
▶ **Cycle control with one hand off the handlebars.** (A skill you need every time you want to signal): Try the game of picking a ball off a stool, cycling over to a bucket, and then dropping the ball in it – all without stopping.
▶ **Precise stopping:** Mark out a square, the child has to stop with the front wheel in it. Hours of quiet occupation for the child with that particular challenge!

Road safety for children

Very young children have no conception of the consequences of their actions, and it's therefore impossible to teach them road safety. Make sure they ride on the pavement, in parks, or in very quiet residential streets. This is a very good reason to live in a cul de sac – in the summer the dead end street where I live is full of kids of all ages riding their bikes.

As soon as children are off 'play bikes' and trikes and on to proper kid's bikes, however, you can easily teach road safety by taking them riding, having them copy what you do and explaining to them why you are doing it as you go. The age at which you can teach children to ride on the open road varies with the particular child's rate of development; nine or ten is about the average, but cases of properly taught eight year olds being able to ride safely in medium traffic are pretty common in the cycling community.

The essential things to teach children are:

▶ To behave predictably and to signal, so other road users know what they are

going to do.
▶ To ride on the left at all times.
▶ To give way where appropriate, that is at junctions where crossing traffic has right of way, and when changing lanes.
▶ To ride out from the kerb between junctions, where they can easily be seen.
▶ To position themselves correctly at junctions depending on which way they are turning.

Proper road safety training

Locally organised cycling proficiency classes are as old as the hills – probably because they have been found to serve a proper purpose. Check out these schemes to have your child taught by a professional. Usually children have to be nine or ten before they can part in these schemes. Contact your local Road Safety Officer at the Council Offices to find out what's on around where you are.

Kids and helmets

It is relatively easy to get young kids to wear helmets, and teenagers who are into cycling as a sport, wear them willingly because they see riders in the bike magazines in helmets all the time. However, in their early teens and just before, many kids get self-conscious about putting on a lid, for all sorts of reasons, mostly to do with image and peer status.

If your child simply will not wear a helmet, don't force the issue. The health and fitness benefits of cycling far outweigh the actual chance of a serious head injury, and children are actually two to three times as likely to sustain head injuries from climbing and jumping than from riding bikes. Kids today get precious little exercise as it is, and lack of exercise in childhood has been linked to a tendency to be overweight in later life. It is far better that children get the benefits of an active, healthy life than that their activities be restricted just because they don't want to wear helmets.

On the road

Contents

The road is where most bikes spend most of their time; suitably shod with slick tyres, even my mountain bikes do a lot of duty as commuters and day-touring bikes. But many people are put off from riding on the road by the volume and speed of traffic and by scare stories of the mortality rates of cyclists. Surely the roads are a dangerous place? Not necessarily. How to be safe on a bike comes under two headings. Firstly, have the right equipment; namely a bike that is well maintained and in proper working order, a helmet, and good lights if it's dark. And secondly and equally importantly, develop some safe riding skills.

The skills safe, experienced cyclists have developed can be summed up very simply; ride with confidence, be predictable and behave like a vehicle. In this chapter we will look briefly at these skills and techniques, at the equipment a road cyclist needs and at all aspects of riding on the road.

There is not sufficient space here to explore all the issues road cycling opens up. An excellent work on the subject – which covers all aspects of cycling in great depth – is 'Effective Cycling' by John Forester.

Equipment for the road

The bike for the road

The definitive machine for riding on the road is the classic drop handlebar road bike. Simply, the road bike is the most efficient machine in existence for the conversion of human power into motion on tarmac. If you need a bike for commuting, road touring, day-riding in the lanes or just getting about, then a

road bike will get you there fastest. If that's so, then why are there so few road bikes about these days? Why do people pound round the streets of our cities on mountain bikes and flat-handlebar hybrids? Why, indeed, do I commute to work by slick-shod mountain bike rather than on a road bike?

Well, my excuse is that it's what I'm used to. I prefer to ride off road, and since that's my main priority I don't want to get used to a different riding position, then have to retrain my reflexes when I ride off road. The problem for most people is that road bikes simply seem un-welcoming and

Road bikes: Ultimate pedal efficiency on tarmac

fragile. The crouched, forward leaning position of a road bike seems unnatural and uncomfortable; the road bike is a tool which takes some getting used to.

In fact, a properly set up road bike is not uncomfortable, which is why riders in the Tour de France are able to spend up to eight hours a day for three weeks in the saddle and competitors in the annual epic Race Across America can ride almost non-stop for ten days. If you need road speed and comfort, get a road bike and set it up properly. If you need a bike that can also be used off road, then look at mountain bikes and think about having a second set of tyres or wheels for the road.

Slick tyres

The type of tyres that you need for getting the best out of a mountain bike on the road are called 'slicks'. These are simply mountain bike tyres without the knobbles. (It is the knobbles on a mountain bike that slow it up on the road). If you can stretch to a second set of wheels for these tyres then do so – interchanging wheels is far quicker than interchanging tyres.

In Chapter 2 we looked at the various types of bikes. To briefly recap, the most suitable bikes for riding on the road are road racing bikes for lightly or unladen riding; touring bikes for long-distance riding or commuting with significant loads and when reliability and toughness is paramount; hybrids for riders who want easy-rolling road bike wheels but mountain bike user-friendliness; roadsters for town cycling in flat places and posing outside Chelsea wine bars, and mountain bikes shod with slick tyres for posers like me, who know better but won't admit it.

Other stuff you need

Topics like helmets and bad weather gear are covered in Chapter 3. The most important factor that a road cyclist has to consider is visibility. A bike is a relatively small object in comparison with most other road users, and it therefore makes sense for you to try and make yourself as visible as possible. This means positioning yourself on the road where other road users expect to see a vehicle, and not hiding in the gutter where you can be easily overlooked. Of course it also means using lights and reflectors at night so that other vehicles can see you.

At night, the law requires you to use a white front light, red rear light and a red rear reflector. The law also requires that these lights conform to the relevant British Standard. Oddly the British Standard actually limits the maximum brightness of the front light you are allowed to use and there are situations where this light is inadequate; if you ride at speed on unlit country lanes at night, you need something brighter, so feel free to ignore the regulations. No policeman will ever stop you for having lights that are too bright. For round-town cycling basic lights are good enough that you will be seen as long as you keep your lights in good condition.

For more on type of lights see Chapter 3. For how to keep your lights in proper working order, see Chapter 22.

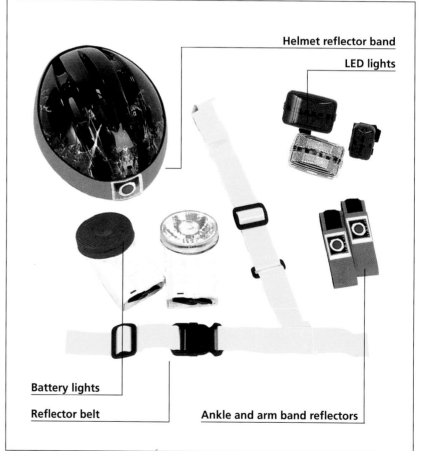

Helmet reflector band

LED lights

Battery lights

Reflector belt

Ankle and arm band reflectors

A complete night-time visibility kit

Road Law

By and large the traffic law in Britain treats cyclists as vehicles, with infrequent exceptions. This is a good thing; road law is there to regulate the flow of traffic along the roads in a way that is safe and efficient for everyone, and obeying road law, and behaving as a vehicle, is the key to safe and efficient riding on the roads. **This, then, means that cyclists have to ride on the left, keep within the speed limit and ride in such a way as not to endanger other road users, whether they are car drivers or pedestrians.**

Cyclists: Their rights on the road

Because bikes do not present as large a danger to other road users or cause damage to road surfaces the way motor vehicles do, we are not required to pass tests or pay road tax, and this is often used by ignorant motorists as an excuse to treat cyclists badly. This argument is baloney. The roads are paid for out of all our taxes because society needs them; motorists are required to take a test and carry a licence because they are in charge of a tonne of metal that is capable of 100mph or more. They must prove their competence before being allowed out on the streets in charge of a piece of kit which can be deadly in the wrong hands, and it must be possible to control bad motorist behaviour by deterrent and punitive measures such as licence points and bans. The unlicensed and untaxed status of cyclists reflects our relative benevolence as road users, and does not imply that we have fewer rights than anyone else on the roads.

Many people believe that the Highway Code requires you to ride as near to the left as possible. Not so. **In traffic moving at the same speed as a bike, which is most rush-hour city traffic in the UK, you are safer taking a position in the traffic rather than grovelling in the gutter.** Riding well out from the left makes you more visible to

motorists and discourages them from attempting to squeeze past when to do so would endanger you, and so the Highway Code contains no instruction to ride on the left-most edge of the road. Of course, you should move aside and let drivers pass when it is safe to do so, but you should ride in such a way as to put your own safety above all other concerns. In fact a close reading of the Highway Code and the Road Traffic Act shows that cyclists are covered by the same regulations as other vehicles, and the sections of those two documents which are specifically aimed at cyclists are, almost without exception, reiterations of the regulations for all vehicles.

What you should avoid doing are the things that routinely get cyclists moaned about: riding the wrong way down one-way streets, jumping red lights, riding on the pavement.

Riding on the road

The basic principles of riding on the road, in or out of traffic, are simple:
▶ Ride on the left side of the road.
▶ Give way when appropriate, that is, at junctions when you are emerging on to a larger road, at traffic lights on red and at roundabouts.
▶ Give way when changing lanes; wait until there is a large enough gap in the traffic for you to be able to change lanes

without impeding oncoming traffic.
▶ At junctions, position yourself according to where you want to go from the junction; near the curb if you want to turn left, at the centre of the road to turn right and in the middle of the lane if you are going straight.
▶ While riding along, position yourself in the traffic stream according to your speed; faster traffic is nearer the centre-line, slower traffic nearer the curb.

On a bike, behave exactly like any other road user.

All of this is very simple; it is the way all other road users behave, after all. But people expect bikes to be different, and **almost all the problems bikes have on the roads are the result of behaving differently from other road users.**

For example, in the US, cyclists are routinely and wrongly taught by non-cyclists to ride facing into oncoming traffic. But a road user coming the other way in their lane is the last thing a motorist expects, and collisions involving cyclists riding against oncoming car traffic are common and often fatal. In Britain riding the wrong way down a one-way street is similarly dangerous.

Commuting

The most common reason to ride, after the sheer pleasure of doing so, is to turn the simple necessity of getting to work into something rather more enjoyable and beneficial from a health and fitness

37

point of view. If your daily commute is less than five miles you could almost certainly do it faster, door to desk, by bike, even allowing for time to get clean and changed. For example, if I get the bus the seven miles to my office it takes about 40 minutes; at least five waiting for the bus, 25 sitting on it, vegetating and ten to walk across town to the office. Riding and showering takes me 35-40 minutes, and I live in a hilly area. Driving takes almost as long as getting the bus, and I have to pay to park my car for the day.

My commute is pretty minor; a colleague who is quite a useful racing cyclist regularly comes into work the long way and does 25 miles before he starts his day. For an ordinarily fit person anything up to ten miles is relatively straightforward.

Your office clothes should be carried neatly rolled up, inside plastic bags in panniers and hung out as soon as you arrive so they have a chance to hang flat a little while you get cleaned up.

If your place of work does not have a shower, ask your employer to provide one; most will if you are persistent. Point out that by riding you are reducing your stress level and improving your overall health and fitness. It has been shown that fit, active people are generally more productive and creative; enlightened employers encourage bike commuting for sound business reasons!

Leisure cycling

Where to go

Our country lanes are Britain's great strength as a place to ride a bike. On a summer weekend there is very little to beat zimming between the hedgerows or dry-stone walls of the English countryside, and our cities, with the exceptions of London and Birmingham, are not so sprawled that getting out of town and into the country by bike is impractical. Dwellers in the big cities should look at hopping on the train with their bikes or driving out of town to find places to ride. Tourist Information offices and the Cyclists' Touring Club are invaluable sources of ideas for places to ride.

Riding with kids

This kind of cycling is ideal for kids; taking your children riding in the countryside can teach them to appreciate the richness of our landscape, and introduce them to sights and smells they would never see otherwise. Plan your rides to have plenty of stops for food, drink and rest and keep in mind that children get tired and overheat quicker than adults. That said, I have seen super-fit 8 year olds who can quite happily ride all day and who cover more miles

pootling round the paddock and spectator areas at bike events than their racing parents do in competition! Children vary a lot.

If you are an adult riding with children, then ride behind them. This means that you can watch them and also any motorist approaching from behind will see you first – you are bigger and therefore easier to spot.

Carrying loads

The best way to carry loads on a bike is in panniers attached to racks which mount firmly on the frame. Small loads, such as your wallet and keys and even your day clothes if your work uniform consists of the tidier items from your t-shirt collection, can be carried in a bum bag round your waist, but anything bigger should go in a pannier. Rucksacks are generally a bad idea because a load on a sloping back is not very good for you. For some situations, such as lightweight off-road touring, a rucksack is the way to go, however; loading the bike is simply impractical when you have to carry it from time to time.

For large loads, put some of the weight into 'low rider' front panniers. These bags sit low on the front fork and do not affect the bike's handling. In fact, expedition cyclist Nick Sanders used just a pair of low riders for his 'Round the

World in 80 Days' trip a few years ago. Handlebar bags are great for a few light items – food, wallet, keys, tickets, passport – but have a severe effect on the handling of the bike if they are heavily loaded.

Fun-rides

Every summer weekend it seems, there's a charity fun-ride going on somewhere. They vary, from a dozen people on a local 'ride for the village hall' to 27,000 people riding from London to Brighton in aid of the British Heart Foundation. If you want to get fit and ride for a good cause then check out what's going on locally (local press, libraries, local cycle clubs, even local bike shops) or alternatively consider one of the big national mass rides. The London to Brighton ride in June is the biggest, but there are others 'biggies' around the country organised throughout the summer. The best place to start to find out about these is to give Bike Events a ring on **0225 480130** and ask for their catalogue.

(A word of warning. If you're thinking of doing the London to Brighton, then book early. A group of people at Haynes wanted to do it, but they were turned away because they sent their booking forms back late and the ride was already full.)

Touring

Every summer, tens of thousands of cyclists pack their essentials into panniers and take off bike touring. Touring is a unique way to get deep into the countryside, whether it's the hills of the Lakes or the mountains of the Alps; on a bike you are part of the countryside, not an intrusion in a steel box, and you can savour the way the landscape unfolds at a human rather than a mechanical pace.

The essentials of touring are a bike – road or mountain – with low gears and capacity to carry luggage. Hardcore tourists camp, so they can go anywhere, less tough types stay in B&Bs so they don't have to carry as much, or travel in organised tours where a van carries the

load and you get to enjoy unladen cycling and relax in good hotels in the evening; this American-invented form of travel is called credit card touring. Nick Crane's Cycling in Europe is probably the best combination of concise but comprehensive advice on touring and a guide to riding most of Europe. Some of his information on countries like Yugoslavia is now sadly out of date, however.

Racing

There are two kinds of road racing widely carried out in the UK. The best known is mass-start racing, where a group of riders start together and the

first to cross the finish line wins. This form of racing is highly tactical and requires very high fitness combined with experience to do well. Since a cyclist in a group expends less energy than a solo rider, there is no point in a rider trying to get away from the others immediately. A racer must bide his time and wait for a moment when he will be able to escape and stay away without being reeled in by the bunch. Sometimes a small group of riders will get away, and then sprint it out in the final few hundred metres; other times the whole bunch will finish together in a 'bunch sprint', in which the riders who are best at going very fast for short periods of time will contest the win.

When a mass start race plays out over a number of days it is referred to as a stage race. The most famous of these, the Tour de France, is the largest annual sporting event in the world, and arguably one of the toughest sporting events in existence.

Time trialling is the most popular form of bike racing in the UK. This solitary discipline consists of racing on your own, against the clock along courses of standard distances of 10, 25, 50 and 100 miles, plus the endurance events of 12 and 24 hour time trials. Riders go off at one minute intervals, so if you have ever wondered what's going on when you've seen a succession of solo riders hammering along early on a Sunday morning, wearing numbers, now you know.

Off the road

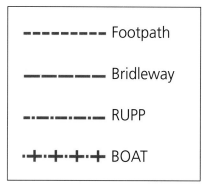

Contents

Be safe and sensible. Take care!

Take care when passing other users, but especially when approaching from behind. Take double care if approaching from behind on a descent. Take triple care if approaching a horse.

Mountain biking is a unique experience. It combines the athletic challenge of cycling with the countryside experience of hill-walking and the skill and excitement of downhill skiing, and this, combined with the sheer pleasure of being away from the urban snarl, is why it is now the largest branch of cycling.

Where to ride?

Byways and bridleways

You can ride a mountain bike on any track where there is a right of way for bicycles, or anywhere that you have the landowner's permission to ride. There are four types of off road right of way in England and Wales:

▶ **Footpath**, a right of way on foot only

▶ **Bridleway**, a right of way for walkers, horse riders and cyclists

▶ **Road Used as Public Path** (RUPP), for walkers, horse riders and cyclists

▶ **Byway Open to all Traffic** (BOAT) open to all the above, plus motorized vehicles too.

On a Ordnance Survey map (pink Landranger series), the above types of trails are marked as such:

---------- Footpath

————— Bridleway

·—·—·—·— RUPP

·+·+·+·+ BOAT

Strictly speaking, it is not against the law to ride a bike on a footpath. However, although it is not a criminal offence, you are trespassing and the landowner could bring a suit for civil trespass if he so desired. To my knowledge, this has never happened in the UK (yet).

On the other types of trails, you have a right to ride a bike, but you must give way to other trail users such as horses and walkers.

Unfortunately these legal designations often have no correlation with the standard of the tracks on the ground. While there are, in theory, minimum widths these trails have to be maintained, this is usually not the case, and there are footpaths with six feet wide gravel surfaces and bridleways that are six inch wide sheep trails. The existence of a bridleway on a map is no indication that there will be a rideable trail at that location when you get there. In some parts of the country where the tracks have not been used for decades, there may not be a trail at all.

How to find places to ride

How, then, do you find places to ride? The adventurous way is to learn to read a map and go find the trails. This needs plenty of time, since you can end up trying to navigate almost non-existent trails and doing quite a bit of walking. If you are new to map-reading and

countryside navigation, pick up Advanced Mountain Biking by Derek Purdy which has a complete guide to this subject for mountain bikes.

The alternative is to pick up a guide book and ride routes where someone else has done the spade work. The Ernest Press's range of guidebooks are excellent and cover the Lakes, Dales, parts of Wales, Northumberland and the Peak District. Other sources of route information include specialist magazines, mountain bike clubs and bike shops.

Basic mountain biking techniques

To a beginning mountain biker the antics of highly skilled riders are daunting. The best mountain bikers can leap their bikes over 3ft in the air, wheelie, bounce the bike on the front wheel, hop sideways and perform other unlikely antics. Fortunately, you don't need to be able to do any of this to simply enjoy riding a bike along a country bridleway or forest road. However, riders who are not used to riding a bike on loose, irregular surfaces can still benefit from a few basic pointers to get them started.

Riding position

The key to proper positioning on a mountain bike is to relax. Keep your wrists, elbows and upper body loose while maintaining a comfortable grip on the handlebar, not a 'death-grip'. A loose upper body will allow your arms to absorb trail impacts and let the bike find its own way along the trail. If, on the other hand, you ride with your arms and wrists locked out and your hands gripping the bars really hard you will quickly get tired and you will find that rather than going where you want it to, the bike will be jarred off line by every little bump.

Some riders like to lower their saddles slightly when they ride off road. For a beginner this is certainly a good idea, since it gives you the psychological cushion of being able to touch the ground when you need to. Don't forget, though that this low position is inefficient; raise the seat back up to its right place as soon as you are confident off road.

Your weight should be equally divided between your arms, legs and bum, and you should be ready to move your weight around the bike at any time. Don't sit with all your weight firmly planted on the saddle; the bike needs to be able to move around under you to handle uneven surfaces. In fact, the best way to tackle, say, rocky and root-infested woodland tracks is to stand on the pedals and let the bike move around under you where it likes, absorbing the movement with your legs and arms.

Looking ahead

Look up and ahead, rather than at the ground right in front of your tyres. It's too late to do anything about a small rock six inches away; you are just going to have to bend your arms and deal with it. What you should be thinking about is steering round the much larger rock fifteen feet down the trail, coping with the tree root after that, then preparing for the corner that follows. You should be constantly scanning the trail ahead; with time, your reactions to obstacles will become automatic.

Turning

Turning on a mountain bike is actually pretty straightforward, and cycling writers make it seem much more complicated than it is by describing advanced techniques that relative beginners don't have the balance and trained reactions to attempt. You steer a mountain bike by a combination of leaning and turning the handlebars, and the amount of each you do depends on your speed, the surface you are on and bike-related factors, like how good your tyres are. Find out how your bike behaves by weaving and slaloming on a loose-surfaced dirt road, gradually increasing your speed, then tackle something more challenging.

'Spin' (pedalling rate) and Shifting (changing gear)

The keys to using all those gears on a mountain bike are shift early and shift lots. You are aiming to keep up an even medium paced 'spin' at around 80-90 rpm. Less is tiring and more is impractical. The fluid, high-speed spin beloved of roadies is impossible on a mountain bike because it can only be maintained for long periods from the saddle; off the seat a 120rpm 'spin' quickly becomes choppy and uncomfortable.

The sheer number of gears on a mountain bike confuses many people, but it's simpler if you think of it as three ranges which overlap somewhat. You will spend most of your time in the middle ring, which provides a range of gears suitable for flat ground and descending and ascending fairly gentle slopes. When you need a lower gear than is available on the middle ring, to get up a steeper slope, then you switch to the small, inner ring, and for descending you use the bigger gears available on the big ring. Strong riders also spend a lot of time in the big ring when riding on the road.

Climbing

The most important part of climbing on a mountain bike is to be in the right gear earlier rather than later. Shift down into the gear you think you will need before you get to a slope, not after you have begun to climb it, and err on the side of selecting a gear that feels too easy. If you are still fresh halfway up an ascent you can always change up. Don't try and storm up a climb in a medium gear unless you are certain that it is short enough that you can do it; modern gear systems are good, but most will still mutiny if you ask them to shift at almost zero miles per hour as you desperately mash the pedals trying to keep going.

Weight distribution is crucial for climbing steep slopes. You can get up gentle climbs in your normal riding position, but as the hill becomes steeper you should gently slide forward on the saddle, and crouch your body down in towards the handlebars. These movements bring your weight forward to keep the front wheel down and stop the bike wheelying. What you are aiming for, and it will only come with practice, is a delicate balance between keeping the front wheel down and keeping enough weight on the rear wheel to maintain traction.
Unless the surface is very good, don't stand up to climb. This is fine on forest roads, but if the trail is a typical British woodland or moorland track the ground will be too loose or slippery (or both) to allow the rear tyre to hook up if you take your weight off it. Another problem is that your pedalling power output is less smooth when you are standing than when you are sitting and you are more likely to break traction by surging at the pedals. Once you lose traction you are unlikely to regain it until you get very good at balancing an almost stationary bike.

Descending

The biggest thrill in mountain biking is flying down an open hill-side with the wind in your ears and the bike soaking up the trail underneath you. You should be careful not to go so fast that you can't stop for an unexpected sheep or walker round a blind bend, and you should be doubly considerate of any other people you meet while descending. You may know that you're in control, but a walker probably doesn't and you don't have the right to spoil their day just for an adrenaline rush.

Weight distribution and calm hands on the brakes are the keys to descending. Your weight should be down and back, so that you can use the front brake without going over the bars. Use both brakes to control your speed; the front brake actually gives you the possibility of twice the deceleration of the rear, but there is the risk that enthusiastic front braking will put you on your face. Nevertheless, for the best control of speed, and for finesse descending of very steep stuff, you need to learn how to use the front brake. Practise going down a fairly steep slope at very low speed, using first one brake then the other to control your speed.

Avoid locking the wheels. A locked front wheel is a major disaster, but a locked, sliding rear wheel is also a problem, since it causes loss of control and trail erosion. You should aim to brake to the limits of wheel traction, not beyond.

Turning while descending involves two separate skills:

Low speed/steep slope turning

At very low speed on steep slopes you have to learn to point the handlebars where you want the bike to go and muscle it round rocks and over tree roots and the like. This can require quite a bit of upper-body work and explains why mountain bikers usually have a bit more arm and chest muscle than road cyclists. Keep your weight back and control the bike with the brakes, trickling it down the slope and actively steering it down the trail.

High speed cornering

At high speed you have to learn to lean, and to trust your tyres. The most likely places that you will get up to significant speeds are on forestry roads – 35 mph is not difficult, and I have heard claims of 50 mph. These roads are good places to practise getting used to a bike at speed, since they usually have consistent surfaces and are nice and wide. The most important thing about high-speed cornering is to approach any corner wide, aim at the 'apex' (the inside

of the curve), then come out again. This straightens out the corner as much as possible and either increases your speed or reduces the amount of leaning you have to do, depending on your nerve.

Brake to a speed you are happy to turn at before you get to the corner; braking in the curve will upset the bike's handling and distract you from the important business of getting round the corner in one piece. As you approach the corner, lift your inside foot, and begin both to lean and steer the bike towards the apex of the turn. Look well ahead all the time; you should be thinking about going through and out of the corner, not about what is in it.

Carrying your bike

Sooner or later you're going to find that you'll have to carry your bike; either

over a stile or similar obstacle, or maybe for longer distances (perhaps if the trail gets too steep to ride). The correct way to carry your bike over your shoulder – as shown here.

Off road equipment

Mountain biking is different enough from road cycling that it is evolving its own unique set of equipment, much of it adapted from traditional cycling, hill-walking and mountaineering designs. *(See chapter 2 for more on the bikes themselves.)*

The off-road essentials: well-ventilated, full-fitting helmet, cycling gloves and hard wearing footwear.

Helmets

The current popularity of helmets is largely down to mountain biking. **Off road, a helmet is an unquestionable essential**, since mountain biking involves more minor tumbles than any other branch of cycling, and there are plenty of potentially dangerous rocks around in the off road environment. Helmets also provide protection against bashing your head on low branches and the like, a minor but useful function.

A helmet for mountain biking needs to be well-ventilated and to wrap around as much of the head as possible.

The minimalist helmets designed for road racing are not really suitable; more protection is needed at the temples and back of the head than these designs provide. It's impossible to recommend models, since manufacturers change their ranges frequently, but Bell, Giro, Specialized and Centurion are all good brands.

(For more general advice about buying and fitting a helmet, refer to Chapter 3.)

Hands and feet

Hand protection is essential and some riders go in for full-finger gloves designed for BMX or motocross. These are very tough, but a bit warm; for most riding, conventional short finger cycling gloves are best.

Mountain bike footwear needs to do double duty. You have to be able to both ride and walk in it, since any mountain bike ride inevitably involves some walking. The range of footwear people use for mountain biking runs from lightweight walking boots to specialist MTB shoes which clip into special pedals and look like road racing shoes that have grown knobbly soles.

Clothing – in summer

In the very height of summer a light jersey and a pair of cycling shorts are all you need. However, the weather on the British hills can change so quickly that it's worth carrying a compact windproof and waterproof jacket and using a lightweight thermal shirt as your upper body garment so that you can add the jacket over it when it gets cold or wet. This combination will keep you warm and dry long enough to get off the hill to shelter.

Clothing – out of summer

From autumn to spring you need to add layers according to the weather, and you run into the fundamental problem of mountain bike clothing: you produce huge amounts of sweat when climbing hills, which then evaporates and makes

you feel cold as you descend, but you need to protect yourself from wet and wind chill.

There is no easy answer to this. None of the current crop of breathable fabrics is adequate to transmit the amount of sweat a cyclist, working hard, produces. The nearest thing to a solution is to wear layers which can be removed and put on according to the conditions and ventilated as much as possible when climbing. A thermal undershirt, a layer or two of light fleece and a *Gore-Tex* or *Sympatex* jacket with long underarm zips is probably the best set-up, combined with warm tights. Experimentation is the only sure way to find out what is right for you.

One alternative system worth looking at is Buffalo's *'Pertex and pile'* clothing. Buffalo's cycling jacket stands conventional wisdom on its head by combining an inner layer of fibre pile with an outer shell of *Pertex*, an unproofed nylon derivative. Because the *Pertex* has a very fine, dense weave water does not easily get through it, and the fibre pile is warm even if it gets wet.

In rain, a Buffalo jacket keeps you warm and comfortable, even if not bone dry. When the rain stops your body heat gradually dries the pile, which doesn't absorb very much water in the first place. It sounds odd, but it works. The only problem is that even the extensively-ventilated cycling jacket – it has full-length zips under each arm and a long neck zip – is a little too warm unless the weather is very cold.

Back-up kit

If things go wrong in the wilds you have to be able to deal with them. See Chapter 23 on 'Roadside repairs' for more on this, but it's worth mentioning here that the absolute minimum you should carry off road is a pump, spare tube, tyre levers if necessary and a good multi-tool like a Cool Tool. I also carry a Gerber hiking multi-tool which has handy things like knives, pliers and scissors that Cool Tool lacks. The last essential is some change and the phone number of someone who will come and bail you out if things go utterly wrong.

The essential back-up kit

Mountain bike racing

Mountain bike racing is very popular because it is much more accessible than any other form of bike racing, and at the entry level you don't need to be super-fit to join in and have a good time, all you need is a bike, helmet and the entry fee. A typical Fun class mountain bike race will consist of two laps of a four or five mile course, and it will be the same course on which the Expert riders will do 20 or 25 miles later in the day. You can find out where races are being held from the racing listings in Mountain Biking UK, or from asking in your local shops. You're better off starting with a smaller, local race than throwing yourself in the deep end with a national points series event.

If all you're interested in is speed, check out downhill racing. This is the original form of mountain bike racing and has undergone a huge surge in popularity in the last few years. The format is simple; riders race down a course on their own, and the fastest time wins. It's fast, exciting and huge fun. The best downhillers are very fit, highly skilled bike riders with superb reflexes, but because all you have to do is point your bike downhill and hang on, it's a sport anyone can have a go at.

Getting splattered like this is all part of the fun

Security

Chapter 7 SECURITY

Contents

Unfortunately bike theft is a fact of life. Bikes are easily stolen, easily re-sold and very difficult to identify. The chances of a stolen bike being recovered and returned to its owner are slim; even if you do everything right, record the frame number and have your postcode stamped on the frame, the police have first to find your bike, and thieves routinely remove identifying numbers by filing them off, and swap components round so that the bike is harder to identify. The answer, quite simply, is not to let your bike get stolen in the first place, and to take out insurance so you can afford to replace it if it does.

Locks

The best locks are heavy and expensive, but, used properly, they work. The Trelock Titan and Kryptonite 2000 have both been proven in independent tests to

be strong enough to stop even a fairly determined thief. Every other lock can be breached by one means or another.

At the bottom of the security heap are cheap chains and cables with flimsy key or combination locks. These are toys, easily opened or cut with the tools your average bike thief routinely carries around and should be avoided.

While cheap cylinder-key 'shackle' or 'U-locks' afford some protection, they can still be opened by a number of brute force methods, and I have opened one very cheap Taiwanese cylinder-key lock by pushing the tumblers in with a pen top. Not recommended. These locks can be opened in a matter of seconds with the right techniques, and should not be relied on for protecting your bike if it will be out of your sight.

There are some very good heavy chain locks and armoured cable locks on the market, intended for motorbikes. These tend to be even heavier and more expensive than top-quality shackle locks but the best ones work well, and they have the flexibility of being able to fit round large, awkward objects like lamp posts.

So the bottom line of all of this is; if you want a decent lock, you'll probably have to pay for it. A cheap alternative is a poor alternative. A good thief will be well versed on his lock manufacturers and will know the ones he can get into and the ones that will give him more hassle (so he'll probably pass by). Some lock manufacturers offer some sort of guarantee if your bike is stolen whilst

the lock was being used correctly. However there are always conditions – make sure you read the small print.

> The most important thing about having a lock is to make sure you use it – **every time you leave your bike.**

Leaving your bike

Using a lock properly

You can significantly reduce the chance of your bike being stolen by using your lock properly. Basically, this means

filling the lock with as many parts of your bike as possible so that a thief can't get tools inside it to attack it, and making the lock mechanism itself as hard to get at as possible so that it cannot be attacked directly.

The best place to lock your bike is in the middle of a set of railings, in a busy public place. The railings provide a barrier to stop the thief getting at the far side of your lock, which is where the lock mechanism should be, and a busy street may provide an amount of deterrence; thieves prefer to work where they are less likely to be seen.

Correct way to lock your bike

Take off the front wheel if it has a quick release and put it in your lock then lock the bike to the railings so that the lock mechanism is on the far side of the railings and therefore awkward to get at.

(This is useless if you can get round the other side of the railings easily; choose a place where there is a big drop to a basement or something like that). Two of the most common methods of opening shackle locks rely on direct access to the lock mechanism itself; deny a thief this access and he will likely go elsewhere.

Would YOU ask what he's doing?

I have just advised you to leave your bike in plain view so that a thief will be discouraged from having a go at the lock by the public nature of the surroundings. This sounds fine in theory and is certainly preferable to leaving your bike out of sight in a dark alley, but unfortunately it cannot always be relied upon for two reasons. The first is that some of the less obvious lock attack techniques just look to a passer-by as if the thief is fiddling with his keys trying to open the lock; the subtler lock breaching methods are also unnoticeable.

The second problem is that people don't care, or don't want to get involved, or generally feel inhibited to go up and confront someone fiddling with the lock on a bike. Many years ago a bike magazine did the following test. A bike was locked to a railing in a busy high street and a 'thief' in a long coat opened the lock with a bolt cropper. The 'thief' got increasingly blatant about what he was doing, but it was only when he practically danced down the street like a silent movie bad guy, brandishing the

bolt cropper, then cut the lock, that anyone said 'Oi, what do you think you're doing?' The moral is that you can't rely on a prominent parking place to protect your bike.

For the same reason I have absolutely no faith in the various alarms sold for bikes, and I don't believe that they are even useful if you expect to stay within earshot of a parked bike. Experienced bike thieves are fast, and the few seconds it will take one to cut your lock may be less than the time it takes you to get to the bike. Why take the risk? In addition, many of the products in this category are so flimsy as to be bad jokes. One alarm I have tested made a suitable ear-piercing screech, but took less than a second to twist off its flimsy plastic mounting. I have yet to see an alarm that would stand a well-aimed hammer blow.

Home security

A very high percentage of bikes are stolen from garages and sheds, and the majority are protected only by the outbuilding's door lock. If this is how your bike is stored, go and look at your outbuilding and ask yourself how long it would take you to get past the door, equipped with a few basic tools, like a crowbar, and whether you'd make enough noise in the process to wake yourself up at 4am. If the answers are 'not long' and 'no', store your bike somewhere else, or fit an alarm to the outbuilding and remember that it's only useful when you're there.

It may be impractical for many people, but the safest place to store your bike is in the house somewhere, which also has the advantage that it is almost certainly covered by your house contents policy when it's in the building.

Insurance

It is becoming increasingly difficult to get stand-alone insurance for bikes. One of the best, but unfortunately most expensive, options is the insurance

provided by the Cyclists' Touring Club (0483 417217). However, the CTC's policy is new for old, and they have a reputation for settling claims quickly and fairly.

It currently seems that the best way to insure your bike is to add it to your house contents insurance. The exact details of the available policies change constantly, so it's worth shopping around and finding out exactly the circumstances under which the bike is covered, how much depreciation the company allows, whether the bike is only covered on the premises or whether it is also covered when you are using it, and so on.

One point relating to claiming on insurance policies if your bike does get stolen is that you can't rely on all firms to cough up if the bike was unlocked at the time. This certainly applies if the bike was stolen whilst left unattended in the street and may even apply if it was stolen from home. So even at home, make sure its locked.

Often brokers are not very clear on how policies apply to bikes. Be a little persistent and get them to phone the underwriter to check things like: is it possible to take out special 'all risks' cover that includes bikes, even though your bike is more expensive than the nominal limit; does the basic household cover include bikes on the premises without further additions; what are the exact security requirements, both in and out of the home; where in the world are you covered, and so on. Amusingly, a couple of my bikes, which are used as product test beds, are insured as 'workmen's tools'!

Don't panic

If all of this seems irretrievably gloomy, don't worry too much. Get a decent lock, insurance and think a little about how and where you leave your bike and you should have no problems. Bikes are stolen from people who are careless about security.

Bike speak

Contents

A Jargon-junkie's bean feast

(A bunch of stuff you just have to know if you want to get seriously into bikes)

As you get into bikes you will come across ideas and terminology with meanings that aren't readily obvious. Just what the heck is a gear ratio? What is double butted tubing and why is it used? (That one had me foxed for almost a year when I was getting into cycling, until I finally plucked up the courage to display my ignorance and ask someone!) This chapter is a sort of dump bin for all the weird stuff that infests bikes and bike speak.

Stuff about gears

Gear ratios

The gear ratio is simply a measurement of a sprocket/chainring gear combination. (Well gee – thanks – that explanation helped a lot!). If you find the gearing on your bike inadequate (perhaps because there are some serious hills around where you live and you need lower gears than you currently have in order to get up them), then knowing what gear ratios you currently have on your bike will help you greatly when you come to shop around for a suitable upgrade.

You'll commonly hear gear ratios expressed in one of two ways, either as "forty-six – twelve" or as "100in". The first refers to the actual sizes of the chainring and sprocket that go to make up the gear, while that latter is derived by an arcane formula that needs a little explaining.

Back in the prehistory of modern cycling the brave pioneers of bikes rode 'Ordinaries', the bikes that everyone except bike history pedants calls penny-farthings. Penny-farthings had a very large front wheel which was driven directly from the pedals, and a tiny rear wheel. The gear, which determined how far the rider would go for one pedal stroke, was set by the size of the wheel, and the rider straddled the largest wheel he could. A penny-farthing with a wheel 54in across was said to have a 54in gear.

When chain-driven safety bikes appeared a way of expressing gears was needed that was familiar to Ordinary riders. If you divide the number of teeth on the chainwheel by the number on the rear sprocket, and multiply by the size of the rear wheel in inches, you get a number in 'gear inches' that is the size of a penny-farthing wheel that gives the same gear. Yes, it's odd and archaic, but it's the way cyclists do things, at least in the English-speaking world. The sensible, modern Europeans have no truck with such antediluvian notions and use a system of 'developement', which is the distance in metres that the bike travels for one pedal revolution.

A typical mountain bike, with a 26in wheel, a top gear of 46 teeth on the big chainring and 12 teeth on the smallest rear sprocket, has a gear of 46 – 12 x 26 = 100in. Alternatively one can express that each pedal revolution propels the bike forward almost 8 metres.

To show the whole range of gears on a bike you will sometimes see a chart like this:

	12	14	16	18	21	24	28
24	X	45	39	35	30	26	22
36	78	67	59	52	45	39	33.5
46	100	85	75	66	57	50	X

– The highest (hardest to push) gear on this gearing set-up is 100in.
– The lowest (easiest to push) gear is 22in.
– The X's indicate gears that should not be used because they put the chain across the sprockets and chainwheels at a severe angle, increasing wear and reducing the efficiency of the transmission.

Gear capacity

Whereas gear ratios refer to the relative number of teeth on sprockets and chainrings, gear capacity refers to your mechs.

Different gear mechanisms are designed to cope with different sizes of sprockets and also with different amounts of loose chain produced by the shift between chainrings at the front of the transmission. For example a typical rear mech intended for a mountain bike will be designed to cope with a largest sprocket that has 30 teeth, and will have a 'total capacity' of 38 teeth. The meaning of the first figure is obvious, but the latter is a bit arcane. Total capacity is the sum of the change in chainring sizes and the change in sprocket sizes that the mech can handle. For example a gear set with 24/36/46 chainrings and a 12-28 sprocket cluster requires a rear mech with a total capacity of at least 38 teeth.

Front mech capacities are also expressed in teeth. A typical mountain bike front mech will have a capacity of 26 teeth, which is simply the difference between the biggest and smallest chainrings that can be used at the same time. Sometimes, because of the shapes of the cage plates, a front mech will also have a manufacturer's specification for the largest chainring it will handle, or for the minimum difference between the big and middle rings.

In practice these capacities are often very conservative. I have run tandem chainsets with 24/40/54 rings and had excellent shifting from mountain bike gear mechs with nominal capacities of 26 teeth, and I have seen plenty of low-capacity rear mechs used on wide-ratio mountain bike systems in an effort to save weight. In the latter case, getting the chain length right is crucial.

Layman's translation

Know about gear ratios if you are unhappy with the gearing on your bike (if you find riding tiring, if the bike can't cope with local hills, etc.) and you want to change. Compare the gear ratios you currently have to the ones you want to upgrade to.

Also, if you're considering playing around with chainrings and sprockets and changing your gear ratios and ranges, make sure you don't exceed your gear capacity or you could get shifting problems because your mech's can't handle the extended gear range.

Cadence

The objective of all those gears is to allow the rider to maintain a narrow range of pedalling rates, referred to by bike jargon-junkies as cadence. This is simply the speed in RPM at which you turn the cranks.

Unlike a car the human engine is only efficient across a fairly narrow range of revs; the optimum cadence for most people seems to be 80-100rpm. You can count your revs if you like – you can even get computers that will tell you it – but in short, if you feel that you are pedalling quite fast, then that is probably about right.

Rookie cyclists often make the mistake of pedalling a big gear very slowly; they think that they can't be doing anything unless it really feels like they are working. In fact a higher cadence is much more efficient and less tiring in the long run, because you are asking your muscles to repeatedly do a small amount of work, rather than to do a large amount of work fewer times.

At first a higher cadence feels unusual, but you soon get used to shifting gear so you can keep spinning at a comfortable pace.

Bike tubing

The tubing used for bikes is usually made from a steel or aluminium alloy, that is a mixture of the base metal with traces of other elements which increase its strength or improve other properties and so make it useful for making bike tubing.

Steel tubing is by far the most common. The most basic bikes have frames made from carbon-steel tubing, often referred to as 'high-tensile' steel. This material is actually a fairly low-strength steel, and so quite a bit of it is needed to make a bike frame that is adequately strong; frames from high-tensile steel tend to be heavy. Much better are steels with traces of alloying elements like chromium, molybdenum and manganese, the most common of which are the chromium-molybdenum steels, usually called chromoly because it's much easier to say. The additional elements in these steels make the metal much stronger, and so allow bike designers to use less of it to make a frame that is still strong. A good chromoly mountain bike frame can weigh as little as 2.1kg/4.6lbs, compared to 3.5kg/7.7lbs for a high-tensile frame.

The very best steels are heat-treated, a method of further increasing their strength that allows frames to dip under 1.8kg/4lbs. Heat-treated tubing is expensive and tricky to weld without weakening, and so is only found on very expensive bikes.

Aluminium tubing is characterised by its distinctive 'fat' appearance. Because aluminium is less strong and stiff than steel, more of it is needed to make a strong frame. However aluminium is also only about one-third as dense as steel, so much more of it can be used before weight starts to become a problem, and for engineering reasons the best way to use aluminium is in relatively large tubes which make for very stiff frames.

(For more on frame materials, see Chapter 21.)

Tyres and how they work

Tyres are one of the most important factors in determining how a bike rides and performs, and a change of tyres can transform a bike, turning a mountain bike into a road rocket, a tourer into a nippier road machine or a racer into a comfy commuter.

Tyre sizing

The most confusing aspect of tyres is size. Tyres are marked on their sidewalls with two sets of numbers which on a typical mountain bike tyre will say something like '26 x 1.95' and '47-559'. The first set of numbers is the tyre size

in the old Imperial system and indicates a tyre that is nominally 26in in diameter from tread to tread. The second set is the European Tyre and Rim Technical Organisation (ETRTO) designation (I am not making this up!) and indicates the width of the tyre in millimetres and the diameter of the rim which it fits, also in millimetres.

This second number is definitive. All rims with a 559mm diameter will take all tyres with this marking. The number is actually the nominal diameter of the tyre bead and of the part of the rim, the bead seat, where it sits when the tyre is inflated.

Road tyres
Tyre sizes
Road tyres are usually designated as 700c, a number which is a leftover from another, French, system of sizing tyres and doesn't actually mean anything at all any more. Originally there were lots of tyres in this system, 700a, 700b, 700c, 650a, 650b, 650c and so on. The number indicated the outside diameter of the tyre in millimetres and the letter designated a particular rim size which the tyre fitted. Modern 700c tyres are narrow road bike rubber and never measure 700mm in diameter, however.

The bead seat diameter of a 700c tyre is 622mm and they range in width from super-skinny 18mm tyres for time-trialling to fat 35mm rubber for commuting, touring and tandems. **The size of a road bike tyre makes a tremendous difference to its feel**, since

fatter tyres can be inflated less hard to give a softer ride. However, softer tyres require more effort to keep them rolling, so you have to decide where to compromise between comfort and efficiency.

Tyre pressures
Narrow road bike tyres (under 25mm) should be inflated at 100psi or more. As a rule of thumb, this can be dropped 5psi for every size above this, so a 28mm tyre can be run at 95 psi, a 32mm at 90 psi and so on. Unfortunately tyre manufacturers tend to mark their tyres a size larger than they actually are, so a 25mm tyre may actually be only 23mm wide. It's worth tinkering with tyre pressures to find out what works best for you.

Roadsters
3-speed Roadster bikes often use 26in tyres; these are a British 26in which is different from mountain bike's American 26in. MTB and roadster tyres are not interchangeable.

Treadless tyres
If you've ever wondered why road tyres have hardly any tread, and sometimes none at all, it's because they don't really need it, even in the wet. Car and motorbike tyres have tread to disperse water, because they are wide and run at low pressure. A treadless car tyre will aquaplane at relatively low speeds, resulting in hazardous loss of control. A high-pressure bike tyre on the other hand, behaves like one of the narrow tread portions of a car tyre and disperses water on its own, cutting through to the road underneath. It has been estimated that a 1in wide bike tyre at 100psi will aquaplane at about 250 mph!

MTB tyres
Tyre sizes
Mountain bike tyres typically have deep treads to grip soft surfaces, but beyond this the variety of sizes and tread patterns is bewildering. MTB tyres are

53

measured in inches, part of the American heritage of their genesis. Off road tyres range in size from skinny 1.5in lightweights intended for light riders racing on smooth forest tracks to 2.5 in monsters that provide lots of traction and cushioning. Manufacturers' markings are not very consistent with the actual tyre width, though – a Specialized 1.95in tyre and Ritchey 2.1in are both 47mm wide. Most riders plump for something around this size, unless they have particular needs.

Tread patterns
Tread patterns reflect the intended use. Shallow, close patterns are good for hard tracks but pack up in mud, while deep, open patterns grip well in mud but are less good on hard surfaces and very dodgy on tarmac. Good bike shops and other riders are an invaluable source of information on which tyres work well in which conditions.

Tyre pressure
MTB tyre pressure really depends on your weight and the surface conditions, but the most common mistake is to inflate tyres too hard, which results in a loss of traction and cushioning. For off road use, with tyres around 1.95in, start at about 35psi – 40psi and adjust the pressure after you've been riding for a while.

Clips, straps and cleats

Many people are wary of clips and straps, the simple but effective devices cyclists use to keep our feet in place on the pedals, but there's no need to be. With a little practice it is very easy to flip up the pedal and quickly get your foot into a clip, and you can get out again just as quickly as long as you don't pull the straps up super tight.

The big advantage of clips and straps is that they hold your feet in the right place on the pedals. You should push the pedals with the balls of your feet, but most people's natural tendency is to let their feet slip forward so they are pedalling with the arch, which is less efficient. You need to choose clips which are the right size for your feet to put them in the right place on the pedals. Small clips are for people with feet below about size 6, Medium for 7-9 and Large for 10 and above, though if you are on the borderline, or, say, mountain biking in big walking boots, you should try the two nearest sizes to see what's comfortable.

Riders who are very nervous of clips can start off with **half-clips**, which are simple toe-cups that help you position your feet but don't hold them at all.

Shoe and pedal systems

For sport, touring and most 'serious' recreational cycling, pedals with clips and straps have been replaced by pedal and shoe systems which attach the shoe directly to the pedal. The shoe has a special plate or **cleat** which clips into a spring-loaded mechanism in the pedal. The rider cannot pull up out of the pedal, but releases from the pedal by twisting sideways, and the system is both more secure and safer than clips and straps. Cleats used to be the sole reserve of the road racer, but new modern systems (Shimano SPD's) have the advantage that the cleats are recessed in the soles of the shoes, so you can walk quite comfortably in them. This makes them ideal for mountain biking, touring and commuting. (The old-style traditional road racing cleats protrude out and make you look and sound like a tap-dancer with bunions when you try to walk on them.)

MTBs on the road

To turn a mountain bike into a road bike, simply fit a set of narrow, lightly treaded or treadless road tyres, generically referred to as 'slicks', and pump them up hard. Some top MTB racers have even won road time trials on mountain bikes with such tyres, much to the consternation of the traditional road element.

And finally...
Double butted tubing is tubing which has thicker walls at both ends than in the middle. (And don't you just feel so much better for knowing that!).

Part Two

Caring for your bike

Pre-ride checks

Contents

Before you go out:
Safety critical pre-ride checks

Lots of books on bike maintenance tell you to perform a certain set of routine maintenance chores every few weeks, or months. This is in fact completely unrealistic. Most people wait for a problem to develop, then sort it out, and given how mechanically simple a bike is there is no reason why this system shouldn't work well.

However, you do need to know what you are looking for, so in the next couple of chapters we will deal with the routine checks that will allow you to spot developing problems before they become major ones. Check your bike over before and after a ride; before for potentially dangerous problems like worn-out brake blocks and damaged cables and afterwards for general wear and tear.

Brake checks

It's vital that your brakes work well. You should be able to stop quickly and to slow down or control your speed downhill. For this you need properly functioning brakes.

The simple test of a brake system is to squeeze the lever. The brake blocks should hit the rim after the lever has been squeezed between 1cm and 2cm from its rest position. Less is OK (though you may find braking with such a finely-adjusted set-up is tiring) but more means you need to adjust the cables or replace the brake blocks. *See Chapter 14 for information on adjusting your brakes.*

Brake test

✓ Squeeze the brake lever. It should move about this much before the blocks hit the rim.

✗ If the brake lever can be easily pulled this far then the brake system needs adjusting.
(See Chapter 14, 'Adjusting the brake'.)

Brake cables

Cables get damaged by neglect, so it's important to keep them clean and lubricated. Any frayed or rusty brake cable should be replaced immediately.

✓ This cable is fine; all the strands are twisted together as they should be and there are no signs of rust or other damage.

✗ Fraying usually occurs where the cable rubs against exposed metal, such as a badly cut outer. Any fraying in the loaded part of a cable (that is, between the lever and the cable clamps on the brake caliper) indicates a cable that should be replaced immediately. If the end of the cable beyond the clamp is tatty, this isn't unsafe but will make adjustments more difficult; the cable should be replaced the next time the opportunity arises.
(See Chapter 14, 'Replacing cables'.)

TIP!

If the reach to your brake levers is too large it may be possible to use a small adjusting screw on the clamp to move them nearer to the handlebar.

Brake blocks

Worn blocks can do irreparable and expensive damage to rims, as well as producing inferior or hopeless braking. **Check them frequently.**

> # TIP!
> *Replace standard brake blocks with harder-wearing varieties like Aztec and Kool-stop. These also give better braking in the wet.*

✔ This brake block is fine; there is plenty of pad material left above the water-dispersing grooves in the face of the block. Some blocks have indicator lines which show the limit to which they should be allowed to wear.

✘ A totally worn-out block. All the pad material is gone and this block is a fraction of a millimetre away from exposing the bare metal core, which will dig deep, damaging grooves in the rim. Urgent replacement is needed.
(See Chapter 14, `Replacing blocks'.)

Tyre checks

The importance of tyre condition depends on what sort of riding you do. Mountain bike racers are fanatical about exactly which tyres they use and how much pressure they have in them, and will always run new or almost new tyres that have not yet lost the edge to their tread. A round-town bike simply needs tyres which are properly inflated, with a full coverage of tread and no cuts or other damage.

Check your tyres are properly inflated

Road tyres will wear out more quickly if they are run under-inflated, and mountain bike tyres will perform best at their recommended pressure (this is marked on the sides of the tyres). A basic tyre pressure gauge, which costs about a tenner, or a track pump with built-in gauge, is indispensable for proper tyre care.

If you don't have a pressure gauge, check your tyre pressure by squeezing the tyre sides. You should be just able to dent a properly inflated road tyre and squeeze your thumb about a quarter of an inch into a mountain bike tyre.

Check for tyre damage

A completely worn out tyre will show its carcass through the tread, like this. A mountain bike tyre with the knobbles completely worn off is almost useless off road and should be replaced.

Tears or cuts in the tyre sidewall are usually a result of abrasion by the brake blocks. A sidewall cut will eventually cause a puncture as the tube bulges out of it. Replace the tyre and adjust the brake blocks.

TIP!
Knobbly mountain bike tyres run much faster on the road at higher pressures. Inflate your knobblies to 80 psi for commuting and road riding.

Wheel quick releases

In the last few years quick release wheels have ceased to be the sole preserve of expensive road racing bikes and become commonplace. At the same time an increasing number of legal cases have been brought against bike manufacturers by riders who claim that quick releases have spontaneously opened while they were riding, resulting in a nasty accident. Almost all of these cases have proven to be the result of incorrect use of the quick release lever mechanism. In fact, used properly, a quick release is a cam-action device which cannot come open on its own. If you have quick release wheels it is vital to learn to use them properly and to check that they are fully closed before riding.

✓ A properly closed quick release looks like this. The lever curves in towards the wheel and the word 'closed' is visible on the outside of the lever. As long as enough force was needed to close the lever to leave a mark in your hand the lever cannot now come open on its own.

✗ This quick release is open, as shown by the 'open' mark visible on the lever. Also the lever curves outwards. A lever that is this way round may appear to be holding the wheel in place because it has been used as a big wing–nut and screwed down, but it is possible for it to rattle open and release the wheel.

For more on correct usage of wheel quick releases see Chapter 13.

Other problems you might find when setting off

If last time you took your bike out, you did the after-ride cleaning, oiling and checks that is described in Chapter 10, then off you go and barring unforeseen occurrences, your bike should run safely and smoothly.

However, if last time you just threw your bike in the garage or shed after riding it, then don't blame us if now you've got problems. At the very least, check the chain for rust and oil it if necessary. Better still, turn to the next chapter and do the cleaning, oiling and checking now.

And when you come back from your ride, don't forget to clean, lube and check all over again.

After a ride

Contents

Use a brush-head that has a soap reservoir and a switch that can change between plain and soapy water (some even have built in sprays as well). They are relatively inexpensive and common in most car accessory shops.

When you come back: Clean, lube and check

A bike that is properly cleaned, and lubricated regularly will last longer, and the clean and lube procedure is an opportunity to look over the bike and keep an eye on its general mechanical condition. One of my friends always has immaculately clean bikes, and they are also always in perfect mechanical order. He rolls into the office the morning after a wet muddy ride on a bike that is completely devoid of even a speck of dirt in the chain, and he never has mechanical problems with his bikes.

Do I need to clean my bike EVERY time I ride?

If it's dirty, yes. You certainly ought to clean you bike every time you come back from riding off-road. If you only ride on the road, then you ought to clean your bike frequently, but to clean it every time you ride would be over-kill. Be sensible; if it's dirty, if it's been ridden through mud, if it's been ridden in the rain, then clean it. Besides, it's much more pleasurable to ride a clean and shiny bike than one that's covered in mud.

Leaving mud, grit, road spray and other assorted crud on your bike can cause the components to wear, rust and generally not work as well or last as long. The overall aim of cleaning should be to minimise the amount of time that dirt and water spends in contact with the parts of your bike. If you're riding during the winter then clean your bike more often. The salts and grits that they put down on the road can do some serious harm to your bearings if not cleaned off promptly.

You ought to lube (oil) your bike frequently, even if it's not dirty enough to warrant cleaning. If you're using WD40 (or suchlike) then you ought to oil your bike more frequently – perhaps once a week. It will take less than a minute to give all the oiling points of your bike a quick spurt of lube. The types of lubricant to use and the places where you ought to oil are detailed later in this chapter.

Cleaning your bike

Cleaning Procedure

I hate cleaning my bike, but it's a necessity, so I have developed a cleaning procedure which involves the minimum effort. Some people go in for cleaning bikes with buckets of soapy water, brushes, lots of clean cloths and four different types of lubricant. I go in for a hose, a couple of different hose attachments and lots of WD-40. After a muddy ride I can be inside getting myself clean in under 10 minutes.

Tip

Do not use a car pressure-wash to clean a bike. The seals on bike bearings are not good enough to keep out high-pressure spray. Water in the bearings is a certain way to destroy them. Don't spray water directly at the bearings, even with a standard hose. Instead, aim to wash bearing areas from an angle – from above for hubs and bottom brackets, from the side for the headset area. Don't use washing up liquid; it contains salt which can corrode your bike.

TOOLS Hose, brush/soap head, spray head.

TIME 10-15 mins.

MATERIALS WD40, car shampoo, degreaser (possibly).

1 Hose off the worst of the mud with the straight spray from the spray gun. This is best done as soon as you get back from a ride, while the mud is still wet. Dried-on mud is very difficult to shift. Keep the water well away from the bearings.

2 Switch to the brush head, and finish off the initial rinse with water through the brush. This gives you a chance to scrub at any lumps of mud that won't shift easily.

3 When you have got all the mud off, fill the soap reservoir in the brush head with car shampoo. Cover the bike thoroughly with soapy water, scrubbing gently to dislodge the remaining well-stuck dirt.

4 Switch to plain water through the brush and rinse off the soap. Repeat these last two steps as necessary to get the bike properly clean.

5 If any parts of the bike are very clogged up with ground-in dirt, spray them with degreaser and leave it for a few minutes to dislodge the grime, then rinse it off with plain water.

6 Let the water drip off, then spray any exposed metal or moving parts with WD40 to displace the water.

Lubricating your bike

Once you have cleaned your bike, you should now immediately proceed to lubricate it.

Lubricants to use

There are a wide variety of lubricants available for bikes, but for most people a combination of WD40 and a heavier oil for chains will do, as long as lubrication is done often. WD40 is fine as a light, clean lubricant, but tends to wash off easily in rain and so needs frequent re-application. However compared to specialist light lubricants it is very cheap. If you see yourself likely to need lots, then buy it in bulk - a 5 litre container and a refillable spray should set you back less than twenty quid, will last for ages and has lots of other uses.

The chain needs a heavier lubricant because it tends to get wet from wheel-spray and the high forces in the chain require a 'tougher' lubricant that WD40. A standard mineral-based medium weight oil (we've used a multi-purpose home oil) will do fine for most people. Mountain bikers might want to check out teflon lubricants like Superspray MTB, which tend to be less sticky and not get dirty.

Avoid vegetable-based lubricants like 3-in-1 which tend to dry out to leave a very unpleasant, sticky residue.

1 Lube the rear brake pivots.

2 Lube the rear mech jockey wheels.

3 Lube the rear mech pivot points.

4 Lube the front mech pivots.

5 Lube the chain (use WD40 first, then a heavier lubricant).

6 Lube the brake lever pivots.

7 Lube the front brake pivots.

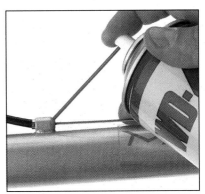

8 Lube all the cable ends at the stops.

Check your bike

While you are cleaning and lubing your bike, check the following areas of the bike for developing problems. It's unusual for much to go wrong spontaneously on a well-maintained bike, but it's worth giving these areas a regular once-over.

A "keep an eye on things" list

1 Cranks

Try and move the cranks from side to side on the axle. If they move at all, tighten them up. *(See Chapter 16.)*

2 Headset

Lift the front wheel off the floor and turn the handlebars to make sure the headset (steering bearing) turns freely and smoothly. Put the wheel back down, jam on the front brake and rock the bike backwards and forwards. A clicking or knocking may indicate a loose headset. If the headset is loose, then adjust it. *(See Chapter 19.)*

3 Pedals

Turn the pedals gently by hand to make sure that the bearings are smooth. If the pedal will move up and down with the crank stationary the bearings are loose and need adjustment. Check that the pedal axle is firmly screwed into the crank. *(See Chapter 16 for pedal adjustments.)*

4 Brakes (front and rear)

Check that the brakes hit the rims in the middle and the blocks are not worn. If the brakes are not right, then correct them. *(See Chapter 14).*

5 Chainrings

Make sure the chainring bolts are tight, either by trying to move the chainrings or by quickly snugging each bolt up with an Allen key.

6 Handlebars and stem

To check that the stem is tight in the frame, grab the front wheel between your knees and try to turn the bars. Also, try to rotate the bars in the stem clamp to make sure it is tight. If the handlebars or stem is loose, then tighten them. *(See Chapter 18.)*

7 Bottom Bracket

Drop the chain off the chainrings and turn the cranks on the bottom bracket. They should spin freely and easily. If you can feel any looseness or roughness in the bottom bracket, adjust it immediately. *(See Chapter 16)*

Also to make sure the bottom bracket isn't loose, grab both cranks and try to move them at 90 degrees to the plane of the bike. If both can be moved the bottom bracket bearing is loose. If just one moves or clicks then the crank is loose on the axle.
(In either case, refer to Chapter 16)

8 Saddle and seat post

Make sure the saddle is tight on the seat post by trying to move it around or up and down, and try to twist the whole assembly to check that the seat post is secure in the frame. If the saddle or seat post can be moved then tighten them. *(See Chapter 17)*

9 Wheels (front and rear)

Spin the wheels through the brakes and check that they are round and true. A small amount of wheel mis-adjustment is OK, but if they are more than a couple of millimetres out they will need truing. *(See Chapter 20.)*

10 Transmission (Gears)

Run through the gears to make sure the gear system is working properly. The gear system should move quickly from one gear to the next and it should not be possible to force the chain off the sprocket cluster.
If there are problems then the gears need attention. *(See Chapter 15.)*

11 Hubs (front and rear)

Drop out the wheels and turn the hub axles with your fingers. They should turn easily without looseness. If they are rough or loose adjust them straight away. *(See Chapter 20.)*

Part Three

Working on your bike

Working tips

Contents

Introduction to bike maintenance and repair

Fixing and maintaining bikes is easy. The way in which bike components work and fit together is generally clear, visible and relatively simple, and this makes working on a bike a much simpler prospect than, say, a car engine. You don't need that mysterious talent called mechanical aptitude, at least not beyond the basic feel for how things work that will develop naturally as a result of working on the bike. As long as you are organised, methodical and have the right tools you can do almost any of the routine jobs on a bike.

Common mechanical systems

Bikes are made up from a number of basic mechanical systems – bearings, cables, bolts and so on – so it's worth taking a little time to become familiar with the things that are common to these systems. For example, all the bearings on a bike are of the same basic design, but differ in their detail. If you understand how that basic design works, you will find all bike bearings easy to handle.

Threads

Almost everything on a bike is held together with threaded parts – simple nuts and bolts or one part that screws into another.

Threads come in two varieties: left and right-handed, depending on the direction in which the thread winds down the bolt. **A right-handed thread tightens clockwise and loosens anti-clockwise and a left-handed thread does the opposite.** A right-handed thread is so named because this is the natural screwing action for a right-handed person, to rotate the hand clockwise whilst pushing. The world being generally arranged for the benefit of the right-handed majority, almost all threads are right-handed.

Left-handed threads

Sometimes, however, a left-handed thread is necessary because a right-handed thread in that location would unscrew itself because of the forces on it. In bikes we find left-handed threads in the non-drive side (left) pedal and drive side (right) bottom bracket cup. The rotational forces on both of these parts are such that a right-handed thread would unscrew itself.

The non-drive side (left) pedal has a left hand thread. It is undone by turning clockwise (not anti-clockwise).

The full explanation of this phenomenon is complicated and really beyond the scope of this book. For more information, interrogate a bicycling engineer.

Thread care

Threads should always be lubricated with some sort of grease or with a locking compound. *(For more on threads; on lubricating and tightening and undoing when stuck, see later in this chapter.)*

Cables

Cables are used in bikes to pull things. A cable always consists of two parts, an inner cable and an outer cover. Both are important, because the inner cable could not pull if the outer did not, in effect, push back to give it something to pull against.

The inner cable is usually made up of a number of very fine wires either twisted or braided together. Since twisted cable has a smoother outer surface and therefore slides through outers more easily, it is generally better for our applications, though in some circumstances the higher flexibility of braided cable can offer advantages.

Outer cable is usually made up of a single piece of wire wound into a tight spiral. Very cheap outer cable uses round

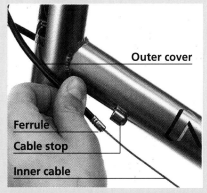

wire which unfortunately makes for a very compressible outer. This produces problems with loss of power in braking systems and unacceptable loss of precision in gear systems. Better outer uses flattened wire, wound edge-to-edge, which does not compress as much when the inner is pulled and is therefore better for brake systems and some gear systems. All outers should have caps over the ends – called ferrules – to protect the frame and provide a solid end to the outer.

Gear cable outer

Some high quality indexed gear systems use an outer which is different to that described above. This 'Shimano SP' outer has many longitudinal wire strands in a harder plastic sheath and is almost incompressible. This outer is necessary to give the high shifting precision necessary for indexed gear systems to work. *(For more on this see Chapter 15, section on 'Gear Cables'.)*

Cable care

Most cables have some sort of low-friction lining between the inner and outer. Despite this, they should be lubricated with a light oil to prevent corrosion. *(For more on lubricating cables and cutting inners and outers without leaving a mashed mess, see later in this chapter.)*

Bearings

Almost everything that moves on a bike does so on some sort of bearing. These may be simple metal-on-metal pivots like those in a gear mechanism, the plastic bushings in a jockey wheel or the full blown bearings with highly-

69

polished, hardened surfaces and hard steel balls found in hubs, headsets, pedals and bottom brackets.

All bearings have in common the fact that one part moves against another, either by sliding or rolling. Sliding bearings are less efficient but are good enough for lightly-loaded applications like pivots and jockey wheels.

Bearing care

Bearings should be kept clean and well-lubricated, since they rely on a layer of lubricant between the sliding surfaces to keep them working. Without it they will corrode and seize.

Cup and cone bearings

Rolling bearings use a round body between two surfaces to reduce friction and ease movement. In a bike a typical bearing uses steel balls between two curved surfaces. Because of their shapes these parts are usually called a cup and a cone, hence the name 'cup and cone' bearings. On a bike, cup and cone

Cone
Cup
Bearing balls

bearings are found in the bottom bracket (shown below), the hubs, the headset and the pedals.

Cup and cone bearings are used because they are very tolerant of bad alignment; a cup and cone bearing will still work if the axle it turns on is bent. Since bike parts are not usually manufactured to the high degree of precision common in, say, aerospace engineering, this is a sensible design, especially when most bike bearings rely

on threaded parts for their adjustment and alignment. It is virtually impossible to cut a thread accurately enough to provide a basis for the alignment of most other bearings.

Cup and cone bearings have the further advantage of being easily serviced, lubricated and replaced with simple tools. **Any bearing should be adjusted so that it turns easily but is not loose;** we'll see how to adjust each particular bearing when we get to it, since the fine details of each are slightly different.

Clamps

The front mech clamp, here being loosened so that the mech can be positioned.

In many parts of a bike one thing is clamped round, or into, another. Examples include the handlebar and stem, frame and seat post, front derailleur and frame and so on. Unless the part being clamped is a cable which can safely be crushed it is essential for clamped parts to be a good fit, usually to 0.1mm accuracy. If clamped parts do not fit properly one or both of them will be damaged.

In practise this means getting correctly sized replacement parts. If you have a seat post which is 26.4mm diameter, for example, do not try to fit a 26.2mm or 26.6mm post in its place. The frame clamp will probably not close properly on the smaller post and may be damaged by the attempt and the larger post will either not fit at all, or will fit only with extreme difficulty and will be damaged in the process.

General maintenance advice

Metal-on-metal surfaces

In many parts of the bike two bare metal surfaces touch. As well as threads, this occurs in bearings, the chain, the seat post and stem in the frame, the crank on the bottom bracket and so on. **Wherever bare metal surfaces touch it is essential that some sort of lubricant is used, both to ease assembly and to prevent corrosion and allow later disassembly.** Appropriate lubricants are recommended in the later sections for each particular job; the essential minimum is good waterproof grease.

Always grease threads on re-assembly, as shown here with pedal threads.

Preventing corrosion

The biggest enemy of the bike mechanic is corrosion. It is extremely unusual for any bike part to simply wear out; rather what happens is that very small areas of the bearing or pivot become corroded, then the corroded areas break off and this eventually produces damage or slop in the part. It is therefore vital to take as many precautions as possible to prevent parts from corroding.

In practice this means three things: preventing water from getting to corrodible parts; displacing it when it does; and minimising the effects of water contamination. These aims can be achieved by using waterproof lubricants, water displacers like WD40 and greases which absorb water when its presence can't be prevented.

We'll deal with the issues of greasing and lubrication in much more detail for each individual part. For the time being it is worth keeping in mind that one of the main things you are trying to do in all bike maintenance and preparation is to keep water away from exposed metal.

Corrosion of metal-on-metal parts

Keeping water out is especially important wherever you have two bare metal surfaces touching, and if the two are different (steel and aluminium for example) then generous lubrication is an absolute necessity. In combination with water, especially salt water, two different

Grease your seat post (and handlebar stem) to ensure you don't find it seized next time you want to adjust it.

metals can produce a chemical effect exactly like that in a battery. This results in rapid corrosion of whichever of the metals is the more chemically active. If you have an aluminium part in contact with steel, the aluminium will corrode to

produce aluminium oxide, the aluminium equivalent of rust. Aluminium oxide is a lot more bulky than the aluminium it replaces and if you have, say, an aluminium seat post in a steel frame the corroded post will seize in the frame and require extreme measures to get it out.

Starting threads

A crossed or stripped thread could ruin your bike, especially if you damage a thread in the frame. Hence, when you screw a bolt into a thread it is vital to have the two parts correctly aligned. It is quite easy to damage large diameter fine pitch threads by forcing together two threads which are not properly aligned.

If you cannot tell by eye whether a part is set to go in straight, try fitting the beginning of the threads together, then turning the internal part the wrong way (usually anti-clockwise) and feeling for the tell-tale click which indicates that the start of the thread has just passed its equivalent. Then screw the parts together. The first few turns of any threaded part should require no more than finger force to assemble them, as long as they are clean, greased and free from corrosion. If this is not the case, check that you are not crossing the threads.

Don't use tools to force threads together unless you are absolutely certain that they are properly aligned and are just simply tight.

Don't over-tighten

Bike parts generally have fine, often quite fragile threads. A mechanic equipped with lots of strength and enthusiasm and a set of big spanners can quite rapidly do a great deal of damage to a bike. When you tighten any bike bolt, it should basically be no tighter than is necessary to hold the part in place. For parts like seat posts, handlebars and so on, this is a simple criterion; tighten it up until you cannot move the part by hand. For larger parts like pedals, bottom bracket lockrings, saddle clamp bolts and so on, tighten them hard with standard tools. This means, for example, using most of your strength with a standard (10cm long) Allen key to tighten a saddle clamp bolt, and being a little gentler if you have long Allen keys.

If in doubt, under-tighten and test the part in a safe situation. If it moves in use, tighten it harder. Use this technique to teach yourself the appropriate tightening for the various parts of a bike, rather than risking over-tightening and stripping threads.

Basic solutions to basic problems

It's stuck, I can't undo it

There are a few problems which crop up again and again, especially on neglected bikes. Here are a few general rules for dealing with them.

Undoing parts that seem as if they just won't come off is possibly the most common and certainly most frustrating problem that you will come across. This problem might arise because the part is corroded, because the nut is chewed up and 'rounded', or simply because it is put on very tight – perhaps because it was last tightened by a gorilla with a six-foot spanner. There are a few tricks you can use to get it undone again. Try them in the order shown; subtle methods first, then more violent ones. Never be too violent. Beware that some of these later methods won't do the nut, bolt or part much good and it might need replacing.

1 Check you're doing it right

First of all, make sure you're trying to turn the fastening the right way. Apart from the left-hand threads mentioned earlier in this chapter, all the nuts and bolts you're likely to come across undo by turning anti-clockwise. **Also make sure that the tool you're using is a good fit.** Using ordinary pliers to undo nuts and bolts, except in emergency situations, is not recommended.

2 'Dowse' in WD40 (or suchlike)

If a part has frozen into place as a result of corrosion, it may be possible to remove it or get it moving again with plenty of lubrication and some patience. **Always, the first thing to do is to spray plenty of WD40, GT85 or Plusgas at the affected area, and leave it to creep in.** This approach needs time to work and therefore patience on your part. Go make yourself a coffee (or something) whilst waiting for the lube to do its job.

3 Get some leverage

Assuming that the tool fits the nut or bolt snugly, it may be possible to apply more leverage by using a piece of pipe. Be careful not to shear off the fastening by abusing this advantage, nor to take the skin off your knuckles if the pipe or spanner slips. Extra leverage can also be obtained by using the appropriate socket spanner (found in most DIY motorists' tool kits) and an extension bar, but

again, be careful not to snap anything off. This sort of tool is designed for working on car parts – it has no way of knowing that bicycle parts are mostly a lot more delicate.

4 Extra tips for undoing a 'chewed up' nut

If the nut or bolt is so badly chewed up that no spanner in creation will get a good grip on it, the next method of attack is to use self-locking pliers (Mole, Vise-grip or similar). Clamp the pliers as firmly as possible onto the fastening and unscrew it. Each failed attempt is liable to take another corner or two off the nut, so take the time to get a good grip before starting to unscrew. **However, using such pliers is not an alternative to having a correctly fitting spanner.**

5 Extra tips for Allen bolts

Use an Allen key extension tube to get extra leverage on Allen bolts.

Allen bolts which won't come undone are particularly frustrating. A good quality set of Allen keys is invaluable, along with a short section of pipe for the judicious application of extra force. However, if someone has already rounded off the inside of the screw head by unsuccessful attempts with a badly-fitting key, you are in fairly deep trouble.

6 When all else fails

When all else fails take your bike down to your local bike shop. No doubt, the bike mechanic there will have seen your particular 'stuck nut' countless times before on countless other bikes. He will have the right tools and probably his own specially perfected way of effectively solving the problem.

The key to the 'it's stuck' problem is to be patient, use the right tools and recognise the limitations that one has with a normal set of home/bicycle tools. It's not worth losing your temper over and it's certainly not worth damaging the bike through ill-guided use of excessive force. Swallow your pride, take it to the bike shop if you have to.

Problems with cables

Sticky cables

Corroded cables show up as slow gear shifting or brakes that require significant force just to get the pads to hit the rim. Again, plenty of light lubricant is the answer; sometimes it is useful to dismantle the entire cable and fill the outer with light lube as shown here.

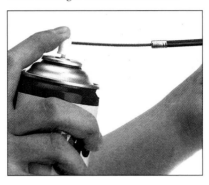

Cutting inner cables

It is essential to use proper cable cutters when cutting gear and brake cables; the so-called cutting edge in combination pliers will usually just produce a mashed, useless mess that cannot be threaded through a cable outer. Without a cleanly cut cable end, you will find any task involving replacing a cable extremely difficult, if not impossible. *(For more on the right cable cutting tools, see Chapter 12.)*

Cable end caps

Prevent cables fraying in the first place. **Always fit a cable end cap.** These cost about 10p and are just pinched on with pliers. If your bike doesn't have them on, go to your bike shop, buy some and fit them on now.

Dealing with frayed inner cable ends

Dealing with frayed inner cable ends. Even with cable cutters it is possible to for the wires of the cable to become spread.

If after cutting a cable you have a slight fraying, do the following.

1 Carefully twist the strands back together with your fingers. Watch out, the strands may be sharp. And then...

2 ...fit a cable end cap.

Cutting normal cable outer

It is important to cut outers cleanly. Otherwise you will have difficulty in feeding inner cables through them. More importantly, rough outer edges will damage and fray the inners. On a brake cable, that is potentially very nasty.

1 To cut cable outer cleanly, bend the outer over the jaws of the cutter so that the cutter goes in between one of the spirals of the outer.

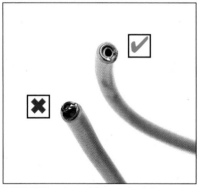

2 If like the cable on the left, you end up with a burr on the cut end, use the cutters to trim it off.

And finally, especially before you go out riding on a bike which you have just finished working on, make sure that you do all the pre-ride safety checks that are outlined in Chapter 9.

Stevenson's top tips

1 Always clean and grease metal on metal surfaces before reassembling them. (Especially threads, seat post and handlebar stem).
2 Always put a cable end cap on a bare cable end.
3 Always use clean hands when handling ball bearings. (Dirt in the bearings will cause them to wear).
4 If bare metal parts get wet, spray them with WD40 to displace the water and prevent corrosion.
5 If a part is stuck, spray it generously with WD40 (and then leave it to creep in) before trying any strong arm tactics.

Safety

It is possible to adjust bike components wrongly in ways that are potentially dangerous, and, through carelessness, to leave parts in a dangerous state by, for example, not tightening them properly during an adjustment. After any repair procedure you should check thoroughly the state of the parts that you have worked on. Make sure that things work as they should and that all bolts are fully tightened. If necessary go over each bolt and nut on a part and gently try to tighten it a little further. You may find a part that you have forgotten to tighten fully.

It is especially important to check that wheels are properly tight in the frame and that brakes work and do not have loose blocks or cable clamps. See the relevant sections for more on these checks and how to put right any problems you may encounter.

Tools

Contents

If you ever get the chance, take a look at the array of tools in the workshop of a really good bike shop, especially one which builds its own frames. Among the obvious spanners, screwdrivers and Allen keys you'll see lots of large, unusually-shaped bits of metal; presses, cutters, special spanners and pulling and driving tools, each with its own very specific job, some so specialized that they do one job on one component or model of bike. Looking at this bewildering array it's easy to get the idea that to work on bikes you need to invest a huge amount of money on specialist tools.

Fortunately this is not the case.

A carefully selected set of spanners, screwdrivers and Allen keys, plus a very few specialist tools, is enough to tackle almost all the jobs in this book. Bike shops need lots of special tools because they need to be able to cope with any job which comes in, be it ever so bizarre, and because time is money in a bike shop workshop they also need to be able to do jobs in the minimum time.

The requirements of a home workshop are simpler. You need only the tools that fit your bike, and you can afford to take the time to do things the longer but cheaper way if this is necessary.

Where to work

If possible, work in a dedicated workshop area such as a garage. Many people don't have the luxury of space and have to make do with a corner of the kitchen or somewhere like that. If this is the case with you, try to give yourself as much space as possible, and as an absolute minimum make sure you have a large, flat table top where you can work on small parts and keep tools at hand's reach. Since I hate working outside in the garage, I cover a little-used kitchen work surface with a thick layer of newspaper to protect it and clean up thoroughly afterwards.

Of course I do have the luxury of a dedicated workshop at the office!

Holding the Bike

The biggest problem with working on bikes is that of holding them steady while you do it. The two simplest and most effective methods are to hang the bike on ropes or hooks from the ceiling of the garage or to turn the bike upside down. The latter may require you to make a couple of wooden blocks with a slot for the handlebar to keep the controls off the floor. However both methods may become deficient if you need to exert any leverage. In these instances you will have to get someone to come and hold the bike.

The very best solution is some sort of workstand. Ideally you should use a purpose-built bike stand like the one above, but alternatively, a simple DIY workmate would just about do. If you are going to do most of your own work on your bike, or your household owns several bikes, a proper workstand will quickly pay for itself in time, reduced hassle and better work, but for the occasional mechanic the initial layout is probably a bit much. Nevertheless, buy one if you can afford one.

Tools and materials

What tools you buy will depend on the amount of different jobs you want to tackle. If all you are ever likely to do is fix punctures and adjust brakes and gears then you really don't need anything more than the ordinary spanners, screwdrivers and Allen keys found in the typical home tool kit. However, there are a few specialist tools, like a cable puller, which make these jobs much, much easier. There are also a few essential 'soft tools' like greases, lubricants and hand cleaner, that are must-haves for anyone working on a bike, and a few spares that it is worth keeping a very small stock of.

Basic tools

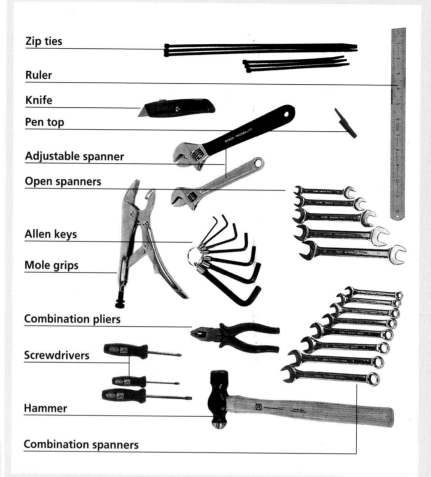

Zip ties
Ruler
Knife
Pen top
Adjustable spanner
Open spanners
Allen keys
Mole grips
Combination pliers
Screwdrivers
Hammer
Combination spanners

Spanners

Bike nuts and bolts are almost always metric sizes (with the exception of very old British bikes which use imperial sizes). An absolute minimum is a collection of 8mm, 9mm, 10mm, 12mm and 15mm open and ring spanners, plus any others your bike might need. The perfect spanner set would consist of two sets of combination spanners, which have a ring on one end and an open spanner on the other. This would allow the best combination of open and ring spanners to be used, whatever the job. If you don't have any spanners at all, the cheapest way to get some is to buy a set; individual spanners are significantly more expensive.

A medium-sized adjustable spanner is invaluable, and there are a couple of jobs for which a very large one is also very handy. Buy a good one; cheap adjustable spanners are rubbish.

Socket spanners are not strictly necessary on a bike, though if you have a socket set with a ratchet driver you may find it very useful, and it can speed up many jobs. By and large, you can get at most nut and bolt heads with conventional spanners. The exception is the bearing locknut in pedals which is inaccessible without the correct socket, and sometimes an extension bar is necessary to get through the pedal cage as well.

Using spanners

The reason why spanners exist in both ring and open forms is that they have different uses. A ring spanner grips the bolt at six points and is therefore much less likely to slip off than an open spanner. Open spanners are good for access to awkward places and for initial snugging down of bolts, but for the final tightening you should use a ring.

Adjustable spanners should always be used in such a way that the spanner rotates toward the movable jaw; this reduces the risk of the spanner slipping, or the load damaging the spanner.

Screwdrivers

A small Phillips screwdriver and an assortment of flat head screwdrivers from ⅛in to ⁵⁄₁₆in will do almost anything you come across on a bike. Screwdrivers are also useful for gentle prying and lifting operations, though it should be kept in mind that they are relatively easy to damage if used as drifts or to pry hard materials. Screwdrivers, like spanners, are cheapest bought in sets (but beware very cheap sets from markets or car boot sales). If possible, get ridged 'engineer's' screwdrivers rather than ones with rounded handles intended for wood-working application, as ridged handles are easier to grip with greasy hands.

Allen keys

It's almost possible to assemble some modern bikes with just a set of Allen keys, so widespread have these handy and easy to use fittings become. You will certainly need a 4mm, 5mm and a 6mm tool, but other sizes like 2mm, 3mm, 8mm and 10mm are not unknown, so once again it is better to buy a set. Get good quality ones; cheap Allen keys tend to be very nasty indeed and will round off just when you are trying to firmly tighten a crucial component. The very best Allen keys are Bondhus tools, with a ball end on the long arm, which allow very quick and easy initial screwing in of bolts because they remove the need for the tool to be absolutely straight. A set will cost about a tenner, but the saving in time and hassle is worth every penny. Also, if you can, get an extension tube to fit your Allen keys; it will give you the extra leverage when needed.

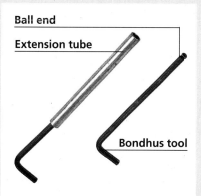

Ball end

Extension tube

Bondhus tool

Pliers and Mole grips

Pliers should never be used to grip bolts; they invariably do damage. They are useful for holding and gripping parts when they need to be held fairly firmly; jobs like pulling cables for example. Get good combination pliers which have flat, rounded and cutting jaws. Phillips do good ones.

A Mole grip is invaluable if you ever need to get a very firm grip on a part which is, for whatever reason, impossible to grip with a spanner or other tool. Stanley make the original Mole grip and it's still one of the best.

Hammer

Pro workshops have a wide variety of hammer and mallets with plastic, rubber and even copper heads. For the couple of jobs in this book that require a hammer an ordinary ball-peen hammer is fine. Resist the temptation to reach for a hammer whenever something seems reluctant to move; 99 times out a hundred it is not the solution and you'll end up damaging something. **If in doubt, don't clout.**

Knife

Where would we be without Stanley knives? Get one with a retractable blade for safety.

Ruler or tape measure

Essential for measuring things!

Biro pen top

Amazingly handy for putting bearings into confined spaces.

Zip ties

Neither tools nor materials really, but zip ties are handy whenever you need to temporarily attach something to your bike, or hold something in place. 'Zippies', re-usable zip ties from Sensible Products, are my favourite, or try Maplin.

Tool-box

Finally get some sort of box to store all your tools and bike bits. Metal ones are sturdy but expensive. Plastic ones are cheap but are unlikely to stand up well to a good beating.

Materials

Barrier cream

Hand cleaner

Anti-seize

Oils

Degreaser

Grease

I like to refer to stuff like oils and greases as 'soft tools'; if a tool is an extension of the human hand, then using the right type of grease on a part is a long term extension of both hand and brain, and will help to keep parts working properly in the long term.

WD40

I've used WD40 extensively as a light lubricant, water-displacer and penetrant in this book. While there are better lubricants for jobs such as lubricating derailleur pivots, WD40 has the advantages of very wide availability, relative cheapness (less than £3 per litre in quantity – some specialist bike lubes cost almost ten times more) and there is a can in everyone's garage. One thing though, don't lose the straw; it is ever so handy for directing the lube just where you want it.

Oil

Where there is a need for a general purpose medium weight oil I have used Duckham's Home Oil. Any mineral-based or synthetic oil will do the job for things like lubricating chains, or you can

use a specialist lubricant like Super Spray Lube, Pedro's or Finish Line. What you use on your chain is less important than that you use something and use it regularly. However, avoid vegetable-based lubricants like 3-in-1 which tend to dry out to leave a very unpleasant, sticky residue.

Solvents (degreasers)

Use a degreaser to clean dirt, oil and grease from components. In this book I've used Pedro's Bio Degreaser and the chain cleaning fluid which comes with the Barbieri chain cleaner. The Pedro's stuff is biodegradable and is very good, though it is helped by liberal application of elbow grease. High-strength petroleum based solvents should be avoided because they are toxic and environmentally lousy.

Grease

For bearings, use a bicycle specific bearing grease like Pedro's or Finish Line or one of any number of others. Greases intended for cars are designed for use at high temperatures and often don't work

as well at the lower temperatures found in bike bearings. If you can, use a grease injector to store your grease; it will keep the grease clean and uncontaminated and is a lot less messy than a tub.

Anti-seize

The use of anti-seize compounds, such as Duckham's Copper Grease, Copaslip, Copper Ease or the zinc/aluminium TQM anti-seize available from bike shops, is one of the secrets of good bike care that is just becoming widely realised. These are very tenacious greases with very fine metal particles mixed in them, which have the effect of making it easier to assemble and disassemble threaded parts, especially where those parts include aluminium or titanium surfaces.

Barrier cream

Use barrier cream before you work on your bike, to protect your skin from solvents, oils and greases, which can cause dermatological problems. More of an issue for pro mechanics, really, but barrier creams do make it a lot easier to wash your hands afterwards

Hand cleaner

A good hand cleaner like Swarfega or Fast Orange will get your hands thoroughly clean after you've worked on your bike.

Spares

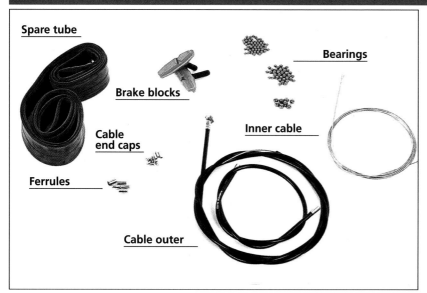

Spare tube

Brake blocks

Bearings

Cable end caps

Inner cable

Ferrules

Cable outer

Cable

For similar reasons I have a spare brake cable which is long enough to be used for front or rear, a spare gear cable and enough cable outers to replace a section of either brake or gear outer. If you have indexed gears, you'll need different outer for brake and gears because of the requirements of indexed gears for incompressible outer. Get Shimano SIS SP outer for gears.

Cable end caps

These little metal cable covers are cheap, and help to keep cables tidy. Buy a handful from a bike shop; they should last ages.

Cable ferrules

A few of the steel caps that fit over the ends of cables to protect the frame from the cut end of the outer are worth having.

Puncture repair kit

Even if you don't have any other spares you should keep a puncture repair kit so that you can fix punctured tubes rather than throwing them away. Done properly a good puncture repair can be treated as permanent and you can continue to use the tube.

Spare tube

Even if you have a puncture repair kit, keep a spare tube handy as well. There might not be the time nor the inclination to repair the puncture straight away. Take the tube with you when you ride, then if you get a puncture you can change tubes immediately and repair the old one in the warm comfort of your own home.

Brake blocks

I usually have a couple of sets of spare blocks in my home tool kit to save me traipsing the seven miles into town if I find I need to replace them.

Bearings

If you are going to do your own work on bearings, then it is worth replacing the balls whenever you service the particular part. Get good quality bearings in the sizes needed for your bike. Components differ, but below is a general guideline for the sizes you will need.

Table of bearing sizes		
component	size	most common alternative
Cup and cone bottom bracket	¼in	none
Front hub	³⁄₁₆in	⁷⁄₃₂in; ¼in (both very rare)
Rear hub	¼in	
Pedals	⁵⁄₃₂in	⅛in
Standard 1in headset	⁵⁄₃₂in	varies (See chapter 19)

Specialist bike tools

Now we come to the tools which are specifically designed and manufactured for use on bikes. Some of these tools simply make bike jobs easier and more convenient, while others are essential; without them you can't do the job. For example my favourite Park cable pulling tool, which you'll see used a lot in this book, is not essential, I could use pliers. But the Park puller makes fine adjustments of cables much easier because its ratchet lock means I can leave it attached to a cable, freeing both hands to do something else. On the other hand the **only** way to remove a crank from an axle is with the proper crank removal tool; other methods, usually involving large amounts of brute force, will damage the crank or the axle bearings.

I have listed these specialist tools in what I consider to be decreasing order of importance, based on how likely you are to need them and how much the full set of tools to do a particular job costs. For this reason a crank remover and the tools to service a bottom bracket are fairly low on the list, because if you only service your bottom bracket every couple of years, and this is all that a summer-only, fair-weather rider needs to do, then you are probably better off taking it to a bike shop.

Key to the cost of special tools

£	Less than £5
££	£5 to £10
£££	£10 to £15
££££	£15 to £20
£££££	£20 or more

Tyre levers

Rating: Essential for sensible people!
Cost: £ (for a set of 3)
Skilled mechanics can remove tyres without tools, and in fact a colleague and I have contests to see who can remove the tightest-fitting tyres without recourse to tyre levers. However, we are very sad; sensible people use tyre levers.

Cable cutters

Rating: Some sort of good cable cutter is essential.
Alternative: Good wire cutters. *(don't use pliers)*
Cost: £££££ (Shimano tool); ££ (wire cutters)

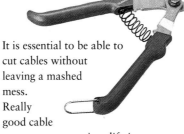

It is essential to be able to cut cables without leaving a mashed mess. Really good cable cutters are a once-in-a-lifetime investment; in home use they should never need replacing. Shimano's are the best, but for about £25 they should be!

For the average person however, normal wire cutters (as shown here) work just as well to start off with. If you're using them everyday (as bicycle mechanics do – that's why they have proper ones) then they won't last as long. However for infrequent home use they are perfectly adequate, they are widely available in all tool stores and more importantly, they cost less than £10. When buying make it absolutely clear that you want them for cutting bike cables, and don't use pliers which will almost always mash the cable and make a mess.

Cable puller

Rating: Extremely handy for adjusting brakes and gears.
Alternatives: Combination pliers. (Although you may feel like you need to grow an extra hand as well).
Cost: ££ (Madison tool)
Cost: ££££ (Park tool)
A cable puller helps with adjustment of brakes and gears and generally simplifies several of the jobs you will do most often. Worth having, even if not utterly indispensable. If you have sidepull brakes then the much cheaper '3rd hand tool' can be used for brake cable adjustment.

Chain cleaner

Rating: Very useful labour saving tool.
Alternative: Toothbrush, tray and a lot of elbow grease.
Cost: £££
Frequent cleaning prolongs the life of chains, but removing the chain to do it is messy and annoying. One of these simple devices makes the job much easier. *(For 'How to use this tool', see Chapter 15.)*

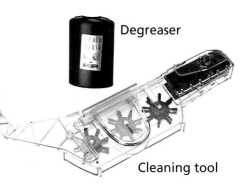

Degreaser

Cleaning tool

Track pump

Rating: Speedy inflater.
Alternative: Normal pump, lot of elbow action.
Cost: ££££
A good floor-standing pump with a built-in gauge is well worth the cost; it will allow you to keep your tyres at the proper pressure, reducing tyre wear and making riding generally more pleasant (pushing under-inflated tyres round the place is no fun at all). Zefal do a wide range of pumps from the inexpensive Rush to the wonderful but expensive Double Shot, which can inflate a road bike tyre to 100psi in seconds.

Assorted extension tubes and drifts

Rating: Tatty (but useful) bits of metal.
Cost: Nothing.
There are a few jobs for which extension tubes that fit closely over spanners and Allen keys are very useful for providing extra leverage, and a few tatty bits of metal to use as drifts can take the place of the right tools in an emergency.

Chain splitter

Rating: Essential for splitting chains.
Cost: £ (standard), **££** (Shimano).

Shimano tool   **Standard tool**

One of those 'the only way to do this is with the right bit of kit' tools. There is no reliable way to join and split chains without one of these. If you have a Shimano Hyperglide chain make sure you get a compatible tool; it will say so somewhere on the packaging. *(For more on chain splitting see Chapter 15.)*

Cone spanners

Rating: Essential for hub adjustments.
Cost: ££

Thin spanners with 13mm, 14mm, 15mm, and 16mm heads, used for adjusting hub bearings – you need two. If you're going to get into adjusting bearings, this is a good place to start as the tools are relatively cheap (less than a tenner a pair) and hub bearings are easy to work on.

Pedal spanner

Rating: Especially useful for extra leverage on sticky pedal threads.
Alternatives: Any 15mm spanner.
Cost: ££

A long, thin 15mm spanner is very handy for fitting and removing pedals. A pedal spanner is usually attached to the other end of one of the tools needed to work on the bottom bracket or headset.

Headset spanners

Rating: Essential for headset. adjustments.
Alternatives: If you chose your spanner combinations wisely, you can combine the spanners needed to take apart a headset with those needed for a cup and cone bottom bracket (see below).
Cost: ££££ (for a set of 2)

Headset end

A good set of headset spanners is essential for the proper adjustment of a headset. This bearing controls the steering and it is vital that it is properly adjusted. Headset spanners are therefore quite important. *(For more on headset spanners, and the correct sizes to have, see Chapter 19).*
As shown here, headset spanners are often found at the other end of bottom bracket spanners.

Headset end

Chain whip

Rating: Essential for Shimano sprocket cassettes.

Other tools needed: Shimano Hyperglide cassette lockring remover.
Cost: ££££
If you've got a Shimano sprocket cassette (part of the freewheel assembly, *see Chapter 20*), you need one of these to take it off. Use with a Shimano Hyperglide cassette lockring remover. Only necessary if you are going to change your own sprocket sets.

Shimano Hyperglide cassette lockring remover

Rating: Essential for Shimano sprocket cassettes.
Other tools needed: Chain whip.
Cost: ££
Essential for removing a Shimano sprocket cassette. *(For more on this see Chapter 20; the section on `Freewheels')*

Freewheel remover

Rating: Essential for freewheel blocks.
Cost: ££

For hubs with screw-on freewheels this tool, along with a vice or large adjustable spanner, is needed to take the complete freewheel and sprocket assembly off the wheel for repair or replacement. The two most common types are a splined remover for Shimano freewheels and their clones, and a four-prong tool for SunTour freewheels and copies thereof. There are also lots of other, slightly different designs for older, more obscure freewheels, so it's a good idea to have the wheel with you when buying.

Crank and bottom bracket tools

This group of tools is essential for removing, fitting and adjusting cranks and bottom brackets. *Refer to Chapter 16 for info on identifying the type of bottom bracket you have*; cup-and-cone bottom brackets and cartridge bottom brackets require completely different tools.

Crank puller

Rating: Essential for removing cranks.
Cost: ££
The only way to get cranks off without risking damage to crank or bearings. Get a remover which is the same brand as your cranks to ensure a good fit between threads and puller.

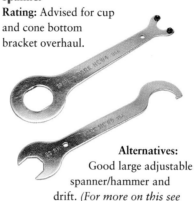

Shimano cartridge bottom bracket tool

Rating: Essential to remove bottom bracket.
Other tools needed: Crank remover (to give access to bottom bracket).
Cost: ££
Essential to fit and remove Shimano cartridge bottom brackets, which are the dominant fitting on bikes over about £250 built since 1992. Needs a big adjustable spanner to drive it.

Bottom bracket fixed cup spanner; bottom bracket lockring spanner; bottom bracket adjustable cup spanner

Rating: Advised for cup and cone bottom bracket overhaul.

Alternatives: Good large adjustable spanner/hammer and drift. *(For more on this see Chapter 16.)*
Cost: ££££ (for a set).
These three tools are the best equipment for removing, fitting and adjusting cup and cone bottom bracket assemblies. It is possible to use a hammer and drift to loosen and tighten the lockring, and a good large adjustable spanner on the fixed cup. However, tools which fit properly are less likely to do damage. There are several shapes and designs of lockring and adjustable cup, which require different tools; the ones here fit Shimano and Campagnolo-pattern brackets, which were very, very common before 1992. Buy from a bike shop, who will be able to advise on exactly what you need.

Workstand

Rating: Very useful if you're likely to do a lot of bike repair.
Alternatives: See 'Holding your bike' earlier in this chapter.
Cost: £££££ and beyond!
If you work on your bike a lot, then a stand which holds your bike securely at a sensible height off the ground and allows it to be rotated so that you can easily reach any part of it is very useful. Such workstands are not cheap; professional quality versions retail for up to £300, and good home-use stands start at about £60, but they make any job on the bike much easier.

Spoke key

Rating: The most dangerous tool in the universe.
Other tools needed: A

wheel jig (to do the job properly).
Cost: £
Vital for adjusting wheel shape, but also the tool which offers most potential for foul-ups. The spoke key is a £3 tool with which you can easily do £30-worth of damage; adjusting wheels should only be tackled by mechanics who have built up a decent level of experience and 'feel' for the way things work. Spoke keys come in a number of sizes because the different thicknesses of spoke have different nipple sizes. Almost all spokes on production bikes use 14g nipples, but European 14g nipples are slightly different from far eastern ones; get the snuggest fit you can.

Wheel jig

Rating: For the serious wheel mechanic only!
Other tools needed: Spoke key.
Cost: £££££ and beyond!
A jig makes working on wheels much, much easier by providing a firm mounting for the wheel and reference points for the shape. Expensive, can pay for itself over the decades in saved time and wheel repair bills.

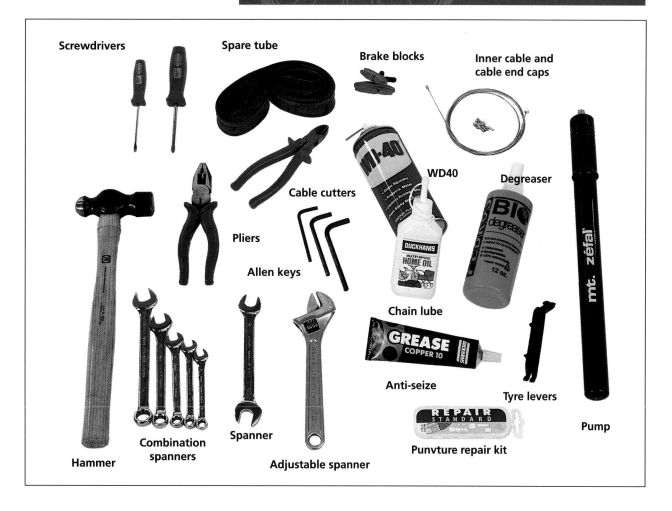

Screwdrivers Spare tube Brake blocks Inner cable and cable end caps WD40 Degreaser Cable cutters Pliers Allen keys Chain lube Anti-seize Tyre levers Pump Hammer Combination spanners Spanner Adjustable spanner Punvture repair kit

A minimum bicycle tool-kit

So of all of that stuff, what do I **really** need? To answer that question we've compiled what we think to be the minimum tool kit needed to keep a bike in good and safe working order. By this we mean being able to fix punctures, adjust saddles and handlebars, brakes and gears; but not necessarily going into the more advanced jobs of overhauling bearings.

Our proposed minimum tool list is as follows:

Basic tools:
- Combination spanners; sizes 8mm, 9mm, 10mm, 12mm, 15mm
- Medium adjustable spanner
- Small Phillips screwdriver
- Small flat head screwdriver
- Allen keys; sizes 4mm, 5mm, 6mm
- Combination pliers
- Hammer

Materials:
- WD40
- Mineral based oil for the chain
- Anti-seize (copper grease)
- Degreaser

Spares:
- Puncture repair kit
- Spare tube
- Brake blocks
- Brake cable
- Cable end caps

Special bike tools:
- Pump
- Tyre Levers
- Cable cutters

That's the basic list; with these you should be able to do all the basic maintenance tasks on a bike. If you want to expand your tool kit then we suggest that the next items you ought to consider are a special chain cleaning tool, a cable puller and a track pump. None of these are essential tools, but, by heck, they don't half make life easier!

83

Spare tube

Lube

Tyre levers

Cool tool

Pump

mt. zéfal

Sealant canister

Frame clip

Portable tools

When you're out on the road or trail, things sometimes go wrong, and you can be faced with a very long walk home if you don't have at least a few tools with you. My minimum tool kit is a multi-tool such as a Cool Tool, which incorporates lots of different tools into one lump of metal, tyre levers, spare tube (sometimes two), pump and a few zip ties. For long wet rides a very small canister of lube is a good idea. Let's look at these in a bit more detail.

Multi-tool

You can lug around spanners, Allen keys, screwdrivers and a chain tool, or you can choose one of the many tools on the market which incorporate multiple functions into one easily carried lump of metal. The original bike multi-tool was the Cool Tool, which includes a chain tool, Phillips screwdriver, 4mm, 5mm and 6mm Allen keys, adjustable spanner, 14mm crank bolt socket, and spoke key in one very usable package. Also worth a look are Ritchey's CPR tool range, and Finish Line's Chain Pup mini chain tool.

Tyre levers

Plastic ones are easier to carry than steel ones and less likely to damage your rims.

Spare tube

I use Presta valve tubes *(See Chapter 13)* because they will fit any other rim and it's not unusual for me to find that I am the only person on the ride with spares.

Pump

A good full-size pump is essential; Zefal's are very good, and durable. Mini-pumps are one of my pet hates. They are light, compact, easy to carry and completely useless when it comes to pumping up tyres, a bit like having a car with low insurance that's easy to park but only does 15mph. Carry a proper pump and put up with the weight.

Alternatively, there are gas canister systems available which inflate the tyre in seconds and which are very easy to carry around, and some versions will even seal small punctures for you. They are expensive, however, and therefore most appropriate for racers and perhaps for commuters like me who always leave home exactly 35 minutes before they have to be at the office (25 minutes riding time plus ten to shower and change).

Lube

A good day out on the trails might well include a couple of stream crossings, a sure way of washing all the lube out of your chain and jockey wheels. When they dry out and start to squeak a few drops of lube from a tiny lube canister will shut them up.

Tyres & tubes

Contents

The most essential skill any cyclist needs is that of fixing a puncture. Unfortunately punctures are a fact of cycling life and are likely to be so for some time. There have been many attempts to produce airless tubes or tyres which are puncture-resistant, but all have suffered from problems of weight, extremely harsh ride, immense difficulty of fitting or, in the case of the most recent example (a tyre made from polyurethane foam) a lack of grip which makes riding them interesting to say the least.

So basically, expect to get punctures and know what to do when you get them. Look upon it as all part of the fun of cycling; if you can!

Special section: Removing and fitting wheels

Many of the jobs in this book require you to remove or fit wheels. Here's a basic guide on how to do that.

Brake release mechanisms

Often the first thing you have to do is release the brake. On a bike with properly adjusted brakes there should not be enough space to squeeze the tyre out between the brake blocks. If you can, then your brake blocks are too far apart and they need adjusting. Luckily however, most modern bikes have some sort of brake release mechanism that will open the brakes and allow the tyre to pass out between the blocks.

Cantilever brakes

Here the brake release is on the brakes themselves. For cantilevers this is done by squeezing together the brake blocks and 'popping' the straddle or link wire out of its slot.

The brake will come apart like so. There is now enough space to take out the wheel.

Side-pull brakes

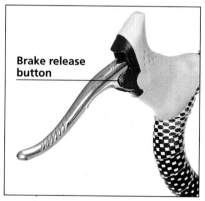

Brake release button

For side-pulls there is usually a button on the lever or a small cam lever on the brake which allows the pads to be moved apart enough to drop the wheel out.

Closing the brake

Remember always to close or re-connect the brake once you have put the wheel back in.

Quick release levers

Quick release levers are cam action devices which move away and towards the wheel to release and lock it to the frame.

They are not wing nuts and you should tighten them in the opposite direction to that in which the wheel rotates.

Warning

It is vitally important that your wheel quick releases are done up tightly. Always have the curved face facing in towards the spokes and the 'closed' mark reading outwards.

Undoing a wheel – quick release

1 To undo the quick release, pull it out and away from the spokes. When the quick release is open the inside of the curved handle will face outwards.

2 Once the quick release is open it may be necessary to undo the nut on the other end of the skewer a few turns to allow the wheel to drop out of the frame.

3 Finally, when the nut is sufficiently loose, drop the wheel out over the lips of the drop-out and out of the frame.

Fitting a wheel – quick release

1 Put the wheel into the drop-out and tighten the skewer nut. Test the lever frequently as you tighten the nut.

2 The nut is tight enough when you start to feel resistance at the lever when the lever is halfway between closed and open.

3 Close the lever fully. This should require enough force to leave a mark in your hand; if it doesn't, open the lever and tighten the nut a little more.

Removing and fitting the rear wheel

The tangle of sprockets, chain and rear mech at the rear wheel gives some people problems, but removing and fitting a rear wheel is simple if you just concentrate on what you are doing. We've chosen an example with nuts to simplify things a bit, *(see above for stuff on quick releases)*. It's easiest if the chain is on the smallest sprocket.

Undoing wheel nuts

1 The easiest way to undo wheel nuts is with two 15mm spanners. This allows you to loosen both nuts simultaneously; using one spanner usually means that the second nut spins with the axle because there is no resistance to hold it in place.

Taking out the wheel

2 Push the mech back out of the way and drop the wheel out of the frame and clear of the chain.

Fitting the wheel

1 Put the wheel in the frame so that the sprockets are in between the two runs of the chain.

2 Hook the wheel up so that the chain sits on the small sprocket.

3 Slide the axle into the drop-outs. It may be necessary to slightly pull apart the drop-outs to fit the wheel in.

4 Pull the axle right to the back of the drop-outs. This should automatically align the wheel in the frame. Nevertheless, check that the tyre is centred between the chain-stays (the tubes that run from the bottom bracket to the drop-outs).

Tightening wheel nuts

5 Tighten the axle nuts. Again, use two spanners and tighten by turning both nuts at the same time. Tightening one at a time could tighten the hub adjustments *(see Chapter 20)* meaning that the wheel won't spin properly. Make sure that tightening has not put the wheel out of alignment and that it is still properly centred between the chain-stays.

Final checks

Before you ride the bike, check the following three things

1. That the wheels (especially the back) are properly aligned in the frame and tyres and rims are not rubbing against the frame or the brakes.

2. That the quick release is properly closed and tight. (If necessary, open and close it again just to check.)

3. That the brakes are re-connected and any brake release mechanisms are closed.

Types of valve

There are two main types of valve used in bikes: Schrader, which is the same as a car tyre valve and is found on all mountain bikes and most 3-speeds, and Presta, which is the thinner type and found on road and racing bikes. Schrader valves require a bigger hole in the rim, and it's not possible to fit a Schrader valve tube into a rim that is drilled for Presta. There's very little to choose between them; I happen to think that the Presta is a better design, if only because as they fit on all bikes, it's possible to loan a Presta valved tube to a rider who has forgotten to bring a spare tube with them *(see section on portable tools in Chapter 12)*. But you could equally argue that if you run Schrader you can scrounge spare tubes from anyone!

Most pumps can be easily modified to fit either Presta or Schrader tubes by swapping round a couple of internal parts or by using this little conversion widget.

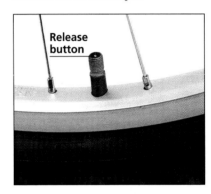

Presta valves

A Presta valve. Both types of valve sometimes have a locknut, as shown here, to hold the valve in place on the rim.
Under the dustcap is a small locking nut on a very thin threaded rod.

Schrader valves

A Schrader valve. Keep the dustcap on; it can act as a secondary seal to keep the air in if the valve malfunctions.

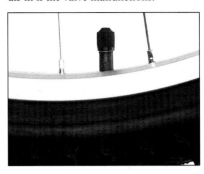

Under the cap is a spring-loaded release button. To open the valve (and deflate the tyre) this button must be pressed, which is why all pump fittings for Schrader have a central pin.

Release button

Locking nut

To open the valve and deflate the tyre, fully unscrew the locking nut and push it in. Also if pumping up the tyre make sure the nut is unscrewed. But also make sure you screw it down again once the tyre is inflated.

Tyre and Wheel Arrangement

Rim

Well

Tyre

Tyre bead

Rim tape

TIP!
Be careful when removing, or inflating tubes with Presta valves, the threaded rod is quite fragile and easy to damage.

Replacing a tube

You should always carry a spare tube. Fixing punctures is a pain, especially out in the field where at the very best you'll keep your riding partners waiting and at worst you will get cold and wet. In wet conditions it is virtually impossible to get a patch to stick anyway. Replace the tube, then fix it at home.

TOOLS Plastic tyre levers, pump.

TIME 5 mins.

DIFFICULTY 🔧🔧🔧🔧🔧

SPARES Replacement tube.

OBJECTIVE To remove a punctured tube and fit a new one.

Removing the tube

1 The first step with any puncture repair or tube replacement is to remove the wheel. *(See the special section earlier in this chapter for tips on wheel removal.)*

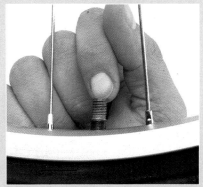

2 Undo the valve cap and put it somewhere safe. Push in the valve to release any remaining air in the tube.

3 Push the valve into the tyre to allow the tyre bead to move into the well of the rim.

4 Put a pair of levers under the tyre bead so that each is next to a spoke.

5 Hook one of the levers under a spoke

6 Push the other lever to lift the tyre. Push it along under the bead to loosen the rest of the tyre.

7 Once you have used the lever to loosen along a little distance, pull the rest of the tyre off the rim with your hands.

8 Reach inside the tyre and pull out the punctured inner tube.

Find the cause

Feel round inside the tyre until you find the cause of the puncture. Search thoroughly; it is possible for a shard of glass to fall out after causing a puncture, but you want to get the problem object out or to be sure that there is nothing there.

Putting in the new tube

When starting to put in a new tube, have the tyre arranged so that one tyre bead is inside the rim and one is out. The general idea is then to put the tube into the tyre and then push the tyre bead onto the rim.

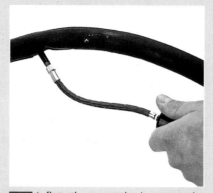

1 Inflate the new tube just enough that it holds its shape.

2 Start with the valve. Push the valve through the hole in the rim and then pull the tyre over the tube.

3 Push the tube into the tyre all the way round the wheel.

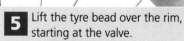

4 Push the tube over the rim so that the tyre bead sits next to the rim all the way round.

5 Lift the tyre bead over the rim, starting at the valve.

6 Push the valve up into the tyre to prevent the bead from pinching and puncturing the tube.

7 Push the rest of the bead over the rim. This will require some force, but it should be possible to do it by hand; you may need strong thumbs.

TIP!
Don't use tyre levers to lever the final bit of the tyre back in. You're only likely to cause another puncture.

Check the tube is seated

8 Work round the rim checking that the tyre is evenly seated on the rim. There should be no parts of the tyre that are high on the rim and there should be no places where the tube is caught under the bead. Pull and push the tyre into place as necessary.

Inflate

9 Inflate the tyre to the correct pressure. This is marked on the tyre side-wall. If you don't have a tyre gauge, check your tyre pressure by squeezing the tyre sides. You should be just able to dent a properly inflated road tyre and squeeze your thumb about a quarter of an inch into a mountain bike tyre.

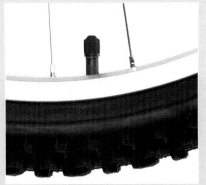

10 Finally put the valve cap back on and refit the wheel. *(See special section above.)* Make certain that your wheel quick release is properly done up.

Changing a tyre

See Chapter 9 for worn tyres and when to replace.

This is exactly the same as replacing a tube except that you will want to take the tyre off as well and fit a fresh one.

First, deflate the tyre and remove the tube as above. Pull the old tyre completely off the rim, and put one bead of the new tyre on the rim. Then replace the tube and inflate the tyre, as above.

(For more on types of tyres and tyre sizes, see Chapter 8.)

Puncture prevention

The only reasonably successful way to prevent flats is to use some sort of tyre sealant such as Slime, TQM or Safe T Seal. These products work by putting a layer of liquid in the tube which contains fibres or rubber particles in suspension. When you get a puncture the bits in the liquid are forced into the hole and block it, a strategy which usually seals the tube at least long enough to get you home. However, because they are water based, these compounds can make it difficult to subsequently repair the tube properly, and the seal often fails if the tube is removed and then re-fitted.

Fixing a puncture

There was a time when bike books recommended treating a puncture repair as a strictly temporary, get-you-home measure and told you to replace the tube as soon as possible. However, modern puncture repair kits are good enough that you really can treat a properly done tube repair as permanent and happily continue to use the tube. The difference is better glues and patches with tapering edges which blend into the tube.

Finding the hole

The first stage is to find the hole. There are a number of ways of doing this: listening for the place where the air is escaping; passing the tube close to your eye so you eventually feel the air rushing out; or the old standby, running the tube through water and looking for a stream of bubbles. The last technique is very good for tiny, pinhole punctures that often elude location by any other method.

Patching the hole

TOOLS Pump, puncture repair outfit.

TIME 10 mins.

DIFFICULTY 🔧🔧🔧🔧🔧

SPARES None.

OBJECTIVE To locate and fix a hole in an inner tube.

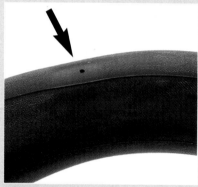

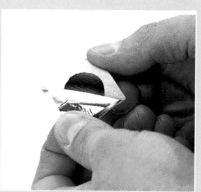

1 Here's a typical large hole such as might be made in a tube by a big shard of glass or a large thorn. Inflate the tube hard enough that it grows to about twice its flat size. Be careful not to overdo it; it is possible to burst a tube.

2 Deflate the tube and roughen the area around the hole with the sandpaper in the puncture repair kit. Get the tube surface good and rough and sand an area about twice the size of the patch that you are going to stick to it.

3 It's not essential, but marking the hole can help keep track of it.

4 Spread a thin layer of glue on and around the hole. You're aiming for a fairly thin layer to speed up the drying process.

5 Let the glue dry until it is tacky. Don't rush this step; go and do something else for five minutes if necessary. The patch won't stick properly if the glue is wet.

6 Peel the backing foil off the patch, leaving the patch mounted on its paper or plastic top cover.

7 Press the patch firmly on to the tube and leave it to set. Stacking a big pile of books on top of the tube to help fix the patch often helps.

8 Flex the patch in the middle to crack the top cover.

9 Peel the top cover off the patch **from the middle outwards**. It is possible to pull a patch off by taking the cover off from the edge, if the patch is not completely stuck down.

10 To test the patch inflate the tube a little, so that it holds its own shape and stretches a bit. Pass it through water and check for bubbles or listen closely for escaping air.

TIP!

Always used 'tapered' or 'feathered patches' with thin edges that will bend into the tyre. These are far superior to a 'normal', non-tapered rubber patch.

95

Brakes

Contents

Good brakes are essential. A bike that won't stop quickly and in control is potentially dangerous. Let's not mince words, a bike with lousy brakes is a potential death-trap. Even if you're not meticulous about anything else on your bike, you should make sure that your brakes are in perfect working order.

Important!

Safety Tip

It's essential that your brakes work well for you to be able to ride safely, so if you are at all unsure that you have set them up right, get someone else to check that your brakes work properly. Whatever you do, don't skimp on maintaining your brakes.

Types of Brake

All brakes work by using friction to slow down the wheels, and therefore the bike. In almost all modern brakes this friction is that caused by a brake block on the rim, which turns the energy of motion of the bike into heat. (This is why the blocks and rim sometimes get hot when you brake from high speed.) You may occasionally come across hub brakes, which have the friction mechanism housed in the wheel hub, or disc brakes that use separate discs on the hubs, but work in much the same way as rim brakes.

However, these designs are rare or expensive (or both!). The most common types of brakes are side-pulls and cantilevers.

Side-pull brake

Side-pull brakes are characterised by the two caliper arms which, as the name suggests, are pulled together by a cable connected to one side.

Cantilever brake

Cantilever brakes are characterised by brake bodies which bolt directly to the forks.

Special tools

The following special tools are useful for dealing with brakes. None are however essential. *(For more on special tools, see Chapter 12.)*

Cable puller

A cable puller makes many of the adjustment and maintenance jobs on brakes much easier, though it is not essential. This Park tool has a ratchet which allows it to be used to lock a cable in position, freeing your hands up to do other things.

3rd hand tool
An alternative to a cable puller is a 3rd hand tool. This tool holds brake blocks against the wheel rim whilst you tighten the cable. **However, it works for side-pull brakes only.** It is much cheaper than a cable puller, costing less than a tenner.

Cable cutter
The importance of good cable cutters cannot be overstressed.

Ordinary cutters, especially those found in pliers, will turn a perfectly good shiny new cable into a mashed, spread, useless mess. These Shimano cutters are professional quality and are designed to cut both inner cables and outers cleanly and tidily. They can also be used on gear cables.

Brake test

There are number of ways you can check that your brakes are working properly. With your weight on the handlebar, squeeze the front brake lever hard and try to push the bike forwards. It should be impossible to move the bike without skidding the wheel or lifting the rear wheel. Then, do the same for the rear brake. The bike should move, but only by sliding the rear wheel along the ground; the wheel should not turn, however hard you press on the saddle to move the bike along.

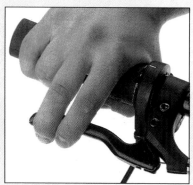

When you squeeze the brake lever the blocks should hit the rim after the lever has moved 1-2cm, and it should be difficult to squeeze the lever so that it hits the handlebar.

If you can squeeze the brake lever this far, then your brakes need urgent adjusting. *Refer to 'Adjusting the brake' for either side-pulls or cantilevers (depending on which type you have).*

Fault Diagnosis
Side-pull Brakes

However, proper bicycle cable cutters are expensive and cheaper general purpose wire cutters like these will do if they are only to be used infrequently.

Cone spanner

Cone spanners are normally used to adjust hub bearings, but are also handy for centring side-pull brakes that are equipped with spanner flats on the spring spacer, or other nut on the centre bolt. Alternatively, a thin spanner of the right size can be used.

SYMPTOM	CAUSE	REMEDY	PROCEDURE
Brakes don't work (or don't work well enough)	Blocks too far from rim	Adjust cable	Simple cable adjustment, or full cable adjustment
	Brake blocks worn	Replace blocks	Replacing worn brake blocks
Blocks rub on rim	Brake not centred	Centre brake	Centring the brake
	Wheel not true	True wheel	*Refer to Chapter 20*
Blocks rub on tyre	Incorrect block adjustment	Adjust blocks	Replacing the blocks (final parts)
Brakes squeal	Wrong type of blocks	Try a different set of blocks	Replacing brake blocks
Brakes stiff	Lever pivot stiff	Lube lever pivot	*See section on brake levers*
	Cable sticky	Lube cable...	Routine care
		If still stiff, replace cable	Replacing the cable
Brakes judder	Brake loose on mounting	Tighten mounting bolt	Brake removal and assembly
	Headset loose	Adjust headset	*See Chapter 19*
	Rim dented	True or replace rim	*See Chapter 20*
Brake blocks worn unevenly	Blocks not aligned properly	Tidy blocks, then align properly	Tidying worn brake blocks
Cable damaged	Wear and tear	Replace cable	Replacing the cable
Outer damaged	Wear and tear	Replace outer	Replacing the outer
	Crash damage	Don't crash; replace cable	Replacing the outer
Brake seized/ crudded up	Neglect/corrosion	Overhaul or replace brake	Brake dismantling and overhaul

Typical side-pull

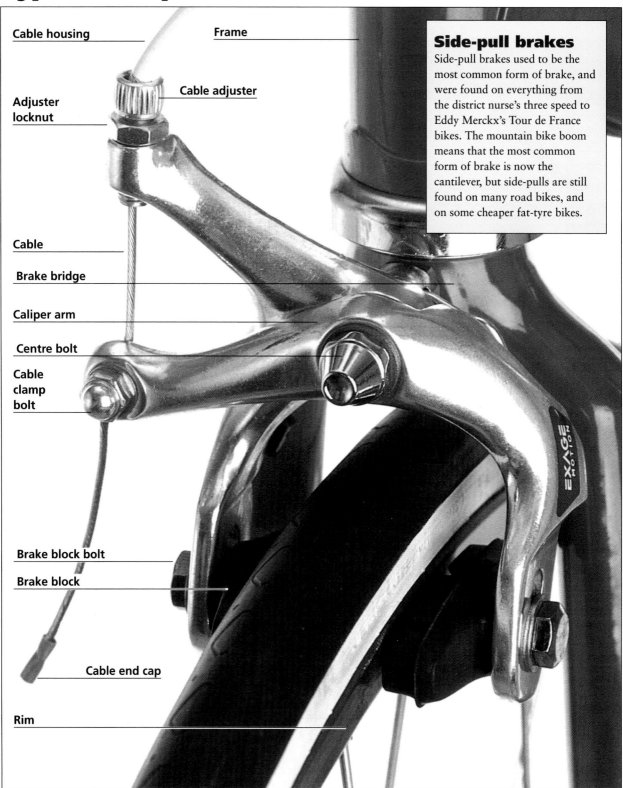

Cable housing

Frame

Cable adjuster

Adjuster
locknut

Cable

Brake bridge

Caliper arm

Centre bolt

Cable
clamp
bolt

Brake block bolt

Brake block

Cable end cap

Rim

Side-pull brakes

Side-pull brakes used to be the most common form of brake, and were found on everything from the district nurse's three speed to Eddy Merckx's Tour de France bikes. The mountain bike boom means that the most common form of brake is now the cantilever, but side-pulls are still found on many road bikes, and on some cheaper fat-tyre bikes.

Routine care and checks

The main thing a side-pull brake needs, like any brake, is to be kept clean and properly lubricated. The only moving parts are the cables and the caliper arms. You should check the condition of the brake blocks at least once a month, more if you ride frequently.

Adjustments

In a properly set up side-pull the following should happen:

▶ The blocks should hit the rim after the lever has been pulled about two centimetres. *(See 'Simple' and 'Full cable adjustments' if they don't.)*

▶ The blocks should be equally spaced either side of the rim. *(See 'Centring the brake' if they aren't.)*

▶ Both blocks should hit the rim squarely with no part hanging over the bottom of the rim or hitting the tyre. *(See the procedures of replacing blocks if they don't.)* This last situation is particularly dangerous; a badly adjusted block will quickly wear through the side of a tyre, eventually causing a blowout. If this happens at speed on the front wheel the results won't be pretty.

TIP!

If your brake has a quick-release lever (either on the brake itself or on the lever – see section on levers for further details), then make sure it is not engaged before beginning to adjust your brakes.

Lubricating your brakes

Frequently lubricate the point at which the two caliper arms meet. Use a light lubricant such as WD40 very frequently, or a heavier oil less often. There are thin washers either side of the caliper arms and between them. All of these need lube. As you oil the pivot, squeeze and release the brake lever, this will open and close the gaps between the caliper arms and allow the lube to run in. Make sure you avoid getting any lube on the rims or brake blocks. If you do, clean it off properly.

Blocks that are properly set up should show signs of even wear all over. If they are worn more at one end than another, or have a lip at the bottom edge, then they should be trimmed to an even shape or replaced. *(See 'Tidying worn brake blocks' and/or 'Replacing blocks' later in this section for details of how to do these tasks.)*

Checking the condition of the brake blocks

1 Drop the wheel out of the frame so that you can clearly see the blocks. *(See Chapter 13 for how to remove a wheel.)*

2 Inspect the surface of the brake block. On grooved brake blocks, the grooves should still be visible in the surface. If the block is worn to the bottom of the groove it should be replaced. Blocks without grooves will have a wear indicator line on the top, and should be replaced when they have worn to this line.

Adjusting the brakes (1): Simple cable adjustment

The most common adjustment to a side-pull is to take up some of the slack in the cable so that the lever activates the brake near the beginning of its travel, rather than near the end. Cable slack develops because cables bed in or stretch slightly from new, and because brake blocks wear and so have to travel farther to reach the rim. Simple cable adjustment is achieved with the adjuster on the top of the caliper arm.

TOOLS Fingers (may need pliers).

TIME 5 mins.

DIFFICULTY 🔧🔧🔧🔧🔧

SPARES None.

OBJECTIVE To take up cable slack in the brake system so that the blocks hit the rim after the lever has been pulled about a centimetre.

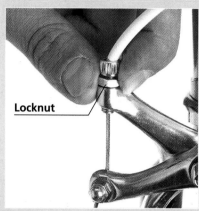

Locknut

1 The cable adjuster is held in place with a locknut. Unscrew the locknut to allow you to move the adjuster. It should be only finger-tight. If you have to reach for pliers to loosen it, be gentle. These are often quite flimsy plastic parts that are easily damaged by over-enthusiastic wrenching.

2 Squeeze the brake blocks on to the rim. This produces some cable slack and makes it easier to move the adjuster. Unscrew the adjuster a couple of turns. Try the brake at this point and unscrew the adjuster more if necessary until the blocks hit the rim after the lever has moved about a centimetre.

3 When you are done the brake blocks should be this far from the rim, or closer. *(We have removed the tyre for clarity.)* Spin the wheel and make sure it turns freely. If the brake rubs one side of the rim, centre the brake *(see below)*. Finally, re-tighten the locknut against the caliper arm.

Adjusting the brakes (2): Full cable adjustment

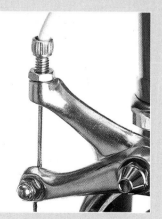

Eventually you will run out of adjustment on the cable adjuster. When you do it will look like this; a large amount of the thread on the adjuster is visible out of the brake, and only a small amount remains in the caliper arm. If you try to unscrew the adjuster much further it will come out of the caliper, and an extended adjuster like this is easily damaged by a fall. It's time to take up the cable slack by pulling it through the clamp bolt.

TOOLS Spanner to fit cable clamp bolt (usually 8mm), cable puller (or pliers).

TIME 10 mins.

DIFFICULTY 🔧🔧🔧🔧🔧

SPARES None.

OBJECTIVE To take up cable slack in the brake system; to set the adjuster screw to the bottom of its travel so it may subsequently be used to adjust the cable.

1 Unscrew the locknut on the cable adjuster and wind it all the way up to the top of the adjuster.

2 Squeeze the brake blocks together and screw the adjuster all the way into the caliper arm.

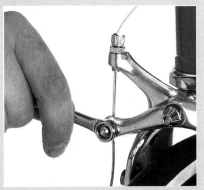

3 Loosen the cable clamp bolt. The blocks will move away from the rim.

If you have a cable puller

4a Pull the cable through the clamp bolt until the lever moves two centimetres before the blocks hit the rim, or the blocks are as close as possible to the rim but still clear when the wheel is spun. Then tighten the cable clamp bolt firmly. If this bolt is loose and the cable slips, your brakes won't work. Potentially nasty.

TIP!

If holding the blocks against the rim while playing with the cable adjustment is fiddly, try holding the blocks in place with a strap, like a spare toe-strap. Alternatively, use a 3rd hand tool.

If you don't have a cable puller

4b Firstly, unscrew the cable adjuster one or two turns so that you have the option to adjust it in both directions after you have tightened the cable clamp.

4c Tighten the cable clamp bolt enough that it grips the cable lightly, but allows it to be pulled through with pliers. Squeeze the blocks hard against the rim with your fingers. Pull the cable through with your other hand, or with pliers.

4d Then tighten the cable clamp bolt hard while still holding the blocks against the rim. Finally, fine tune your brakes by making a simple adjustment if necessary, *(this has been described previously),* and then tighten down the locknut again.

103

Centring the brake

TOOLS 13mm or multi-size cone spanner.

TIME 5 mins.

DIFFICULTY 🔧🔧🔧🔧

SPARES None.

OBJECTIVE To adjust the brake so that the blocks are evenly spaced either side of the rim (or the rim is centred between the blocks, depending on how you look at it).

 1 A common fault with side-pulls is that they sit off-centre to the rim; one block hits the rim before the other and may even rub as the wheel turns.

2 To centre the brake it is necessary to turn the whole brake unit around the centre bolt. To allow this, brakes have spanner flats on the spacer which holds the return spring. A thin spanner is needed to reach in the narrow space between the brake and the frame, and a cone spanner (intended for adjusting wheel hub bearings) is ideal.

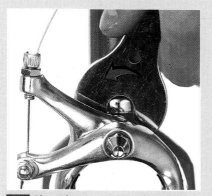

3 Place the spanner on the return spring spacer and turn it in the direction of the widest spaced block until the blocks are evenly spaced either side of the rim. Squeeze the brake lever to check that the adjustment was as much as necessary.

4 This is what you should end up with – blocks that are evenly spaced. Repeat step three until this is the case both before and after you squeeze the brake lever.

TIP!

If the blocks persistently rub on the rim and centring doesn't help, then check that it's not the actual wheel that's out of true.

Repairs and replacements

Replacing worn brake blocks

Sooner or later your brake blocks will wear to an extent that they need to be replaced. You should replace them with either the original manufacturer's parts or with high-quality third party blocks. Aztecs and Kool Stops are the best ones.

TOOLS 10mm spanner or Allen key (depending on make of blocks).

TIME 20 mins.

DIFFICULTY 🔧🔧🔧🔧🔧

SPARES New brake blocks.

OBJECTIVE To replace worn-out brake blocks.

1 Screw the cable adjuster all the way in *(see 'Adjusting the brakes')* and undo the cable clamp bolt. Since you will have adjusted the cable to take up the slack produced by the worn blocks, replacing the blocks will mean that the cable also needs to be adjusted.

2 Undo the bolt which holds the brake block in the caliper arm and pull out the blocks. Check the condition of the block. When the block gets worn it is possible for this core to protrude through the block and do irreparable damage to your rims, so it is important to replace blocks well before they get that bad.

3 Fit the new block, tightening the bolt up finger-tight. Push the block against the rim and position it so that it is parallel to top and bottom of the rim, hits the rim in the middle, and doesn't rub on the tyre or hang over the bottom of the rim.

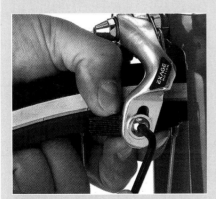

4 Tighten the bolt while holding the brake block firmly in place. It may be necessary to hold the block with an adjustable spanner, pliers or a Mole grip to keep it from turning. Make sure you tighten the bolt hard; **it is vital the brake blocks are tight.**

5 Finally, pull the cable through and adjust the brake as detailed in *'Adjusting the brake(2): Full cable adjustment'*. **Make sure that you re-tighten the cable clamp bolt afterwards.**

TIP!

Various types of synthetic blocks work well on alloy rims, but for steel rims get leather-faced blocks. These produce much better braking in the wet; if you have standard rubber blocks, replace them with leather-faced ones immediately.

Tidying unevenly worn brake blocks

Blocks that have worn unevenly, for whatever reason, can be tidied up by careful use of a sharp knife; a Stanley knife is ideal.

TOOLS Mole grip or pliers, Stanley knife.

TIME 5 mins.

DIFFICULTY 🔧🔧🔧🔧🔧

SPARES None.

OBJECTIVE To trim worn brake blocks so that they have a square face.

1 Remove the brake blocks as described above. Then hold the block firmly in pliers or, even better, a mole grip.

2 Cutting away from yourself, trim the block a thin sliver at a time until the braking surface is smooth, flat and square to the body of the block. Finally, replace the brake blocks squarely to the rim. *(See the previous procedure.)*

SAFETY TIP!

Do not hold the block in your fingers. A slip while trimming a hand-held block will inevitably result in a trip to Casualty and a five-hour wait for a tetanus jab in the bum. Think how much better your time could be spent.

Replacing the cable

Brake cables are cheap enough and safety-critical enough that they should be replaced if there is the slightest hint of anything wrong with them. This includes damaged outers, frayed cables or just old, sticky cables that no longer pull smoothly.

TOOLS Pliers; WD40; 8mm spanner; cable cutters.

TIME 20 mins.

DIFFICULTY 🔧🔧🔧🔧🔧

SPARES New inner cable, new cable end cap.

OBJECTIVE To replace a damaged inner cable and lubricate the cable outer while you are about it.

TIP!

You can make a dramatic improvement to the performance of budget brakes by replacing the cables with better quality ones. Shimano's cables for their SLR brake systems are excellent, as are Clarks'.

Tips on Cables: *See Chapter 11 for general advice on dealing with cables.*

Removing the old cable

1 Slacken the Cable Clamp Bolt. Then cut the cable between the clamp bolt and the adjuster. This way you can pull the frayed end down out of the clamp instead of trying to drag the messy bit through the clamp and cable outer. (Alternatively, pull or cut off the cable end cap.)

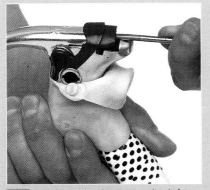

2 Pull the rubber lever cover back from the top of the lever. Some levers have a plastic cover round the top of the lever blade. Carefully prise this off. It should come off fairly easily, but may need some gentle working and wiggling to remove it. Once off, put it somewhere safe!

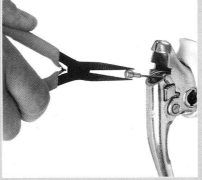

3 Remove the cable from the lever. Push it out from the brake end until you can see the nipple in the lever, then pull it out with pliers or your fingers. Throw it away.

Putting in a new cable

4 Types of brake cable nipple – pear-shaped (for drop handlebar levers) and barrel-shaped (for flat handlebar levers). If you have a universal cable, cut off the one you **don't** need.

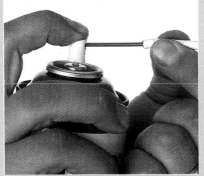

5 While you have the cable out, squirt WD40 inside the outer to lubricate it and protect the cable from corrosion.

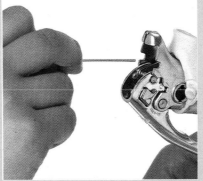

6 Deep inside the lever there is a hole which the cable runs through, and above that the cable anchor in which the nipple sits. Thread the new cable through the cable anchor and into the guide hole in the bottom of the lever.

TIP!

Where the cable is routed under the handlebar tape, the cable outer is right under the cable guide hole, and it's not unusual for the cable to need an amount of wiggling to get it in, since the outer and guide hole may not be perfectly aligned.

7 Thread the cable right through the outer and into the adjuster (which should be screwed right down), and into the clamp. Pull the cable all the way into the brake so that there is no slack in the cable and the cable pulls the lever shut. Screw the clamp down finger-tight.

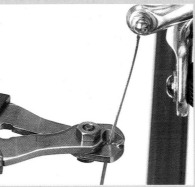

8 Cut the cable to length, leaving about 5cm of excess cable after the clamp so that you can adjust it later.

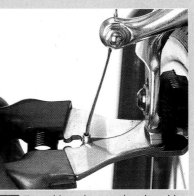

9 Fit a cable end cap so that the cable doesn't fray, and to cover the sharp end. Finally, adjust the brake as previously described. Remember to refit the plastic lever cover and to tighten the cable clamp bolt when finished.

Replacing the outer

A damaged outer cable can be removed without removing the inner wire. The techniques in this procedure are also needed if you are going to replace the whole inner and outer combination.

TOOLS Pliers; WD40; 8mm spanner; cable cutters.

TIME 25 mins.

DIFFICULTY 🔧🔧🔧🔧🔧

SPARES New cable outer, new cable end cap, (maybe new handlebar tape).

OBJECTIVE To replace a damaged outer cable.

Note: Under-tape cable routeing
On the bike that we're working on in this sequence, the brake outer goes completely under the handlebar tape to the brake lever. Hence to replace the outer we also have to replace the handlebar tape. *(See Chapter 18 for how to do this.)*

1 Undo the cable clamp bolt, pull off the end cap with pliers, and pull the cable out of the brake.

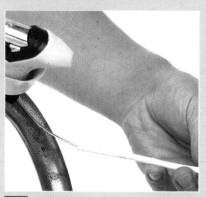

2 Undo the handlebar tape (if you have to). Pull the outer off the inner.

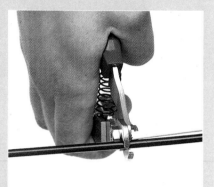

3 Cut the new outer to the same length as the old one.

4 Feed the new outer with lube. Then thread the inner cable back into the outer and push the outer up against whatever it stopped against (brake lever, cable stop, under-tape cable channel, etc.).

5 Thread the inner and outer back into the adjuster, making sure that outer is properly pushed into the adjuster. Then feed the inner through the cable clamp. Set up and adjust your brake as previously described.

TIP!

For a host of tips on cable outers see page 121.

Dismantling and overhauling a side-pull brake

Removal

If your brake gets extremely gunked up, after, say a winter commuting in a big city (how do they manage to get diesel engines to turn out so much ultra-fine crud?) then you may want to completely strip it down to clean it.

TOOLS 5mm Allen key, pliers, 8mm spanner, 10mm spanner, 14mm cone spanner.

TIME 45 mins.

DIFFICULTY

SPARES None.

OBJECTIVE Completely dismantle brake, clean and rebuild.

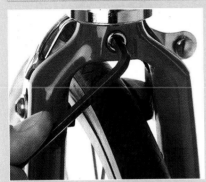

1 First, remove the cable end cap so that the cable can be pulled out of the brake. Undo the cable clamp bolt. Then unscrew the nut which holds the brake in the frame.

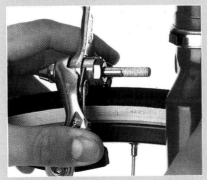

2 Pull the brake out of the front and the nut out of the back of the frame. With the caliper off the bike, the unit can now be broken down into its component parts.

The brake unit dismantles from the back, so it is not possible to disassemble it and leave the bolt in the frame. Remove the parts, noting the order in which they came off (lay them out in sequence). Clean all the parts with degreaser. You should (give or take a washer) find yourself with bits looking very similar to these:

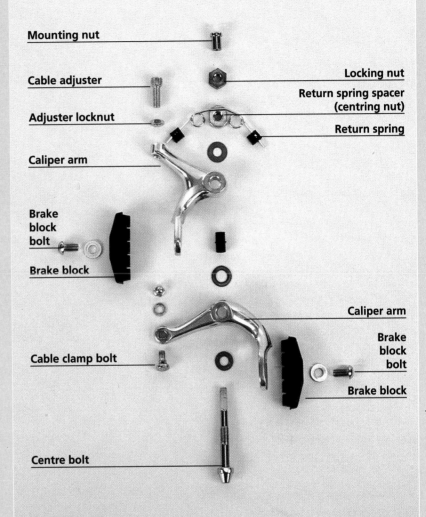

Mounting nut

Cable adjuster

Adjuster locknut

Caliper arm

Brake block bolt

Brake block

Cable clamp bolt

Centre bolt

Locking nut

Return spring spacer (centring nut)

Return spring

Caliper arm

Brake block bolt

Brake block

Reassembly

Reassemble the brake in the reverse order to the way it was taken apart. Place the parts back on the centre bolt in the correct order *(refer to the picture if you have to)*. Smear grease on all surfaces that have to slide against each other. Make sure you replace the springs in their stops.

The caliper arms need to be screwed down until they pivot freely around the brake bolt but cannot be moved in any other direction. Then this position needs to be locked off. Holding the spring spacer with one spanner, tighten the nut hard against it to lock them together. Fit the brake back into the frame and tighten the brake nut. Finally reattach the cable and brake blocks as detailed in previous procedures.

Cantilever brakes

Cantilever brakes are used where there is a need for powerful brakes, but because of fat tyres or large frame clearances a side-pull brake would be very weak. Cantilevers mount on special bosses which are welded to the frame either side of the rim and each side of the brake has its own return spring.

Cantilever brake designs

There are two types of common cantilever brake designs. They are essentially the same, except for straddle cable differences.

On one type, the brake cable (via a straddle yoke) pulls on a small extra bit of cable (called a straddle cable) which joins the two sides of the brake and pulls them together equally when the lever is pulled. This is the traditional design of cantilever brakes, and in this chapter we shall be calling them **straddle cable (cantilever) brakes.**

On newer bikes there is a slightly different design. Here the main brake cable goes through a cable guide to one side of the brake and is bolted directly to the brake body. A short cable – called a link wire, though strictly speaking it's a cable – which is part of the cable guide pulls the other side. This type of cantilever brake we shall be referring to as **link wire brakes**.

Bikespeak: Cable? Wire? What's the difference?

A cable is made up of lots of thin metal strands, while a wire is a single piece of metal. A cable is made up of lots of wires, therefore. However, these terms are used pretty loosely and are virtually interchangeable unless you are talking to a pedantic engineer!

Cantilever brake with link wire

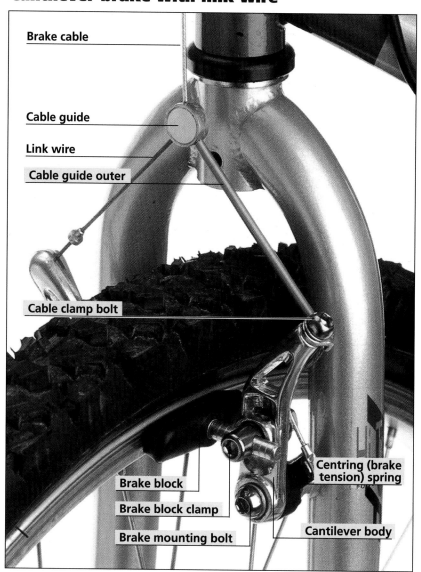

- Brake cable
- Cable guide
- Link wire
- Cable guide outer
- Cable clamp bolt
- Brake block
- Brake block clamp
- Brake mounting bolt
- Centring (brake tension) spring
- Cantilever body

Brake levers ▶

With cantilever brakes, you will find the cable adjusters not on the brakes themselves, but on the levers.

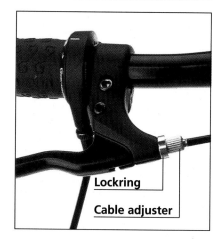

- Lockring
- Cable adjuster

Cantilever brake with straddle cable

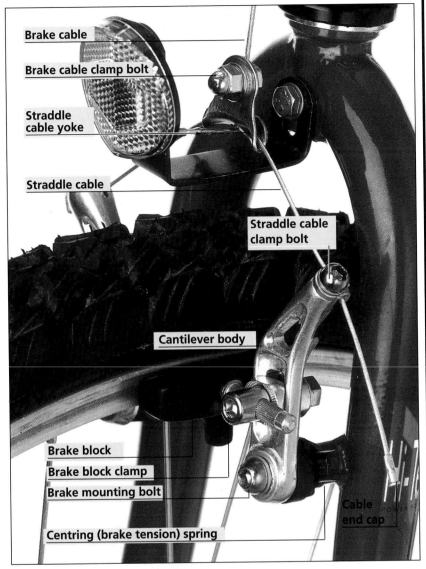

Brake cable

Brake cable clamp bolt

Straddle cable yoke

Straddle cable

Straddle cable clamp bolt

Cantilever body

Brake block

Brake block clamp

Brake mounting bolt

Centring (brake tension) spring

Cable end cap

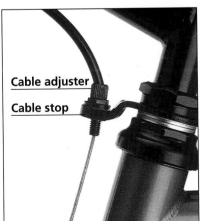

Cable adjuster

Cable stop

◀ Front brake cable stop

The outer cable for the front brake will stop either at the handlebar stem or at a guide which is mounted in the headset like this. In some cases (as here) the stop incorporates a cable adjuster.

Routine care and checks

Like any brake a cantilever needs to be kept clean and properly lubricated. The only moving parts are the cables and the cantilever arms. You should check the condition of the brake blocks at least once a month, more if you ride frequently.

Lubricating your brakes

Frequently lubricate the point at which the cantilever bodies rotate on the frame mountings. Use a light lubricant such as WD40 very frequently, or a heavier oil less often. As you oil the pivot, squeeze and release the brake lever, this will allow the lube to run in. Be careful not to get lube on the brake blocks or rim.

Also lube the cables in their stops to displace any water in the cable housing and keep your cables from getting sticky. As you oil, squeeze and release the brake lever to work lube up inside the cable outer.

Check the condition of your blocks

1 To check the condition of the brake blocks, first open the brake so that you can clearly see the blocks.

2 Inspect the surface of the brake block. There should still be grooves visible in the surface; if the block is worn to the bottom of the groove it should be replaced. Blocks without grooves will have a wear indicator line on the top, and should be replaced when they have worn to this line.

Blocks that are properly set up should show signs of even wear all over. If they are worn more at one end than another, or have a lip at the bottom edge then they should be trimmed to an even shape or replaced.

See 'Tidying worn brake blocks' in the section on side-pull brakes for details of how to trim unevenly worn blocks. See 'Replacing blocks' later in this section if the state of the blocks is beyond tidying.

Fault Diagnosis
Cantilever Brakes

SYMPTOM	CAUSE	REMEDY	PROCEDURE
Brakes don't work (or don't work well enough)	Blocks too far from rim	Adjust cable	Simple cable adjustment, or full cable adjustment
	Brake blocks worn	Replace blocks	Replacing worn brake blocks
Blocks rub on rim	Brake not centred	Centre brake	Centring the brake
	Wheel not true	True wheel	*Refer to Chapter 20*
Blocks rub on tyre	Incorrect block adjustment	Adjust blocks	Replacing the blocks (final parts)
Brakes squeal	Incorrect block set-up	Adjust blocks	Toeing in the blocks
Brakes stiff	Lever pivot stiff	Lube lever pivot	*See section on brake levers*
	Cable sticky	Lube cable...	Routine care
		If still stiff, replace cable	Replacing the cable
Brakes judder	Brake loose on mounting	Tighten mounting bolt	Brake removal and assembly
	Headset loose	Adjust headset	*See Chapter 19*
	Rim dented	True or replace rim	*See Chapter 20*
Brake blocks worn unevenly	Brakes not aligned properly	Tidy blocks, then align properly	Tidying worn brake blocks (*in side-pull section*)
Cable damaged	Wear and tear	Replace cable	Replacing the cable
Outer damaged	Wear and tear	Replace outer	Replacing the outer
	Crash damage	Don't crash; replace cable	Replacing the outer; Plus *see Chapter 6 'Off the road'* for riding tips
Brake seized/ crudded up	Neglect/corrosion	Overhaul or replace brake	Brake dismantling and overhaul

Adjustments

In a properly set up cantilever the following should happen:

▶ The blocks should hit the rim after the lever has been pulled about two centimetres. *(See 'Simple' and 'Full cable adjustments' if they don't.)*

▶ The blocks should be equally spaced either side of the rim. *(See 'Centring the brake' if they aren't.)*

▶ Both blocks should hit the rim squarely with no part hanging over the bottom of the rim or hitting the tyre. *(See the procedures of replacing blocks if they don't.)* This last situation is particularly dangerous; a badly adjusted block will quickly wear through the side of a tyre, eventually causing a blowout. If this happens at speed on the front wheel the results won't be pretty.

Adjusting the brakes (1): Simple cable adjustment

The most frequently needed adjustment is to take up some of the slack in the cable so that the lever activates the brake near the beginning of its travel, rather than near the end. Cable slack develops because cables bed in or stretch slightly from new, and because brake blocks wear and so have to travel farther to reach the rim. Simple cable adjustment is achieved with the adjuster on the brake lever.

TOOLS Fingers (may need pliers).

TIME 5 mins.

DIFFICULTY 🔧🔧🔧🔧

SPARES None.

OBJECTIVE To take up cable slack in the brake system so that the blocks hit the rim after the lever has been pulled about two centimetres.

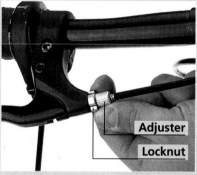

Adjuster
Locknut

1 Screw out the cable adjuster and locknut on the lever. If these are tight or seized first squirt them with some WD40. You may also need to gently use pliers or a Mole grip to free them. Unscrew the adjuster a couple of turns, then try the lever.

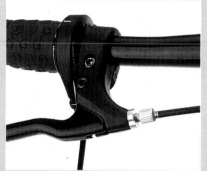

2 When the lever moves about 2cm before activating the brake, screw the locknut back down against the brake lever body to fix the adjustment.

3 When you are done the blocks should be about this far from the rim. (We have removed the tyre for clarity.) Spin the wheel and make sure it turns freely. If the brake rubs one side of the rim, centre the brake *(see below)*.

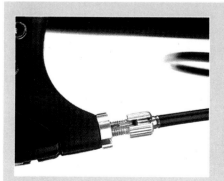

Adjusting the brake (2): Full cable adjustment

Eventually you will run out of adjustment on the cable adjuster. When you do it will look like this; a large amount of the thread on the adjuster is visible out of the lever, and only a small amount remains in the lever body. If you try to unscrew the adjuster much further it will come out of the lever, and an extended adjuster like this is easily damaged by a fall. It's time to take the cable slack up by pulling it through the clamp bolt.

This procedure is slightly different depending on whether you have a brake with a straddle cable or a link wire; we will deal with a full adjustment on a link wire brake first, then afterwards show the differences that occur on a straddle type design.

Full cable adjustment – link wire brakes

TOOLS Tool to fit cable clamp bolt (usually 5mm Allen key or 10mm spanner); cable puller or pliers.

TIME 10 mins.

DIFFICULTY 🔧🔧🔧🔧🔧

SPARES None.

OBJECTIVE To take up cable slack in the brake system; to set the adjuster screw to the bottom of its travel so it may subsequently be used to adjust the cable.

1 Undo the locknut and screw the cable adjuster all the way in.

2 Loosen the cable clamp bolt on the cantilever arm.

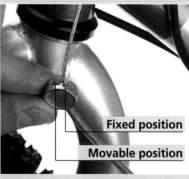

Fixed position

Movable position

3 Pop the brake cable from its normal, fixed position in the cable guide to the movable position in the larger, left hand slot.

If you have a cable puller

4a Pull the cable through the clamp bolt until the lever moves two centimetres before the blocks hit the rim (or the blocks are as close to the rim as shown above). Then tighten the cable clamp bolt firmly. If this bolt is loose, the cable will slip through it and your brakes won't work. Potentially nasty.

If you don't have a cable puller

4b Firstly unscrew the cable adjuster one or two turns so that you have the option to adjust it in both directions after you have tightened the cable clamp.

4c Tighten the cable clamp bolt just enough that it grips the cable lightly, but allows it to be pulled through with pliers. Pull the cable through until the blocks almost touch the rim, then tighten the cable clamp. Then adjust the block spacing with the adjuster on the lever, as necessary.

Final step

5 When the adjustment is complete, pop the brake back into its normal (fixed) position in the cable guide.

Variant – straddle cable brakes

Making a full cable adjustment on this design of cantilever brake is identical except for the following points.

▶ There is no cable guide and therefore no slots to move the cable in and out of. Hence, steps 3 and 5 of the above procedure do not apply.

▶ You can make **small cable adjustments** and move the blocks tighter to the rim by pulling through the straddle wire. Don't try adjusting the brake cable on the straddle yoke unless you are totally re-setting the cable set-up *(see below)*.

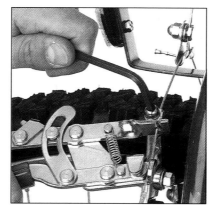

Warning

However, by doing this you may upset the position of the straddle yoke above the tyre. **If it touches the front reflector mounting**, you now need to re-set the straddle cabling by undoing the straddle cable and yoke and setting them up again. *For how to do this, see 'Setting up a straddle wire brake' later in this chapter.*

Centring the brake

TOOLS Spanner to fit tension spring (Varies – 10mm spanner/ 13mm/multi-size cone spanner); 5mm Allen key.

TIME 5 mins.

DIFFICULTY 🔧🔧🔧🔧

SPARES None.

OBJECTIVE To adjust the brake so that the blocks are evenly spaced either side of the rim.

Variant: Centring screws

Many Shimano cantilevers use a screw in the right hand brake arm to adjust the spring. Turning the screw in (clockwise) increases the spring tension and moves the block away from the rim.

1 The brake blocks should be evenly spaced either side of the rim. If they look like this, then one block is probably rubbing on the rim as you ride, and the brake needs centring. This is achieved by increasing or decreasing the tension of one of the springs; an adjuster behind one of the cantilevers allows this.

2 Loosen the brake mounting bolt, adjust the spring with a spanner so that the blocks are centred, then tighten up the bolt while holding the adjustment with the spanner. In this example, turning the spanner clockwise increases the spring tension and moves the block on the right-hand side away from the rim.

3 This is what you should achieve: Blocks that are evenly positioned either side of the rim make for even braking and no annoying rubbing noises as you ride. If it hasn't worked the first time, repeat this procedure until it does.

Toeing in the blocks

The commonest problem with all brakes is that they squeal when used. In busy city streets full of less than attentive pedestrians, this can be a bonus, but out in the peace and quiet of the countryside it's deeply annoying. Brake squeal usually happens because the brake vibrates at high frequency as the block hits the rim; this can usually be cured by toeing in the brake block, that is, adjusting the angle of the block so that the front of the block hits the rim slightly before the rear. Sometimes this doesn't work, in which case try switching to a different brand of block or even, if all else fails, switching to different brakes. Exactly how the blocks toe in varies with the particular brake block clamp design. However, almost all current cantilever brakes use the following system.

TOOLS 5mm Allen key; 10mm spanner.

TIME 10 mins.

DIFFICULTY

SPARES None.

OBJECTIVE To adjust the blocks so that the front edges hit before the rear.

1 Hold the front of the brake block clamp with the Allen key while loosening the nut at the back. Loosen the nut just enough that the clamp assembly and block will move with pressure from the Allen key. Twist the clamp in towards the rim so that the front edge of the block is 1mm nearer to the rim than the back edge. Then tighten the nut hard.

2 This is what you are aiming for, exaggerated a bit for clarity. The block on the right is toed in, the one on the left is not. Push the block against the rim with your hand; when the front edge touches, the rear should be about 1mm from the rim. Much more and braking will become mushy and it will be difficult to adjust the brake so that you get a combination of full braking power and no brake rub.

Repairs and replacements

Replacing blocks

TOOLS 10mm spanner; 5mm Allen key/6mm Allen key.

TIME 20 mins.

DIFFICULTY 🔧🔧🔧🔧🔧

SPARES New brake blocks.

OBJECTIVE To replace worn-out brake blocks.

1 First, screw the cable adjuster on the brake lever all the way in.

2 Pull the straddle cable out of its slot to release the brake and allow it to open clear of the rim.

3 Loosen the nut at the back of the brake block clamp to release the block. This nut is almost invariably 10mm.

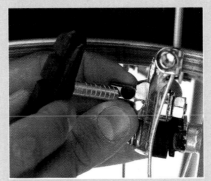

4 Pull the old block out of the brake and fit a new one in its place. While you are here, check the condition of the block surface.

5 Fit a new block into its clamp and adjust so it hits the rim in the middle, is parallel with the rim and misses the tyre.

6 Adjust the toe-in *(see 'Toeing in the blocks')* then tighten the block hard. **It is vital that brake blocks are tight;** if they are not, your brakes won't work, possibly with disastrous consequences.

7 You should now properly adjust your brakes. *See 'Adjusting the brakes (2): Full cable adjustment' for this procedure.*

TIP!

When replacing blocks, get good quality replacements such as Aztec, Kool Stop or Shimano M-System.

Replacing the cable

Brake cables are cheap enough and safety-critical enough that they should be replaced if there is the slightest hint of anything wrong with them. This includes damaged outers, frayed cables or just old, sticky cables that no longer pull smoothly.

TOOLS Pliers, cable cutter, WD40, 5mm Allen key or suitable tool to fit cable clamp.

TIME 20 mins.

DIFFICULTY 🔧🔧🔧🔧🔧

SPARES New inner cable, new cable end cap.

OBJECTIVE To replace a damaged inner cable and lubricate the cable outer while you are about it.

1 Undo the cable clamp bolt. In a straddle cable brake, undo the brake clamp in the straddle yoke.

Removing the old cable

2 Cut the cable above the clamp bolt or alternatively pull off the cable end cap. **If you're cutting, do not cut the cable cover in a link wire system.**

Fixed position

Movable position

3 Pop the cable out of the fixed position in the cable guide and over into the movable position. Pull the cable out of the cable guide.

4 Unscrew the locknut and cable adjuster and align the slots with each other and with the slot in the brake lever body if there is one. Pull the cable out of the slots. Throw it away.

Putting in a new cable

5 Types of brake cable nipple – pear-shaped (for drop handlebar levers) and barrel-shaped (for flat handlebar levers). If you have a universal cable, cut off the one you **don't** need.

6 Put the new cable into the brake lever. In some levers this nipple housing is accessed by pulling the lever against the bar.

7 Screw the locknut against the end of the cable adjuster, then screw the adjuster all the way into the lever.

8 While you have the cable apart, squirt WD40 into the outer to lubricate it and protect it from corrosion.

9 Thread the cable through the outer, and through whatever guides or stops your bike has, to get it to the brake.

Straddle wire brake

10a In a straddle cable system, the brake cable threads through the straddle yoke, between the bolt and washer. **If you have this sort of brake system, proceed now to the next procedure;** *'Setting up a straddle wire brake'.*

Link wire brake

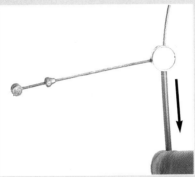

10b In a link wire system, the cable now threads through the cable guide to the cable clamp on the brake arm.

11 Thread the cable through the cable clamp bolt on the brake arm.

12 Hook the link wire back on the other brake arm (it probably fell off when you pulled out the old cable).

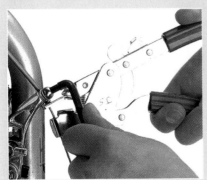

13 Pull the cable through the cable clamp bolt with a cable puller (or pliers). Adjust the cable position. *(see 'Full cable adjustment')* and tighten the clamp bolt.

14 When adjustments are complete, push the cable from the movable position in the cable guide to its fixed slot (as shown).

15 Finally, cut the cable to length and fit a cable end cap to stop it from fraying.

Setting up a straddle cable type brake

Typical straddle yoke arrangement

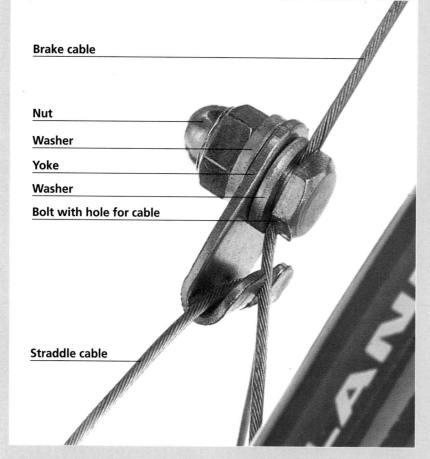

Brake cable

Nut

Washer

Yoke

Washer

Bolt with hole for cable

Straddle cable

1 Position (and clamp) the straddle wire yoke on the brake cable so that it is about 2cm above the tyre, higher if necessary to clear the reflector bracket.

2 Hook the end of the straddle wire into the other side of the cantilever and thread the bare end through the yoke and straddle cable clamp.

3 Pull the cable through the clamp and tighten the clamp bolt. Tighten the cable clamp bolt just enough that it grips the cable lightly, but allows it to be pulled through with pliers. Pull cable through until the blocks almost touch the rim, then tighten the cable clamp. Adjust the block spacing with the adjuster on the lever, as necessary.

In a link wire system, the short length of outer between the cable guide and the cable clamp determines the positions of the parts of the brake. In a straddle cable set-up, this is determined by the position of the straddle yoke, **which should be fairly close to the tyre.**

Most bikes have a reflector bracket mounted in the front fork, which also acts as a safety device to prevent the straddle cable from snagging in the tyre if the brake cable should break. While this is a highly unlikely accident it is a potentially fatal one. **It must be left in place.**

TOOLS Spanners for straddle yoke bolts (usually two 9mm or 10mm spanners); tool for cable clamp bolt (usually 5mm Allen key or 10mm spanner); cable puller or pliers.

TIME 10 mins.

DIFFICULTY 🔧🔧🔧🔧🔧

SPARES None (possibly replacement straddle cable).

OBJECTIVE To reset the straddle arrangement; (either after brake cable replacement, or to replace a straddle cable, or as part of adjusting the brake procedure).

Replacing the outer

A damaged outer cable can be removed without removing the inner wire. The techniques in this procedure are also needed if you are going to replace the whole inner and outer combination.

TOOLS Pliers, cable cutter, WD40, 5mm Allen key or suitable tool to fit cable clamp.

TIME 25 mins.

DIFFICULTY 🔧🔧🔧🔧🔧

SPARES New cable outer, new cable end cap.

OBJECTIVE To replace a damaged outer.

1 Pull the cable end cap off the cable. You did fit one didn't you? Undo the cable clamp bolt, pull the brake cable out of the cable guide. (Or, if you have a straddle cable brake, undo the brake cable from the straddle yoke).

2 Once the inner cable is free of the brake and all stops, pull the outer off the inner.

How to cut cable outers properly

It is important to cut outers cleanly. Otherwise you will have difficulty in feeding inner cables through them. More importantly, rough outer edges will damage and fray the inners. On a brake cable, that is potentially very nasty.

Brake cable outer is made up of a narrow, flattened steel sheet, wound in a spiral. To cut cable outer cleanly, bend the outer over the jaws of the cutter so that the cutter goes in between one of the spirals of the outer.

If like the cable on the left, you end up with a burr on the cut end, use the cutters to trim it off.

3 Cut the new outer to the same length as the old one. **Important:** *See accompanying tips on cable cutting and cable lengths.*

Cable Lengths

Cable outers should be cut so they take short, smooth, curved paths between the points they connect, and they enter and leave stops and guides along the centre-line of those guides. Excess brake cable causes mushiness in a brake system, too little increases cable friction by pulling the inner against the inside of the outer. *For more tips on cables, see Chapter 11.*

TIP!

If you have a file, or, even better, access to a grinding wheel, file or grind the ends of the cable outer flat, then use a needle to open up the end of the cable (the heat generated by grinding may melt the cable's inner lining).

4 Fill the outer with lube. Then thread the inner cable back into the outer and reconnect the inner cable to the brake as detailed in *'Replacing the cable'* if you have a link wire brake, or *'Setting up a straddle cable brake'* if you have one of those types.

Dismantling and overhauling a cantilever brake

There is very little that can go wrong with cantilever brakes. In time the brake action can become sticky because of corrosion in the pivots.

If this happens the brake should be removed and the pivots cleaned up with very light emery cloth and lubricated with grease.

TOOLS 5mm Allen key, solvents, emery paper and grease as needed.

TIME Disassembly: 5 mins; cleaning and overhaul, up to 30 mins.

DIFFICULTY

SPARES None.

OBJECTIVE To dismantle and clean brake and pivots, re-lubricate everything, remove corrosion from pivot if necessary.

Disassembly

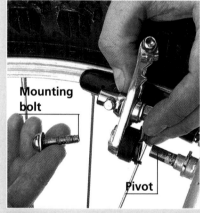

Mounting bolt

Pivot

1 Undo the cable clamp bolt, and then the brake mounting bolt. Remove the bolt and lift the brake off the pivot. If the pivot is corroded, gently sand off the rust with fine emery cloth.

2 **The parts come apart as shown.** Clean all the parts with degreaser.

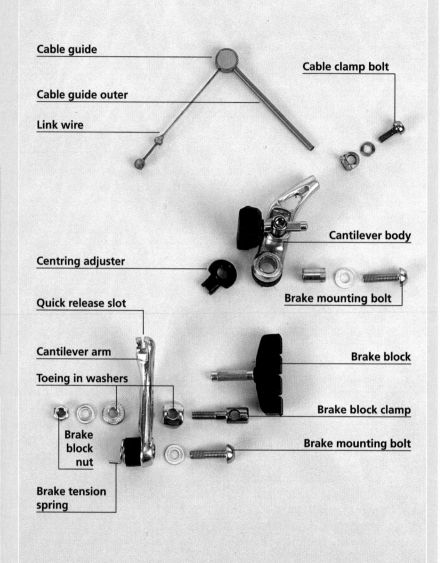

Cable guide

Cable clamp bolt

Cable guide outer

Link wire

Cantilever body

Centring adjuster

Brake mounting bolt

Quick release slot

Cantilever arm

Brake block

Toeing in washers

Brake block clamp

Brake block nut

Brake mounting bolt

Brake tension spring

Reassembly

3 Putting it back together again is the reverse of the way you took it apart. *(Use the picture to guide you if necessary.)* Smear grease on all surfaces that have to slide against each other. Reconnect the brake blocks (if you removed them) and the cable as shown in previous procedures.

Brake Levers

Not much can go wrong with a brake lever: It's possible to damage one by crashing, in which case it will need replacing, and very old brake levers do become loose and rattly; again, the cure is replacement.

Flat-handlebar (MTB) levers

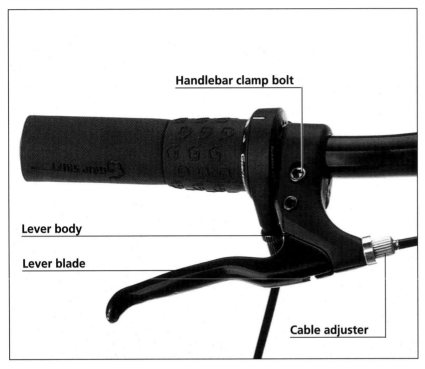

Handlebar clamp bolt

Lever body

Lever blade

Cable adjuster

TIPS!

● *The levers should be positioned so that you can comfortably reach the ends of the lever blades with your hands at the ends of the handlebar. This position gives maximum control and braking power on descents.*

● *The clamps which attach brake levers need to be tight enough to hold the lever in place and no tighter. It is possible to damage some very light-weight handlebars by getting too enthusiastic with the brake lever clamps.*

Routine care

The only routine care levers need is an occasional spray of light lube into the pivot to keep it moving freely.

Adjustments

Adjusting lever position
The position of the brake lever can be adjusted by unscrewing the Allen key bolt which clamps the lever to the handlebar and rotating the lever round the bar, or moving it sideways on the bar. Brake levers should be angled down at about 45 degrees.

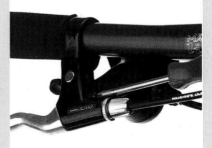

Adjusting lever reach
Some brake levers have provision for you to adjust the reach of the lever blade. A screw in the lever body can be turned in to move the lever nearer to the handlebar, and out to move the lever further away.

Drop Handlebar brake levers

A common type of drop handlebar brake lever is the 'aero' design, which routes the brake cable under the handlebar tape for a sleek look. Older levers route the cable out of the top of the lever.

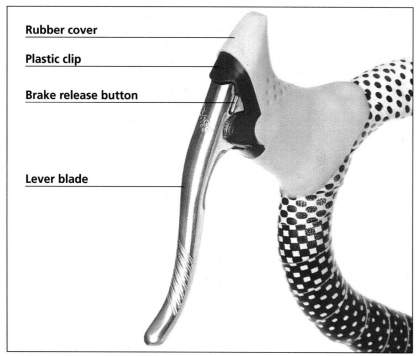

Rubber cover

Plastic clip

Brake release button

Lever blade

Brake Release Button

The brake release button has the effect of allowing the lever to move to this position, feeding more slack cable into the brake system and letting the brake open wider; this is handy for removing the wheel to put the bike in a car or fix a puncture.

Brake release button

From the position of the brake lever it should be obvious that the brake release is on. **Makes sure it is off** when adjusting your brakes and most certainly before going out riding.

Routine care

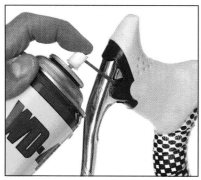

The only routine care levers need is an occasional spray of light lube into the pivot to keep it moving freely.

Adjusting Drop-bar Brake Levers
Adjusting lever position

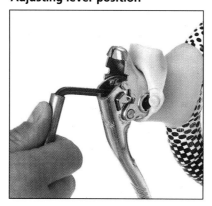

To remove the lever from the handlebar, first remove the cable *(See relevant 'Replacing the cable procedure'.)* Then use a 5mm Allen key to loosen the bolt inside the lever body. Now you can position the levers.

Setting brake lever position

To set lever height, place a ruler on the bottom of the handlebar so that it projects forward from the bar. The end of the brake lever should be within half an inch of the ruler.

When adjusting lever position, lay a long ruler across the top of the levers. Adjusting the levers so this ruler is parallel with the handlebar will ensure that the levers are at the same height. The bodies of the brake levers should be parallel to the centre line of the bike when viewed from above with the handlebar straight ahead.

Removing the levers
To take the levers off, undo the bolt completely. The levers are attached to the bar by this type of clamp. Slide the clamp off the handlebars (you'll have to remove the tape) if you need to.

Warning

Extension Levers

Brake systems with 'safety' or extension levers, which allow the brakes to be activated from the centre of the handlebar, should be checked more frequently. These extensions reduce the total movement of the main lever and so require more frequent cable adjustment to keep everything working properly. Since safety levers also provide less stopping power than the main levers, and allow you to brake from a position which gives less control of the bike, my advice is that you remove them, or switch to conventional levers.

Other brakes

Centre-pull Brakes

The most common 'alternative' brake design on road bikes is the centre-pull. These used to be very popular on touring bikes, and you may therefore come across them on bikes like the classic Dawes Galaxy tourers of the early eighties. They have fallen out of favour in recent years because good cantilever and side-pulls offer better stopping power. They work best with as short a straddle wire as is reasonable, and frequent lubrication on the pivot point on either side of the brake.

Hub brakes and Drum brakes

These are built into the wheel hub and therefore sealed from the elements. Occasionally they are found as an additional brake on tandems. They are not widespread and are not covered in this book.

Disc Brakes

Making something of a comeback at the moment are disc brakes, which, like motorcycle brakes, use separate discs that are not part of the rim. Because the disc is always perfectly straight, the brake blocks can run very close to it and as a result this design offers the possibility of very high mechanical advantage and lots of stopping power. Discs are therefore becoming popular with downhill mountain bike racers who need to be able to stop their bikes from 50 mph.

Transmission

Contents

Types of Gears

Hub gears

One of the earliest types of gear system used an arrangement of cogs inside the rear hub shell to provide differing drive ratios. In a hub gear the drive from the chain is geared up or down by the internal mechanism which in turn drives the hub shell and therefore the wheel. The classic Sturmey-Archer three-speed hub gear is still in widespread use all round the world today, and is perfect for utility bikes that are used where there are no serious hills. It is reliable, simple to maintain and relatively cheap. However its limited range of gears and mechanical losses of a few per cent of the rider's energy make it unsuitable for touring and sporting use.

Adjusting and maintaining Hub gears are dealt with at the end of this chapter.

Derailleur gears

In the search for more gears, bike designers soon began to experiment with systems which used multiple sprockets on the rear wheel and devices to move the chain from one to another. They were called by the French term; derailleur. The derivation really is that obvious – it derails the chain from one sprocket to the next. Early derailleur systems used three or four sprockets and in recent years we have seen this grow through five to six, seven and even eight. In addition, similar systems on the front gear have produced two and three chainrings, each of which can be used

with all the sprockets at the back, so a typical modern bike has anywhere between 10 and 24 gears.

Derailleur gears are by far the most common type of gears found on modern bikes today. All mountain bikes are equipped with them. Consequently this chapter will deal in the main with derailleur gears.

Why so many?

The reason for this proliferation of gears is to do with the range of effort at which the human engine is comfortable. The objective of gears is to allow you to work at about the same rate whether you are climbing a one in six at 5 mph or hurtling down the other side at 40 mph; you can see that this requires a very wide range of gears, and typical gear systems for mountain and touring bikes give a range of almost five to one between the highest and lowest gears. In between those extremes the rider needs as many gears as possible to keep the effort level more or less constant at any speed, hence the development of 21 and 24 speed systems.

As you'd expect, there are trade-offs. Chains aren't really meant to be shoved unceremoniously from one sprocket to the next, or to be used in anything but a straight line from chainwheel to sprocket. Because of the extra friction that comes from running out of line, a chain in a derailleur system will last for

10,000 miles at the very most, and in practise you will be lucky to get more than 5,000 miles of use. By comparison, chains in well-aligned hub gear systems last for years. And of course all those extra mechanisms are exposed to the elements and to knocks and bumps; derailleur gear systems need quite a bit more care and feeding than hub gears, or – the ultimate in simplicity – a one-speed.

Fortunately modern derailleur gears work exceptionally well and are easy to fix and adjust when they do go wrong. At first sight it's pretty surprising that derailleur gears work at all. That they work as well as they do is a testament to the skill and intelligence of the engineers who produce them.

Indexed gears

Almost all modern bikes except the very cheapest now have indexed gears. The principle is simple: you push the gear lever and the gear guides the chain precisely from one sprocket to the next. To tell you this has occurred there is a mechanism in the shift lever which produces an audible and tactile click. Introduced by Japanese component giant Shimano in the mid-eighties, indexed gears are one of the crucial refinements of recent years and have made a previously fiddly operation – changing gear – into a very simple one.

Derailleur gears

The front mech

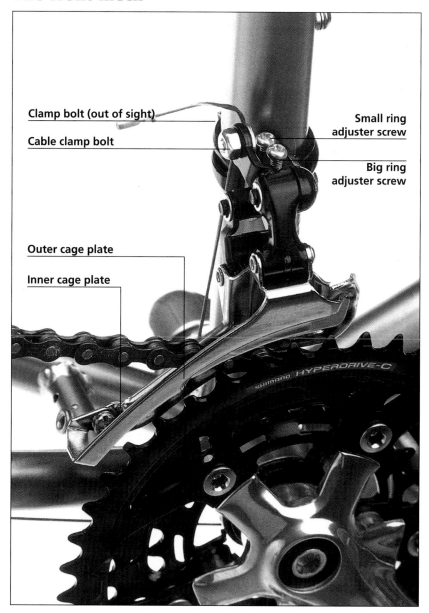

Clamp bolt (out of sight)

Cable clamp bolt

Small ring adjuster screw

Big ring adjuster screw

Outer cage plate

Inner cage plate

Routine lubrication

1 Keep a front mech clean and well lubricated and it will last years. The important places to lube are the pivots on which the mech moves to push the chain. WD40 or other light, penetrating lube is good.

2 Also lubricate the cables. Sticky cables are the enemy of good shifting. Spray a little WD40 into the cable ends frequently to keep them from corroding.

If, after you have lubed the cables, the shifting is still very slow, you may have to lube them more thoroughly. *For techniques on this refer to the section on gear cables later in this chapter.*

Fault Diagnosis
Front mech

SYMPTOM	CAUSE	REMEDY	PROCEDURE
Chain falls off outwards or chain won't shift up to big ring	Mech stop screws not adjusted correctly	Adjust outer stop screw	Shifting adjustments
Chain falls off inwards or chain won't shift down to small ring	Mech stop screws not adjusted correctly	Adjust inner stop screw	Shifting adjustments
Shifting is vague or imprecise	Mech too high	Move mech down	Positional adjustments
	Mech not parallel to chainrings	Adjust mech position	Positional adjustments
	Mech inner plate worn out	Replace mech	Removing and replacing the front mech
Chain rubs on mech in more than one chainring	Mech not parallel to chainrings	Adjust mech position	Positional adjustments
	Chainrings bent	Replace Chainrings	(See Chapter 16)
Chain rubs on mech in middle or big ring	Indexing not adjusted properly	Adjust cable tension	Adjusting the indexing
Shifting is slow, especially shifting down	Cable sticky	Lubricate cables	Routine cable care (or cable replacement) (Refer to 'Gear cables' section)
	Mech sticky	Lube mech	Routine lubrication
	Mech corroded	Remove mech and soak in lube	Removing and replacing the front mech
		Replace mech	Removing and replacing the front mech

Positional Adjustment

Most of the problems people have with shifting across the chainrings are due to an improperly positioned front mech. It is very rare for it to go out of adjustment on its own, though the friction of rubbing against a hardened steel chain to shift it will eventually wear through the inner plate. The position of the front mech is adjusted by undoing the clamp bolt on the left-hand side of the frame and moving the mech up, down and rotationally.

TOOLS 5mm Allen key or 9mm spanner, possibly pliers as well.

TIME 5 mins.

DIFFICULTY 🔧

SPARES None.

OBJECTIVE To correctly position the front mech around the seat-tube and above the chainrings.

1 To adjust the position of the front mech, loosen the clamp bolt at the back of the mech and move it by hand. Make small adjustments and test the clearance of the mech over the chainrings after each one.

2 Height above the chainrings

❌ **Mech too low.** When you try to shift up the outer cage plate fouls the big chainring.

✔ **The correct position** for the front mech is so that the outer cage plate clears the big chainring by about 2mm when it swings up over the ring.

❌ **Mech too high.** If the mech is too far up the seat tube the chain will shift up only very reluctantly or not at all, because the rear cage plate is too far from the chain

3 Correct rotation around the seat-tube

The front mech must also be parallel to the chainrings so that the chain does not rub in some of the gears or catch on the crank. Rotate the mech around the seat tube so that the outer cage plate is parallel to the big ring. When you tighten the clamp bolt this adjustment may change. If it does, note how far out of adjustment the mech ends up, loosen the bolt and rotate the mech back a little to take account of the positional drift caused by tightening.

OUTER CAGE PLATE

BIG RING

Adjusting the cable tension

If you are adjusting the height of the mech, it may also be necessary to adjust the cable tension. Slacken off the cable clamp bolt before starting, and once the mech is finally positioned, pull the cable through with pliers and tighten the cable clamp bolt again. *(Note: if adjusting the cable, check also that it now correctly shifts. If this has been put out see 'Shifting adjustments'.)*

Shifting adjustments

If the chain has difficulty shifting onto one of the rings or if it shifts too far and therefore off the rings then it needs adjusting. The movement of the mech across the chainrings is controlled by the two screws on the top of the mech body.

It is also possible for the cable to prevent the mech from moving far enough inward to drop the chain on to the inner ring. In this case, the cable clamp has to be adjusted. *(See tip below.)*

> **TOOLS** Cross head screwdriver.
>
> **TIME** 5 mins.
>
> **DIFFICULTY** 🔧🔧🔧🔧🔧
>
> **SPARES** None.
>
> **OBJECTIVE** To correctly set the limits of movement for the front mech.

If shifting to the small ring is poor adjust the inner screw. Turn it anti-clockwise to allow the mech to drop the chain to the inner ring and clock-wise to stop the chain from dropping too far and missing the ring entirely.

If the chain falls off the big ring when you try to shift up, turn the outer screw clockwise. If it won't shift up to the big ring, turn the screw anti-clockwise to allow the mech to push further. Make adjustments a quarter or a half turn at a time, then try the shift.

If adjustment not successful

If you have undone the inner screw and the chain will still not drop cleanly to the inner ring, try slackening the cable slightly. Undo the cable clamp bolt and let the cable slip through. The mech will probably spring to a lower position. Adjust the screw so that the chain runs cleanly on the small ring, between the cage plates, then take up the cable slack and tighten the clamp bolt.

Adjusting the indexing

Many triple ring systems have indexed front shifting. To adjust this, use the cable tension adjuster on the shifter. To correctly adjust the indexing, turn the adjuster until it is possible to shift the mech up from the inner ring to the middle ring so that the chain no longer rubs on the cage plates once the middle ring is achieved. Once this is set, then the indexing is adjusted for shifting to all the chainrings.

TIP!

Sometimes a bike shifts perfectly in the workshop, but still isn't quite right when the chain is under load. Test ride front mech adjustments as soon as possible.

Repairs and replacements

Removing and replacing the front mech

A neglected front mech may become so sticky that it requires removing from the bike and soaking in penetrating oil to get it moving again, and a very old and worn out mech needs replacing, so you need to know how to get the mech off the bike.

It is not necessary to split the chain. It may be easier to remove a mech by taking off the chain first, but this is not advisable with Shimano chains which do not take kindly to being split and rejoined.

TOOLS 5mm Allen key or 9mm spanner or as required for cable clamp and frame clamp; small crosshead screwdriver.

TIME 10 mins.

DIFFICULTY 🔧🔧🔧🔧🔧

SPARES New front mech if required.

OBJECTIVE To remove the front mech from the frame and, if necessary, fit a new one.

1 Undo the cable clamp bolt.

2 Undo the frame clamp bolt at the back of the mech.

3 Lift the mech off the seat tube and undo the screw that holds the two cage plates together. Sometimes there is a small tube bridging the two plates and the screw goes through it.

4 Finally, flex the two cage plates apart and take the mech off the chain.

Replacing the cable

Damaged gear cables are rare, but it is possible for them to get mashed in crashes, or for cables without end caps to fray. A frayed front mech cable is a serious irritant because it will continually snag the inside of your right leg, and the ends are sharp enough to cut. *(For how to replace a front mech cable, see the section on gear cables later in this chapter).*

Clean, inspect, replace

5 Once off the bike, thoroughly clean the mech with degreaser. If necessary allow the mech to soak in penetrating oil overnight. Try to get the pivots moving freely by hand. There should be no 'stickiness'. If the mech is so seized that it is a lost cause, throw it away and purchase a replacement.

Refitting the mech

6 Refitting the mech is the reverse of removal. The last step of refitting is to re-attach the cable. The cable needs to be taut, hence the cable clamp bolt needs to be tightened whilst the cable is being pulled through either with pliers or by using a special cable pulling tool.

After the mech is attached it will need to be adjusted. *See 'Positional adjustments' and 'Shifting adjustments', above, for details of how to set up a new mech.* **Make sure that once adjusted, you generously lube the mech pivots.**

Derailleur gears
The rear mech

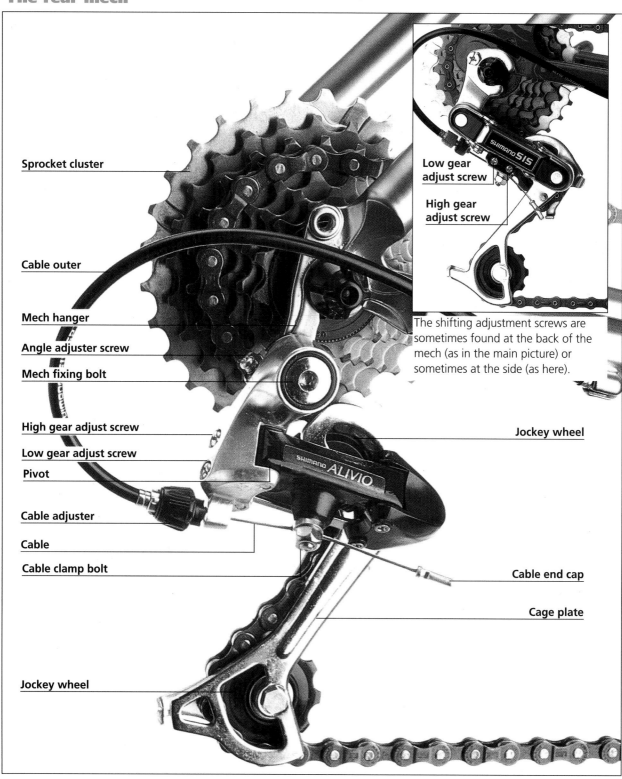

Sprocket cluster

Cable outer

Mech hanger

Angle adjuster screw

Mech fixing bolt

High gear adjust screw

Low gear adjust screw

Pivot

Cable adjuster

Cable

Cable clamp bolt

Jockey wheel

Low gear adjust screw

High gear adjust screw

SHIMANO SIS

The shifting adjustment screws are sometimes found at the back of the mech (as in the main picture) or sometimes at the side (as here).

SHIMANO ALIVIO

Jockey wheel

Cable end cap

Cage plate

134

Fault Diagnosis
Rear mech

SYMPTOM	CAUSE	REMEDY	PROCEDURE
Chain falls off into spokes or chain won't shift up to biggest sprocket	Stop screws misadjusted	Adjust 'L' stop screw	Shifting adjustments
Chain falls off toward frame or chain won't shift down to smallest sprocket	Stop screws misadjusted	Adjust 'H' stop screw	Shifting adjustments
Mech does not shift accurately with shifter	Indexing out of adjustment	Adjust cable tension	Adjusting the indexing
Chain noisy on sprocket	Indexing out of adjustment	Adjust cable tension	Adjusting the indexing
Adjustment fails to get indexing right	Mech bent or damaged	Replace mech	Removing and replacing the rear mech
	Mech hanger on frame bent	Straighten mech	*(Refer to Chapter 21; 'The frame')* **Note:** this really is a job for a pro mechanic
Shifting is poor	Cable damaged by crash or neglect	Replace cable	Replacing the cable *(See next section on 'gear cables')*
Shifting, especially to higher gears, is poor	Cable sticky	Lube cable	Routine cable care (or cable replacement) *(See next section on 'gear cables')*
	Mech sticky	Lube mech	Routine lubrication
Shifting, especially to lower gears, is poor	Outer damaged	Replace outer	Replacing the outer *(See next section on 'gear cables')*
Mech is very sticky or corroded	Neglect	Remove, soak in lube or replace	Removing and replacing the rear mech

Routine lubrication

The exposed position of the rear mech makes it quite prone to crash damage, to corrosion from road salt and to just generally getting gunked up. It's essential to keep this complex component clean and well-lubricated, since its proper function relies on six pivots, three springs (two of them internal) and a pair of jockey wheels, all of which need to move easily and smoothly.

1 Lube any point where the mech moves. This basically means all the pivots.

2 Give the jockey wheels a regular squirt of lube as well. It's rare for their plain bearings to actually seize, but they can get very squeaky if allowed to run dry.

Adjustments

Rear mechs can be adjusted four ways. There are limit screws on the back of the mechanism to control the range of movement across the sprocket cluster, the angle adjust screw changes the position of the mech around the mech hanger and the cable adjuster is used to trim the gear indexing.

Shifting adjustments

If you have problems shifting into all the gears on the bike, (or if you are able to shift too far and the chain goes off the sprockets), then the range of movement of the mech needs adjusting. This is done by adjusting the two screws at the back (or side) of the mech. Between them, these two screws control the movement limits of the rear mech. Make adjustments a quarter to a half a turn at a time and test the shift each time.

TOOLS Cross head screwdriver.

TIME 5 mins.

DIFFICULTY 🔧🔧🔧🔧🔧

SPARES None.

OBJECTIVE To correctly set the limits of movement for the rear mech.

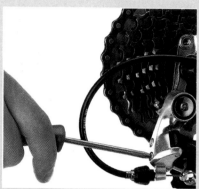

1 Use the lower screw – marked L for low gear – to adjust shifting to and from the largest sprocket. If the chain will not move up to the big ring, turn the screw out (anticlockwise) to allow more movement. If the mech moves too far and rubs against the spokes, turn the screw in (clockwise) to adjust the movement limit away.

2 Use the upper screw – marked H for high gear – to adjust shifting to and from the smallest sprocket. If the chain will not drop into the small sprocket, turn the screw out (anti-clockwise) to allow the mech more movement. If this does not work, it is possible that the mech or cable needs lubrication, or that the cable is too tight and is limiting the mech's movement. If the mech overshoots the small sprocket, turn the adjuster screw clockwise to limit the movement.

3 Also lubricate the cables. Sticky cables are the enemy of good shifting. Spray a little WD40 into the cable ends frequently to keep them from corroding.

136

Adjusting the indexing

An indexed gear system has click-stops built into the shifter which correspond to the positions of the mech on the rear sprockets. If the cable is not precisely adjusted, the shifter and the mech get out of synch and the indexing doesn't work, which usually shows up as a very noisy drive or the chain skipping between sprockets. Fortunately, adjusting the indexing so that it works reliably is very simple.

TOOLS Fingers.

TIME 5 mins.

DIFFICULTY 🔧🔧🔧🔧

SPARES None.

OBJECTIVE To adjust the rear mech cable tension so that the gears index accurately.

1 To adjust the indexing, shift into the second sprocket and unscrew the cable adjuster whilst turning the pedals. This will move the mech across the sprockets towards the largest sprocket.

2 Eventually, the chain will begin to rub on the third sprocket and become noisy. When this happens, screw the adjuster back in until the chain just stops rubbing on the third sprocket. The indexing should now be perfectly adjusted for all gears.

Fine tuning on the road

Indexing adjustment

You can also fine tune your indexing by turning the adjuster at the shifter. This is especially useful whilst riding for making any small adjustments which may be necessary. Alternatively, some shifters have buttons which disable the indexing completely.

TIP!

In Shimano gear systems, reliable indexing is very dependent on Shimano's floating 'Centeron' top jockey wheel, which moves slightly from side to side and allows the chain to self-align on the sprocket. If you have to replace this jockey wheel, be sure to get a genuine Shimano replacement part.

Adjusting the mech's angle

A rare problem is that the top jockey wheel catches on the largest sprocket, usually when the chain is on the smallest sprocket. Screwing in the angle adjust screw pulls the mech back and will sometimes cure this problem. However, the fault is usually caused by using a sprocket which is too big for the mech to cope with. *(See Chapter 8 'Useful Info'.)*

Removing and replacing the rear mech

If a mech has become sticky to the point where simply spraying lube at it doesn't get it moving, then it should be removed, cleaned and soaked in light, penetrating lubricant overnight. When the lubricant has thoroughly penetrated the mech, try to get the pivots moving freely by hand; eventually they will free up.

Alternatively you may simply wish to upgrade to a lighter or better quality rear mech, or one with more gear capacity to allow you to run lower gears, or your rear mech may have been damaged. Here's how to remove and replace the mech.

Note that the procedure below does not involve splitting the chain. With Shimano chains especially, splitting them is not a good idea, and is best avoided if at all possible. *(See 'Chains' later in this chapter.)*

TOOLS 9mm spanner; 5mm Allen key / 8mm spanner.	
TIME 30 mins.	
DIFFICULTY 🔧🔧🔧🔧🔧	
SPARES Replacement rear mech if required.	
OBJECTIVE To remove and replace the rear mech.	

Removing the mech

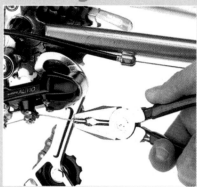

1 Start with the mech and shifter in a small sprocket position. Pull off the cable end cap or, if the cable is frayed at the end cut off the frayed portion.

2 Undo the cable clamp bolt. Pull the gear cable away so that it is free from the rear mech.

3 Undo the bolt which holds the bottom jockey wheel in place. This usually has either an 8mm hex head (as shown) or a 3mm Allen key fitting and is often very tight. **Care is needed not to damage this bolt.**

4 Lift the jockey wheel out of the mech, taking care to keep the parts – two dust covers, a bushing and the wheel – together.

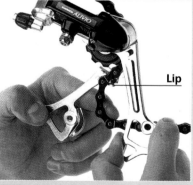

Lip

5 Pull the rear cage plate backwards to allow the chain to come out. It might be necessary to slacken the top jockey wheel nut. The chain will need to be pushed over a lip on the rear cage plate.

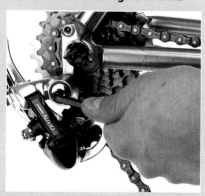

6 With the chain out of the mech, undo the mech fixing bolt. This is almost always a 5mm Allen key bolt.

138

Hanger stop

7 The mech is now free of the frame. Note the protruding stop on the bottom of the gear hanger.

Clean and inspect

Now if necessary undo the upper jockey wheel nut and remove the jockey wheel and the cage plate. The parts disassemble as shown. Clean all the parts thoroughly with degreaser. If the mech pivots are seized, soak the mech body in penetrating oil overnight. Then, by hand, try to get the mech pivots moving freely. If still no joy, the whole mech may need to be replaced.

If the existing mech is to be reassembled, remember to lube the jockey wheels and their bushings.

TIP!

8mm jockey wheel bolts are often of poor quality and a high quality adjustable spanner may fit better than an 8mm spanner.

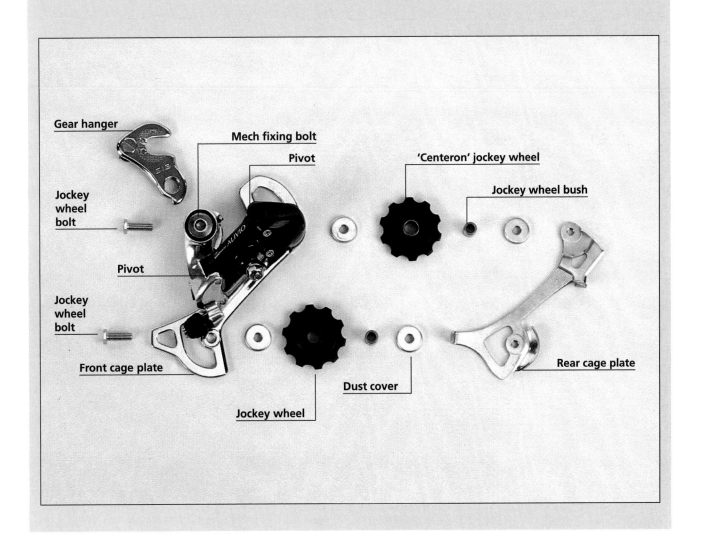

Gear hanger

Mech fixing bolt

Pivot

'Centeron' jockey wheel

Jockey wheel bush

Jockey wheel bolt

Pivot

Jockey wheel bolt

Front cage plate

Jockey wheel

Dust cover

Rear cage plate

Replacing the rear mech

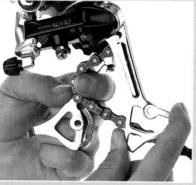

9 Hold the mech as shown so that the angle adjuster screw on the mech does not foul the stop in the hanger. Carefully align the fixing bolt thread with the hanger thread. If necessary, turn the mech bolt backwards in the hanger until you feel the threads click together. *(See Chapter 11 for advice on starting threads).* The bolt should screw in with only light pressure on the Allen key. **Tighten the bolt down hard.**

10 Pull the cage plates apart and thread the chain into them. Lift the chain over the lip in the rear cage plate. The chain goes over the top of the upper jockey wheel and round the back of the bottom one.

11 Put the bottom jockey wheel into place, with the chain running behind it as shown, then fit the bolt and tighten it hard.

12 Moving the cage plates loosens the top jockey wheel bolt, so it is vital to re-tighten this bolt as the final step in attaching the mech.

13 Pull the gear cable back through the mech, and whilst holding the cable taut with pliers or a cable pulling tool, tighten the cable clamp bolt. Cut the cable leaving a couple of inches free for later adjustments. Lastly fit a cable end cap. *(For more on cable fitting see the section on gear cables later in this chapter).*

14 Finally, set the mech up by making the necessary shifting and indexing adjustments (see above). Also remember to lube the mech pivots and the jockey wheels.

Gear cables

In this section we will deal with all the issues of gear cabling – for front and rear mechs – together. Given that there will be different routeing, the cabling for both front and rear mech is identical

Routine cable care

Sticky cables

Sticky cables are the enemy of good shifting. Always keep them lubed. Spray a little WD40 into the cable ends frequently to keep them from corroding.

Special tools

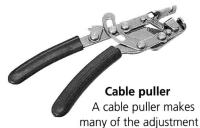

Cable puller
A cable puller makes many of the adjustment and maintenance jobs on gears much easier, though it is not essential. Essentially it enables the cable to be kept taut and in place whilst the clamp bolt is tightened. This Park tool has a ratchet which allows it to be used to lock a cable in position, freeing your hands up to do other things.

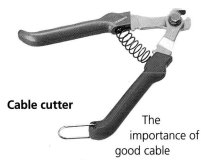

Cable cutter
The importance of good cable cutters cannot be over-stressed. Ordinary cutters, especially those found in pliers, will turn a perfectly good shiny new cable into a mashed, spread, useless mess. These Shimano cutters are professional quality and are designed to cut both inner cables and outers cleanly and tidily. They can also be used on brake cables and outers, and have jaws for shaping the cut end of special index gear outer cable.

Lubing cables more thoroughly

If the shifting gets very slow, the problem is usually sticky cables. If a squirt of lube into the end of the cable doesn't cure the problem, and your bike has cable stops with slots to facilitate cable removal, then it's easy to lubricate the whole cable. This is often enough to get a badly-shifting system working again.

1 Pull the cable out of its slots. To do this you need to create some cable slack. This can be done by putting the mech in the big ring and then dropping the shifter to its small ring position, without turning the pedals.

2 Move the outer along the cable and spray the whole cable with lube. This procedure is worth doing from time to time even if your system seems OK; it's amazing how slow cables can get over time.

141

Replacing a cable

For replacing a cable, we will deal with replacements on the rear mech. The sequence is almost identical for replacements on the front mech cable, except that the cable routeing between shifter and mech will be different.

Refer to Chapter 11 for general hints and tips on cables, especially regarding cutting cables and dealing with frayed ends. Remember, always fit a cable end cap.

Before you start

Before starting, look at your shifters and check that you can see how the cable is going to come out of them. With gripshift shifters (for more details on these see the next section), the cable end is buried inside the shifter and it will not pull out without dismantling the mechanism. This is, to say the least, awkward. If you have shifters like this and are unsure on how they work, then cable replacements are probably best left to the dealer.

TOOLS Cable cutters; pliers/ cable puller; 9mm spanner/5mm Allen key.

TIME 20 mins.

DIFFICULTY 🔧🔧🔧🔧🔧

SPARES Replacement cable, cable end cap.

OBJECTIVE To remove a damaged or corroded gear cable and fit a new one.

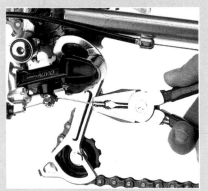

1 Start with the mech and shifter in a smaller sprocket position. Pull off the cable end cap or, if the cable is frayed at the end, cut off the frayed portion. If the cable is damaged elsewhere, cut out the damaged section to make it easier to pull the cable out of the outers.

2 Undo the cable clamp bolt.

3 Pull the cable out of the guides and push it back through the outer so that it pops out of the hole in the shifter. Some Shimano Rapidfire shifters have a rubber bung in this hole; in others it is permanently open. Pull the cable completely out and discard.

TIP!

If the hole in the shifter does not perfectly line up with the internal cable carrier and it is difficult to get the cable head out, try waggling the larger of the two levers to move the cable around until it pops out.

Types of cable nipple. The right-hand nipple is required for almost all derailleur gear systems, while the left-hand nipple fits in Sturmey-Archer three speeds.

4 If you have a universal cable (a cable with a cable nipple on each end), cut off the nipple that you don't need.

5 Take the opportunity to fill the dismantled cable outer with light lube.

6 Thread the new cable through the shifter and into the cable outer.

7 Thread the cable through the twists and turns of the cable routeing. The cables may either run through cable outers along the top tube or through a plastic guide under the bottom bracket (as shown here). The rear mech cable is on the right, the front mech cable is on the left.

Replacing a cable on the front mech

8 Thread the cable through the outer at the rear mech. Then, with the mech and shifter still in a small sprocket position, thread the cable through the clamp bolt. Gently pull it snug, either with a cable puller or pliers, and tighten the cable clamp bolt.

TIP!

Especially if you're using a cable puller, take care not to pull the cable so tight that you actually push the mech and upset its adjustment.

The procedure is identical to that described above, except that the routeing between the shifter and the mech will be different. The cable is attached to the front mech by a 9mm cable clamp bolt as shown here.

Follow on adjustments

After you have fitted the new cable you may still find that the mech now needs to be adjusted in order to shift across all the sprockets/chainrings. For this, refer to the 'Shifting adjustments' in the relevant section.

9 Cut off the excess cable, leaving a couple of inches spare for later adjustments.

10 Finally, fit a cable end cap.

Cable outers

Shimano SIS SP outer

Most quality indexed gear systems now have a type of outer which is different to the normal wire spiral type. Instead this variety has many longitudinal wire strands in a harder plastic sheath and is almost incompressible. This outer is necessary to give the high shifting precision necessary for indexed gear systems to work. To find out if your bike has this type of cabling, look for the SIS SP label on the actual outer.

Replacing an outer

Outer cables (especially the outer by the rear mech) can get damaged in crashes and often simply by abrasion on the frame. SP cables for Shimano SIS systems are particularly vulnerable because without their hard plastic outer sheath the longitudinal wires that make up these outers simply spread out. When this happens shifting becomes very mushy and imprecise and eventually fails altogether.

Outer cable can be bought as individual sections long enough for either the run between shifter and frame or between frame and rear mech. Alternatively, it can be cut to length from a workshop roll.

TIP!

When replacing gear outers, whatever sort of gear system you are fitting outer to, use Shimano SP type. This low-compression outer improves shifting in any gear set-up.

Cutting Shimano SP outer

Normal outer

SIS SP outer

1 The difference between SP outer and normal outer is shown here. Note the longitudinal wires instead of the wire spiral. After cutting, these outers need special attention.

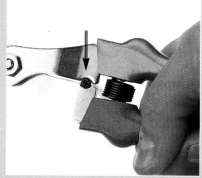

2 SIS SP cable must be re-shaped so that the end is round. Shimano cable cutters have a special part in the jaws to do this, or it can be done, carefully, with pliers.

3 Alternatively, to re-shape the outer, push the gear cable through, then rotate it in the end to push the liner back into place.
(For tips on cutting normal wire spiral outers, see Chapter 11).

TOOLS 9mm spanner / 5mm Allen key, cable cutters.

TIME 20 mins.

DIFFICULTY 🔧🔧🔧🔧🔧

SPARES Replacement outer and ferrules, cable end cap.

OBJECTIVE Replace damaged cable outer.

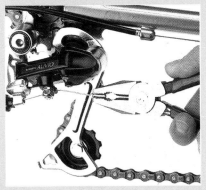

1 Pull off the cable end cap.

2 Undo the cable clamp bolt, pull the cable out of the mech and remove the damaged outer(s) from the inner cable.

TIP!

The outers between the shifter and frame on mountain bikes and hybrids are often unnecessarily long. The bike can be tidied up considerably by trimming them so that there is just enough cable to run in smooth, even, curves and enough that the cables do not get bent or pulled when the steering is turned all the way.

3 Cut the replacement outer to the same length as the original if necessary.

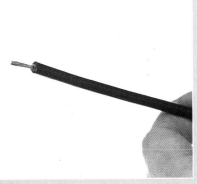

4 Re-shape the squashed end of the cable so that it is round. If the lining of the cable is squashed use a thick needle (or the inner cable itself) to pry it open.

Ferrule

5 Fit a ferrule to the outer. These can be bought with the cables, or may come fitted. Push them on as far as you can by hand, then tap them on the rest of the way by banging the outer and ferrule against a hard surface. Ferrules are absolutely essential for SP cable to work properly.

6 Thread the inner cable into the outer. Note that if the stop on the chainstay has a slot it isn't necessary to thread the inner through it first. If the stop is not slotted, the inner wire must be threaded through the stop before the outer is fitted to it.

7 Thread the outer and inner into the stop and into the cable adjuster on the mech. Tighten the cable as in the final steps of cable replacement.

145

Gear Shifters

Types of shifter

There are four common types of gear shifter systems in common use:

▶ Down tube-mounted gear levers (on road bikes).

▶ Thumbshifter gear levers mounted above the handlebar.

▶ Shimano Rapidfire Plus shifters, a pair of levers under the handlebar.

▶ Gripshift, a twist grip shifter like a motorcycle throttle.

Another type, used on expensive road racing bikes, incorporates the gear shifters in special brake levers, but these are still relatively uncommon.

Routine care and lubrication

Most gear shifters attach to their mountings by obvious clamps. The only maintenance they need is likely to involve replacing cables, dealt with above, and lubrication.

Gripshift shifters

Gripshift are an increasingly popular type of shifter. Maintenance and cable changes are awkward and best left to a dealer. All the internal parts are self-lubricating, so no routine maintenance is necessary.

Shimano Rapidfire Plus levers

Shimano Rapidfire Plus levers have two gear shift triggers, one for upshifts and one for down. Some models have an indicator to show which gear you are in. The shifter is mounted directly on the brake lever. These shifters should not be dismantled.

Lubricate Rapidfire Plus shifters by getting a thin lube right into the body of the shifter, through the cable fitting hole.

Thumbshifters

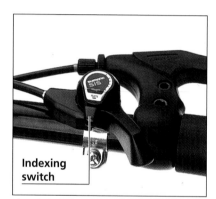

Indexing switch

Thumbshifter gear levers are very simple. They mount on a clamp which wraps round the handlebar and some models have a switch which allows the indexing to be disabled if it goes out of adjustment while you are riding.

Thumbshifters should be lubricated in the pivot on which they turn.

Down tube (road bike) shifters

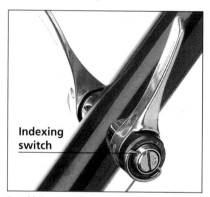

Indexing switch

Road bikes usually have the gear shift levers mounted on the down tube. By turning the D ring on the lever it is possible to disable the indexing of some models.

Lube the gaps where the shifter pivots on its mounting.

The chain

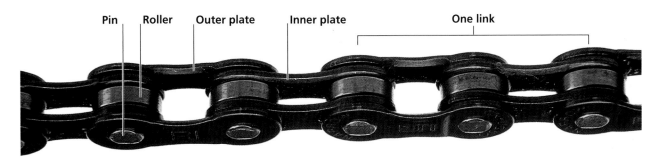

Pin   Roller   Outer plate   Inner plate   One link

Fault Diagnosis

Chain

SYMPTOM	CAUSE	REMEDY	PROCEDURE
Old chain slips on sprockets or chainwheels	Worn chain	Replace chain	Removing and fitting the chain
New chain slips on sprockets or chainwheels	Sprockets or chainwheels worn	Replace parts as necessary	*See Chapter 16 (chainrings) or Chapter 20 (sprockets)*
Chain 'crunchy'	Dirt in chain Chain twisted	Clean chain Remove twisted links	Cleaning the chain
Chain broken	Trail disaster!	Rejoin chain	Removing and fitting the chain. *(See also Chapter 23, 'Roadside repairs')*
Chain skips once per chain rotation	Stiff link	Loosen link	Removing and fitting the chain. *(See also Chapter 23, 'Roadside repairs')*
Chain stiff because of obvious rust	Neglect	Lubricate; loosen links as necessary	Dealing with stiff links
Chain too slack. (on hub gears or single geared children's bikes).	Rear wheel not properly positioned	Reposition rear wheel	Cleaning and lubricating; dealing with stiff links *See Chapter 13, special section*
	Chain has stretched through wear	Replace chain	Removing and fitting the chain

Chain wear

Chains wear out. Of all the moving parts of a bike, the chain is the one which needs to be monitored most closely for wear, because a worn chain will damage all the other parts with which it comes into contact.

Chain wear is often described as 'stretch' because the chain gets longer. However, nothing actually stretches in the strict sense of the word, rather what happens is that very small amounts of wear occur on the hundred and some tiny bearings that make up the moving links of a chain; the sum of these small amounts of wear is that the chain appears to get longer. Once a section of chain that should be 12in long (that is, 12 full links – each link should measure exactly 1in) measures 12⅛in long then the chain should be replaced.

A worn chain unevenly loads the other components it runs on and dramatically increases their rate of wear. Chainrings and sprockets are designed to use a chain that is exactly half an inch between pin centres. A fresh new chain loads all the chainring and sprocket teeth that it is in contact with evenly, because the rollers touch and load all the sprocket teeth. But a worn chain loads only one tooth at a time, because the chain is too long and the next roller overshoots the next tooth. With sprocket clusters costing up to £25 a set and chainrings starting at £15 each it makes economic sense to keep an eye on your chain.

Cleaning the chain

Special tool: Chain cleaning tool
This is a useful device that will thoroughly and quickly clean the chain whilst the chain is on the bike. Given a lot more elbow grease and the possibility of getting splattered with gunk in the process, a toothbrush, solvent and tray underneath will do the job just as well. Make sure you clean out this tool after each time you use it.

TOOLS Chain cleaning tool, degreaser, (alternatively toothbrush and tray).

TIME 5 min
(10 min with toothbrush).

DIFFICULTY

SPARES None.

OBJECTIVE To thoroughly clean the chain of grit.

1 Pour degreaser into the chain cleaner up to the fill level indicated on the tank and clip it to the chain. The arm on the cleaner hooks behind the rear mech to hold it in place. Close the top of the cleaner to attach it to the chain.

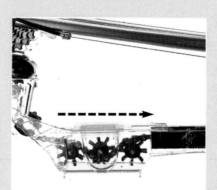

2 Turn the pedals gently backwards. The brushes and solvent will scrub out the chain and the solvent will get very dirty. If the chain doesn't seem to be adequately clean with one pass, repeat the process until it is clean. Don't throw away the solvent; filter it into a jar and re-use it.

TIP!
If possible, use a non-toxic, biodegradable, environ-mentally friendly solvent for cleaning chains, such as Cyclon or Pedro's . If you must use petrochemical solvents like diesel, handle them carefully – they are toxic and skin irritant – and dispose of them through the solvent disposal system of a garage.

TIP!
Shimano Hyperglide chains do not lend themselves well to splitting and they need a special replacement part in order to reconnect them. (For more on this, see later in this section.)

TIP!
Try to clean the chain whilst it remains on the bike. (The chain cleaning tool does this.) Avoid if you can having to split the chain, although this may be unavoidable if the chain is severely gunked up and needs to soak in cleaner overnight.

Routine care and checks

Chain wear can be reduced dramatically by keeping the chain clean and well-lubricated. The best way to wash a chain is to rinse it with lots of hot, soapy water from a brush and bucket arrangement or a car washing hose, then to degrease it with a chain cleaning tool (as shown below). The objective is to get out as much as possible of the very fine grit which tends to penetrate chains and do the most damage.

Lubricating the chain

If you use a water soluble solvent like Pedro's the excess can be washed off the chain and the chain allowed to dry, or treated with WD40 to drive out the remaining water. WD40 is usually not recommended as a chain lube because it is pretty light and tends to wash out. However, as long as you use it very frequently WD40 has the advantage of being very clean and not at all sticky, so it doesn't pick up dirt easily, and of cleaning the chain if you use a lot and allow it to drip off. Most people prefer to use a medium weight mineral household oil (here we're using a general purpose home oil), or one of the spray lubricants specifically marketed as a chain lubricant.

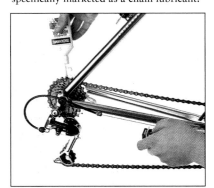

Lube the chain by dripping or spraying lube into the links of the chain while turning the pedals to pass the chain by the lube container. Don't try to run the container along the chain; this is a sure way to waste lube, especially if you're using a spray.

Types of chain

Time was, all chains could be split and rejoined with relative ease. However, because of the details of their construction, many Shimano chains need special treatment.

Standard chains

A standard chain like this can be split and rejoined with the same pin, and any pin can be used to split it.

Shimano Hyperglide chain

Black pin

These are appearing very frequently now, and are now the norm on all but the very cheapest of new bikes. These chains need a special replacement pin to rejoin them after being split. They are identified from the markings on the chain – either HG (for Hyperglide) or 'UG' (Ultraglide) and 'NARROW'.

If these chains are split and rejoined in the traditional manner (as for standard chains), then although they will appear to join, the joined pin will, over time work loose, causing your chain to suddenly break apart. This is because all the pins are slightly peened to prevent them from coming out of the side-plates, so when they are removed they leave an oversize hole which requires an oversize pin to reconnect it. Such an oversize pin is used when the chain is first fitted, and similar ones are needed if it is to be split and rejoined. **The chain should not be subsequently split again at this black pin** because it will be virtually impossible to rejoin successfully afterwards.

Checking chain length

Check the length of your chain every couple of months, more if you ride a lot. A chain should be measured with the chain under tension from the pedals, so that the links are pulled apart as far as they will go.

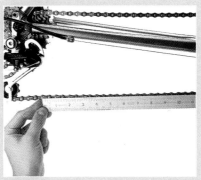

1 Using a good quality steel rule – these measurements need to be accurate – measure 12 full links of chain.

2 The centre of the last pin should be on the 12 of the rule. This is a new chain.

3 **Replacement time**. When the pin overshoots the 12in mark by ⅟₁₆in, then it's time for a new chain.

Removing and fitting the chain

Sometimes, the only way to get a chain really clean is to take it off, soak it in solvent and get very enthusiastic with an old toothbrush. **This is not advised with Shimano chains, because they are such a pain to refit**, but it is perfectly possible with other chains. The only other reason you will have to remove and join a chain is to fit a new one.

Replacement chain lengths

To replace a chain, remove the old one from the bike as described below. Then lay the two chains side by side and trim the new chain to the same length as the old one. Remember that the old chain may be slightly stretched; you want the new chain to have the same number of links as the old one.

New Hyperglide chains have a joining pin installed and should be trimmed from the other end.

Setting a correct chain length

If you don't have the old chain, cut the new chain to the minimum length necessary to allow the bike to sit in the big chainring and big sprocket at the same time. Thread the chain through the mechs and over the big ring and big sprocket, pull the chain as tight as possible, so that the rear mech is pulled to its limit, and add one full link (an inner and outer) to this length.

On some mountain bikes with short cage rear mechs, this will cause the chain to hang loose when you are in the small chainring and small sprockets. Avoid using these gears. The alternative, with a shorter chain is a gear set which can jam if you accidentally shift into the big/big combination. Such jams can be very difficult to sort out.

Special tools

Chain splitting and joining tool

From here on in, this will be referred to as a chain splitter, though of course it is used to join the chain too. All chain splitters have a threaded driver with a hardened steel pin to push the chain pin

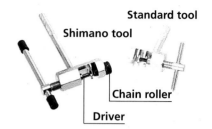

Standard tool
Shimano tool
Chain roller
Driver

in and out. All chain splitters can be used on standard chains, but some splitters are designed with ridges or adjustable, hollow support screws to prevent damage to the shaped outer link plates of Shimano chains. Some splitters have two sets of plates to support the chain, some only one. The plates furthest from the driver are for use when splitting and joining the chain, while the nearer plates can be used, with a little skill, to loosen stiff links. My preference is for the larger single plate designs; they are slightly more expensive than the good old Cyclo tool, but the long handles make them a lot easier to use.

A chain splitting tool is essential for splitting a chain. Fortunately, these tools are cheap – costing around the £5 mark.

Splitting and joining a standard chain

TOOLS Chain splitter.

TIME 20 mins.

DIFFICULTY 🔧🔧🔧🔧🔧

SPARES Replacement chain if required.

OBJECTIVE To remove the chain and refit it after cleaning or fit a replacement.

Caution: Make sure you have identified what sort of chain you have before embarking on splitting it.

Splitting

1 Place the chain in the chain splitter as shown. The chain roller should be well fitted on to the plates and the driver pin should be pointing right at the pin in the chain.

Driver

2 Screw the driver in to push the pin. **You are aiming to push the pin through most of the way, but not to push it out of the plate.** If in doubt, proceed half a turn at a time, backing the driver off each time and trying to part the chain.

3 When the pin is far enough through the chain will come apart with, at most, a little flexing. **Don't push a standard chain's pin all the way out**; they are almost impossible to get back in.

TIP!

If you have mistakenly pushed the pin all the way out (although we did tell you not to), try talking nicely to a bike shop with regards scrounging a few chain links. They usually have them lying around, and it's a far better option than buying a new chain.

Joining

4 Thread the chain over the chainset and through the front mech. Note that it's easiest to lead with the inner link end of the chain; threading a protruding pin through mechs is awkward.

5 Thread the chain through the rear mech as shown; over the top of the upper jockey wheel and round the back of the bottom jockey.

6 Place the two ends of the chain in the splitter so that the pin is protruding toward the driver. Screw the driving pin on to the chain pin.

7 Drive the pin into the chain, pushing it until the head of the pin just protrudes from the outer plate.

Dealing with stiff links

After a chain has been joined it's quite common for the link to be stiff. It will click as it passes through the rear mech and stay bent if flexed.

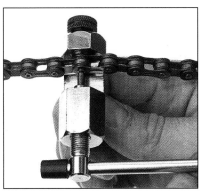

The pin is often slightly further out than it should be and should be driven in a little further. Sometimes this is enough to free the link.

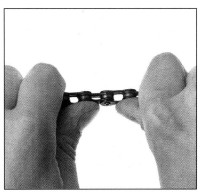

However, the simplest way to sort out a stiff link is to press it as shown. Put your thumbs on the plates either side of the pin and press very hard. This should free up the link.

Splitting and joining a Shimano chain

TOOLS Shimano chain splitter (Not one with a plain flat back).

TIME 20 mins.

DIFFICULTY 🔧🔧🔧

SPARES Shimano pins or replacement chain as required.

OBJECTIVE To remove the chain and refit it after cleaning or fit a replacement.

Splitting

1 Place the chain in the splitter and align the driver pin with the chain pin.

2 Adjust the support screw so that it presses on the back of the chain. It is vital that the side-plate of a Shimano chain is supported by the back of the splitter. **Do not use a splitter with a plain flat back on Shimano chains;** you need either a large, hollow screw fitting as shown or a splitter with ridges for the chain.

Support screw

3 Drive the chain pin all the way through and out of the other side of the chain. These pushed-out pins are believed to be among the most useless objects in the known universe.

Joining

When new, Shimano chains have a short joining pin already installed. Use this pin to join the chain; the procedure is exactly the same as for a standard chain. The procedure below shows you how to rejoin a Shimano chain that has been removed from the bike, or that has split in the field.

To reconnect a Shimano chain a special joining pin is needed. (They can be bought from all bike shops.) This special pin is about twice the length of a normal pin and is scored so it can be broken.

4 Thread up the chain through the front and rear mechs as has been shown for rejoining standard chains. Bring the chain ends together and fit a Shimano joining pin into the chain. The pointed end goes into the chain first, leaving the flat end protruding for the driver to push.

5 Drive the pin through the chain with the chain splitter. The pointed end should go right through the chain and out the other side. Stop when the flat end of the pin is almost flush with the outer link plate.

6 Snap off the pointed end of the pin with pliers. **Don't attempt to remove this pin at a later date.** You can recognise it because it's black; the others are silver.

3-speed hub gears

Routine care

Sturmey Archer's internally geared 3-speed hub is still a very common system on 'roadster' bikes. It has the great virtues of ease of use and little or no need for maintenance; older versions should be lubricated through the oil port in the hub shell with a few drops of Sturmey's own oil, or motor oil.

Vegetable based multi-purpose oils, like 3-in-1, should not be used as they leave sticky residues which eventually gum up the internal workings of the hub.

More recent Sturmey hubs have no oil port and cannot be lubricated; they are pre-lubricated at the factory and sealed for life.

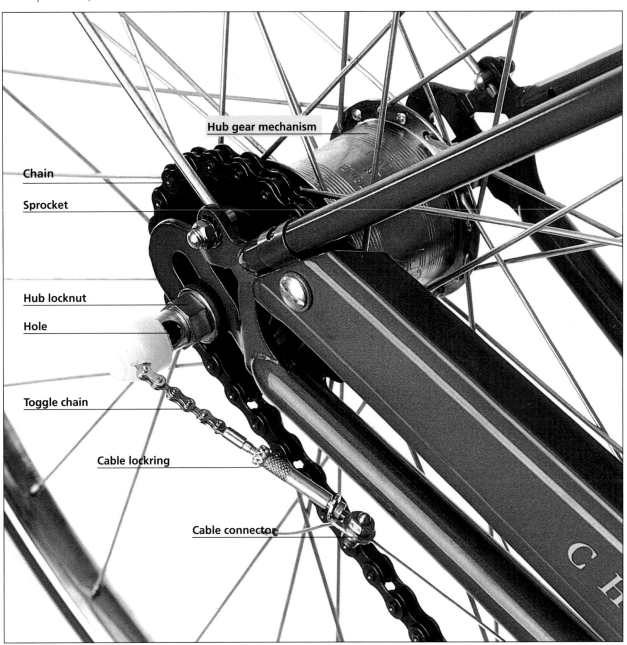

Hub gear mechanism

Chain

Sprocket

Hub locknut

Hole

Toggle chain

Cable lockring

Cable connector

Adjusting 3-speed hubs

A 3-speed hub is very simple to adjust so that the gears correspond to the stops in the lever.

TOOLS Fingers.

TIME 5 mins.

DIFFICULTY 🔧🔧🔧🔧🔧

SPARES None.

OBJECTIVE To adjust a 3-speed hub so that the gears index properly.

1 Put the hub into second gear at the lever.

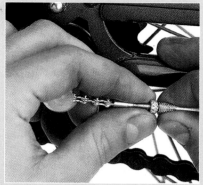

2 Unscrew the lockring on the cable connector.

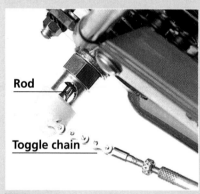

Rod

Toggle chain

3 Look through the hole in the hub locknut. You will see that the chain goes into the hub and attaches to a rod. **The shoulder on this rod should be flush with the end of the axle.** Screw the connector in or out as necessary until this happens.

4 This is how it should look. Tighten the lockring against the connector. If the adjustment on the connector is not enough to get the gears working right, loosen the cable clamp and pull a little cable through.

Chainset

Chainset, bottom bracket and pedals

Contents

One of the most tricky things about the chainset are left hand-threads (ones that undo the wrong way). This symbol in a picture denotes such a thread. For more on this, see Chapter 11.

As the first link in the train which gets power to your rear wheel, the system of pedals, cranks, bottom bracket and chainrings is a crucial one. Mechanically, it's a fairly simple and obvious system; you push on a pedal, which is attached to a crank, and the crank turns on a bearing mounted in the frame.

Problems arise with the chainset if its components are badly assembled in the first place, or if they are neglected for long periods of time. The bottom bracket bearing is particularly vulnerable to water-damage, since it is quite possible to get plenty of water sprayed at it from the front wheel. Because the area around the bottom bracket tends to get filled with mud it is also a favourite area for abuse by enthusiastic riders equipped with jet-washes. As we saw in Chapter 10, the area around the bottom bracket should be washed carefully to prevent this problem.

Noises

Mysterious creaking noises from the crank area are the bane of every mechanic's life. Almost any noise which emanates from the bottom of the bike can appear to be coming from the area around the cranks, even though the cause may be problems as widely separated as loose toe-clip bolts and slack spokes. The only thing to do is to work through all the possible causes until you find the actual problem, and this can be a long job. If you take your bike into a shop and get a large bill for sorting out what you thought was a minor creak, don't be too surprised.

Fault Diagnosis

Chainrings, cranks and bottom bracket

SYMPTOM	CAUSE	REMEDY	PROCEDURE
Mysterious creaking or clicking noise when pedalling	Loose toe-clip bolt	Tighten toe-clips	Toe-clips and straps (See pedals section)
	Loose pedal cage	Tighten pedal cage	Pedal maintenance (See pedals section)
	Pedal loose in crank	Tighten pedals	Removing and fitting pedals
	Chainring bolts loose	Tighten chainrings	Removing (and fitting) chainrings
	Crank loose on bottom bracket	Tighten crank bolts	Removing (and fitting) cranks
	Bottom bracket cups loose in frame	Tighten and adjust bottom bracket	Adjusting bottom brackets
Cranks don't turn freely; grinding noises when pedalling; regular clunking whilst pedalling	Bottom bracket cups too tight in frame	Adjust bottom bracket	Adjusting bottom brackets
	Water in bottom bracket; bottom bracket worn	Overhaul and re-grease bottom bracket; (replace if cartridge unit)	Removing and replacing a bottom bracket
Chainrings rub against front mech	Front mech out of adjustment	Reposition mech	*See Chapter 15*
	Chainrings bent	Replace chainrings	Removing (and fitting) chainrings
	Spider arm bent	Replace crank	Removing (and fitting) cranks
Chainrings worn	Age and use	Replace chainrings	Removing (and fitting) chainrings
	A worn chain (see Chapter 15)	Replace chainrings **and** chain	Removing (and fitting) chainrings, **plus** see Chapter 15 for replacing a chain

More on Pedals: *For remedies to further problems regarding pedals, refer to the separate fault diagnosis guide in the pedal section of this chapter.*

Basic special tools

Working on the bottom bracket requires quite a few special tools, and the ones you need depend on the type of bottom bracket you have. Rather than introduce all the special tools at the start of this chapter, we will introduce them as we go along. However, as so many of the tasks described involve either removing the cranks or the pedals, we will introduce two of the most important and useful special tools now.

Crank puller

Internal pusher

Threaded end

Outer part

Socket end

This tool is essential to remove the crank arms from the bottom bracket axle. The threaded outer part fits into the thread in the crank arm and must be a good fit. Shimano's own model, shown here, works extremely well with Shimano cranks. In general the best option is to use a tool from the same manufacturer as the crank. A socket head in the back of the tool fits hexagon head crank bolts.

Pedal spanner

You can use a conventional 15mm spanner, but a proper pedal spanner is longer and the thin jaws fit more easily into the sometimes confined space between the pedal body and the crank arm. Occasionally pedals requiring a 17mm spanner are encountered.

Chainset assembly
Pedal, crank and chainrings

Chainring

Spider arms

Crank bolt

Chainring bolt

Crank arm

Toe-clip

Toe-strap

Reflector

Pedal

Bottom bracket

Special section Removing and fitting the pedals

For many jobs on a bottom bracket or chainset you need to remove the pedals, or it is handy to have them out of the way. You also need to remove the pedals if ever you want to take your bicycle on an aeroplane (as well as covering the chain, letting down the tyres and turning the handlebars sideways on).

The important thing to remember is that the right-hand pedal is normal, but the left-hand pedal has a left-hand thread (and is therefore undone by turning the other way).

TOOLS Pedal Spanner (or 15mm normal spanner), grease or anti-seize (for reassembly).

TIME 5–10 mins.

DIFFICULTY 🔧🔧🔧🔧

SPARES None.

OBJECTIVE To remove the pedals for whatever reason.

Right-hand pedal

1 The right-hand pedal unscrews normally (i.e. anticlockwise). You should be able to get it off, and tighten it sufficiently, with a conventional 15mm spanner.

Assembling pedals to the crank

1 Apply plenty of grease – copper grease is best – both to the pedal thread and to the crank thread. This will prevent corrosion, and ease assembly and future disassembly.

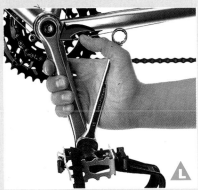

2 Screw the pedal into the crank **by hand**. If it is stiff, check first that you have the correct pedal, then make sure the threads are clean and properly aligned.

2 If the pedal is put on very tight – shop mechanics often get very enthusiastic with pedals – spray the axle with penetrating oil such as WD40 or Plusgas and leave it for a while. Then try again.

3 Finish off tightening with a spanner. There is no need to use too much force; pedal threads are actually self-tightening because of the forces produced by pedalling.

3 If still the pedal will not undo easily, slip a thick steel tube over the spanner to get more leverage. If this doesn't loosen the pedal, take it to a professional.

4 Don't forget that the left-hand pedal tightens anticlockwise.

Left-hand pedal

4 To undo the left-hand pedal, unscrew the pedal clockwise. This feels very odd if you are used to right-hand threads, but it is the correct way to do it.

Seized pedals

The pedal/crank thread is the most vulnerable on the whole bike to bimetallic corrosion because it is a steel on aluminium joint which spends the winter getting doused with salt water. **It is essential that these threads are thoroughly greased.**

If one does become seized it is not unusual for the attempt to remove it to destroy the thread in the crank; the only remedy is replacement, both of the pedal and the crank.

The chainrings

Bikes have one, two or three chainrings. With the prominence of mountain bikes in the marketplace, three is now probably the most common number. They are always attached to the right-hand crank, and are either held in place with bolts so they can be removed and replaced, or fixed in place by being part of the crank arm.

Chainsets with fixed rings tend to be heavier and cheaper, sets with removable rings are lighter and more expensive.

Chainring sizings and gearing

bolt circle diameter

The sizes of rings which can be fitted to a chainset with removable rings, and the degree of interchangeability between them, is determined by the bolt circle diameter of the chainset. For example, a bolt circle diameter of 110mm – very common on mountain bikes before 1994 – will allow the fitting of a ring that has 34 or more teeth. Any fewer and the teeth will overlap the bolt holes, an arrangement which is obviously untenable.

Many chainsets actually have two different bolt circle diameters, a larger outer one for the middle and big ring, and a smaller one for the inner ring. This allows large and small rings to be used together, but mounts the large rings on a larger spider which better supports them. The 110mm bolt circle for mountain bike chainrings is invariably

accompanied by a 74mm inner ring, and this arrangement is referred to as a 110/74 pattern chainset.

Removing chainrings

Chainrings need replacement because they are bent or broken, or simply worn out; or because you want to change the stock gearing of your bike for something different. You may even simply want to take them off to get out ingrained muck from between the rings. The two outer rings of many triple sets and both rings of most doubles can be removed without taking the crank arm off the bike. To get at the inner ring of a triple, the crank must be removed from the bike. This is also necessary with the middle ring of many current Shimano triples. The following sequence shows such a chainset.

TOOLS 5mm Allen key, (+ crank puller and spanner to fit if needing to remove the cranks).

TIME 10–20 mins.

DIFFICULTY 🔧🔧🔧🔧🔧

SPARES New chainrings as required.

OBJECTIVE To remove one or more chainrings for replacement (if worn or upgrading to a different set), or cleaning.

TIP!

Be careful; it is possible to round cheap Allen keys quite easily by using extra force on them. Getting this chainset apart also seemed to require lots of swearing.

Removal

1 Flip the chain off the chainrings and undo the chainring bolts. Chainring bolts are often very tight. If you need more leverage, slip a steel tube over the Allen key to increase its length, or use a longer Allen key.

Chainring bolt

2 Pull the chainring bolts out of the bike. Here you can see the last of the five being removed. The nut part is still in the crankarm (and will stay there until the middle ring is removed). However on some types of chainsets (especially 'doubles'), the chainring nut can be pulled out at this stage.

3 The outer ring will now simply lift off the crankarm, and can be replaced or cleaned as required.

Spacer

4 Many recent chainsets have spacers between the outer pair of rings. Take these off and put them somewhere safe. The middle ring attaches to the inside of the spider arm, the outer ring attaches to the middle ring and the two are held apart by spacers.

4 **VARIANT.** On older triples and many doubles there are thin spacers behind the spider arms and the chainring bolts attach the chainring by clamping through a hole in the spider arm.

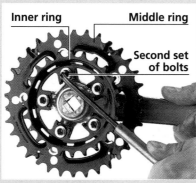

Inner ring   Middle ring

Second set of bolts

5 To remove the inner ring, take the crank off the bottom bracket axle *(see later)* and undo the set of bolts on the reverse side of the chainrings which hold the middle and inner ring directly into the crank.

Reassembly

Assembly is the reverse of disassembly. A little grease on the threads of chainring bolts is essential to ease assembly and subsequent removal. Avoid greasing the outside of the nut, however. This part needs to 'stick' in the rear chainring so that it is easy to unscrew the bolt without the whole part turning in the hole (otherwise, trying to undo the bolts is a real nightmare).

Chainguards

If you have a damaged or rattly chainguard (an extra outer, un-toothed ring that protects the big chainring) you need to undo these screws to remove it, or tighten them up. It is not necessary to remove the cranks from the bike. You will need a cross-head screwdriver.

The cranks and bottom bracket

Bottom bracket problems

It is not unknown for cranks to become loose on the axle, or for the bottom bracket bearing to become loose with use. In such cases, it will become necessary to tighten the cranks or readjust the bottom bracket.

It is also not unknown for dirt and water to get inside the bottom bracket bearing and with time, attack the grease and cause the internal components to wear. Hence it is important to make sure that this area of the bike is regularly cleaned of dirt and mud. (However, if you are using a jet-spray to clean the bike, make sure that the spray is not aimed directly into the bearings because that in itself could force water inside.)

A worn bottom bracket may be evident from various grinding, crunching, and creaking noises and a general 'not-working-as-well-ness'. In these cases, the bottom bracket needs to be overhauled and regreased (if it is not a sealed unit and the components are in good shape), or alternatively, replaced.

What follows is a complete strip-down of a set of cranks and both common types of bottom bracket bearing. If you take care of it, you may never need to remove or adjust a bottom bracket, in which case you can simply skip those steps. However, whatever you are likely to do with the cranks and bottom bracket, it's in the following set of sequences.

161

Removing the cranks

(For 'How to refit a crank' see later in this chapter.)

TOOLS Crank puller (see beginning of chapter for description of this tool), spanners to fit puller, 8mm Allen key (possibly), small screwdriver.

TIME 10 mins.

DIFFICULTY 🔧🔧🔧

SPARES None.

OBJECTIVE To remove the cranks from the bottom bracket axle.

1 There is usually a dustcap in the centre of the crank. It will either pop out, or require a 5mm Allen key or needle nose pliers to unscrew it.

Crank bolt

2 The bolt which holds the crank on is usually a 14mm hex head. A very few chainsets use 15mm bolts, particularly Italian manufacturer Campagnolo.

3 Put the socket end of the crank puller over the crank bolt. Use a spanner on the crank puller to undo the crank bolt as shown. Note that the size of spanner required may vary with the brand of crank puller.

3 VARIANT. On more expensive Shimano-equipped bikes the crank is held on with an 8mm Allen key bolt. A long 8mm Allen key is needed to remove and tighten this type of bolt.

4 Take the bolt out of the crank. If there is a washer under it, as is often the case, make sure you remove the washer as well.

Threaded end

Internal pusher

5 Screw the internal pusher of the puller out all the way (so that the puller is extended as far as it will go), and then fit the threaded end of the crank puller into the crank.

6 Screw the puller into the crank thread until it stops. It should be loose enough to screw in by hand, but nevertheless be a good enough fit that it does not rattle after it has been screwed in four turns or so.

7 Make sure the puller is all the way into the thread by tightening it gently into the crank with a spanner. Note that I am tightening the outer part of the puller into the crank, NOT turning the internal pusher.

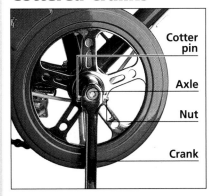

8 With the puller securely in the crank, screw in the internal pusher. This will push on the axle and so pull the crank off the axle. It's not unusual to find that the crank is very tight and requires considerable force to shift it. You may have to rotate the cranks and re-position the spanner on the puller to get enough leverage as the crank comes off.

9 As the crank comes loose, move the chain on to the bottom bracket shell (it's a convenient place to hang it) and lift the crank off the axle.

10 Finally unscrew the crank puller from the removed crank. Then repeat the process for removing the other (left-hand) crank.

Cottered Cranks

Cotter pin
Axle
Nut
Crank

On very inexpensive bikes and on most 3-speeds, the cranks may be made of steel and held in place by cotter pins. To get these out, support the crank on wooden blocks, undo the nut and hammer the pin loose, then remove the pin.

Hammering the pin loose may wreck the pin. If it has, you must purchase some replacement pins. To re-fit them, push in the pin and fit and tighten the nut.

Types of bottom bracket

Essentially there are two types of bottom bracket; **cartridge** bottom brackets (which are sealed units and cannot be adjusted or serviced), and the traditional **cup and cone** variety (which can be serviced).

Identification

From the outside, the difference between the two types can be hard to spot. Look at the bearing parts under the left-hand crank to tell them apart.

Cartridge bottom bracket

Shimano cartridge bottom brackets are characterised by a very 'tidy' appearance with a visibly recessed bearing behind the crank.

Cup and cone bottom bracket

Lockring

Cup and cone bottom brackets have a lockring on the bearing cup under the left-hand crank. The lockring usually has notches so that a special spanner can be used to undo it.

Lockring variant

Some cheaper cup-and-cone bottom brackets use large lockrings with hexagonal spanner flats which require a large adjustable spanner, capable of opening so that the jaws are over 40mm apart.

163

Shimano cartridge bottom brackets

Removal and replacement

Bikes with Shimano equipment built since 1992 are likely to have a cartridge bottom bracket, in which the axle and bearings are contained in one sealed unit which cannot be serviced. These bottom brackets require a special tool to remove and fit them, but have the advantage that it's simple to do so, and no adjustment of the bearing is necessary.

Large spanner flat

Dogs

Shimano bottom bracket tool

This special tool is essential to remove and fit Shimano cartridge bottom brackets. Note that it is simply a big lump of metal with dogs to fit the bottom bracket and spanner flats.

Removal

TOOLS Shimano cartridge bottom bracket remover, large adjustable spanner.

TIME 20 mins.

DIFFICULTY

SPARES New bottom bracket if necessary.

OBJECTIVE To remove the bottom bracket and fit a new one if necessary.

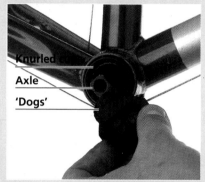

Knurled cup
Axle
'Dogs'

1 Start on the right-hand side of the bike. Place the removal tool over the axle. See how the 'dogs' of the removal tool will fit into the knurled, recessed cup of the bottom bracket.

2 Undo the right hand cup. A big adjustable spanner is pretty much the only tool in the average workshop that fits. It doesn't have to be as battered as mine! **The right-hand side of the bottom bracket unscrews clockwise.**

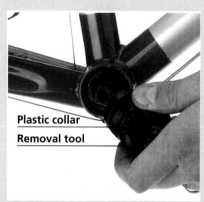

Plastic collar
Removal tool

3 Pull out the plastic collar. Note, in some more expensive Shimano bottom brackets, the axle and bearing cartridge comes out of this side and an alloy cup is removed from the other (left) side.

4 Now apply the tool to the left-hand side of the bike. The left-hand cup unscrews anticlockwise in the normal way.

5 Once undone, remove the single axle and bearing cartridge of the bottom bracket.

Clean and Inspect

Clean all the removed parts with degreaser. Also clean the threads in the frame. Inspect the cartridge unit. It is sealed and cannot be adjusted. If it isn't turning freely then all you can do is chuck it away and get a new one.

Fitting a cartridge bottom bracket

The plastic or alloy collar section of a cartridge bottom bracket acts as a guide when assembling the unit to the frame. It should be partially inserted first. More expensive Shimano cartridge bottom brackets have an alloy collar rather than a plastic one, and the alloy collar fits in the left-hand side of the frame. On cheaper models, the plastic collar fits in the right. However assembly is the same regardless of which side; **the collar goes in first**. Markings on the bottom bracket indicate which side is which.

6 All bottom bracket threads require plenty of grease or anti-seize to ease assembly and subsequent disassembly. Grease the thread of the collar and the thread in the frame. The smaller collar part of the bottom bracket should be inserted first.

7 Using the tool, screw the collar in by hand until it is about **two-thirds** of the way into the frame. The threads in the frame and on the bottom bracket should be cut accurately enough to ensure that this is relatively easy. If not, back the collar out and try again, and if it just won't go in by hand, have a bike shop clean up the threads with a thread chasing tool.

8 Grease the thread of the bottom bracket cartridge and insert it into the other side of the frame. Make sure that the threads are carefully aligned. *(See Chapter 11 for tips on threads.)*

9 Screw the bottom bracket cartridge into the frame with the fitting tool, getting it as far as possible by hand. It should be relatively easy to get most of the thread into the frame without using a spanner.

10 Tighten the bottom bracket cartridge until the shoulders on the thread are flush against the frame.

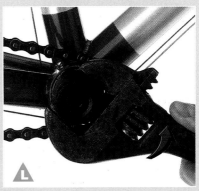

11 Switch sides and tighten the collar until it is flush against the bottom bracket cartridge; it will end up almost flush with the frame.

12 Now replace the cranks. *(To do this refer to later in this chapter.)*

Cup and cone bottom brackets

Until about 1992 almost all bikes came with bottom brackets which could be completely dismantled and serviced. These have now largely vanished from bikes above about £200, where they have been replaced with cartridge bottom brackets, because they are easier to assemble at the factory. However, many cheaper bikes and plenty of older machines still have serviceable cup and cone bottom brackets.

Fixed cup (including bearings)

Axle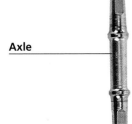

Bearings in cage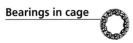

Adjustable cup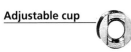

Lockring

The name 'cup and cone' comes from the type of bearing used, which has outer bearing surfaces – cups – that fit in the frame, and inner bearing surfaces – cones – on the bottom bracket axle. The left-hand 'adjustable' cup is held in place by a lockring and is used to adjust the bearing. The right-hand 'fixed' cup screws tight against the bottom bracket shell and has a left-hand thread, just to keep things nice and confusing.

Special tools

Various large special spanners are required to overhaul a cup and cone bottom bracket.

Lockring spanner

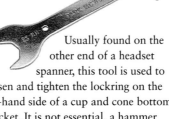

Usually found on the other end of a headset spanner, this tool is used to loosen and tighten the lockring on the left-hand side of a cup and cone bottom bracket. It is not essential, a hammer and drift (carefully used) can be employed instead.

Adjustable cup spanner

Also called a peg spanner, this tool fits into the holes in the outside of the left-hand adjustable cup of **some** cup and cone bottom brackets (but not the one shown here, that has spanner flats instead). It is used to remove the adjustable cup and adjust the bearing.

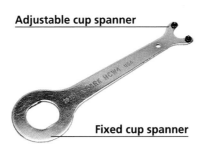

Adjustable cup spanner

Fixed cup spanner

Fixed cup spanner

The right-hand side cup of a cup and cone bottom bracket usually has 36mm spanner flats. This special closed spanner allows maximum force to be exerted to lock this cup in place. A very high quality, large adjustable spanner could be used as an alternative to this tool.

Removing a cup and cone bottom bracket

TOOLS Lockring spanner or hammer and drift, spanner to fit adjustable cup, fixed cup spanner or very large, high quality adjustable spanner.

TIME 20 mins.

DIFFICULTY ✔✔✔✔✔

SPARES None.

OBJECTIVE To remove the bottom bracket from the frame for cleaning, overhaul or replacement.

1 Start on the left hand side. Unscrew the lockring anti-clockwise with the lockring spanner.

1 **ALTERNATIVE.** If you don't have a lockring spanner, the lockring can be loosened by careful application of brute force. Tap it with a hammer and drift, applying medium blows; too hard and you could damage the lockring, too soft and you won't move it.

2 Take the lockring off the cup and put it somewhere safe and obvious. (I usually hang it on my workstand, then forget where it is and waste five minutes later looking for it.)

3 Unscrew the bottom bracket cup with a spanner. This particular adjustable cup has spanner flats, but alternatively some cups have small holes for a peg spanner.

Axle
Bearings
Cup

4 Take the cup off the frame. Here you can see the bearings, held in a retaining cage, inside the cup.

5 Pull the axle out of the frame and put it with the cup and locknut.

6 Switch to the other (right-hand) side of the bike and unscrew the fixed cup **clockwise** with a fixed cup spanner.

7 The fixed cup should be very tight. You may need to tap the spanner to get it moving; hold it in place firmly to stop it slipping off.

7 **ALTERNATIVE.** If you don't have a fixed cup spanner, use an adjustable that is capable of opening to the 36mm width of most fixed cups. You will need a spanner that is in good condition, with nice square edges to the jaws.

Flange

8 Take the fixed cup out of the frame. It looks very similar to the adjustable cup, except for the flange which stops it from disappearing into the bottom bracket shell.

TIP!

All work on the innards of a bearing should be done in a completely clean environment.

Cleaning the bottom bracket and replacing the bearings

Bottom brackets almost always have 9 balls per side, held in steel cages. However, there is room for 11 balls if cages are not used, and it is possible to obtain cages with 11 balls, though they're not easy to find and tend to be expensive. An 11 ball rig is better because the pedalling loads on the bearing are spread over more contact points and the bottom bracket therefore runs slightly more smoothly. I tend to chuck away 9 ball cages and replace them with either 11 ball units or 11 loose balls, though the latter is fiddlier to assemble.

TOOLS Degreaser, new grease, clean rags.

TIME 10 mins.

DIFFICULTY 🔧🔧🔧🔧🔧

SPARES New bearing balls or bearings and cages.

OBJECTIVE To clean the bottom bracket and install new bearings if necessary.

TIP!

Getting the correct replacement parts for bottom brackets is notoriously difficult because there is a huge range of sizes. Always take the original parts with you.

Clean and inspect

1 There is often swarf (little shavings of metal) left over from the manufacturing processes inside the bottom bracket shell. Clean it out; you don't want this stuff getting into your bearings.

3 With degreaser, clean out the old grease from the cup. Thoroughly clean the cage and balls if you are going to re-use them. If they show no signs of damage and pitting, it's fine to refit them.

✗ This cup has had it. The surface is severely pitted. If yours is like this, replace it. *(See later tip on replacements.)*

2 Remove the bearing cages from the cup.

4 Check the condition of the bearing surface inside the cup. It should be shiny or evenly matt with no pits or rust. A polished track where the bearings run is OK.

5 Thoroughly clean the axle so you can inspect the bearing surfaces.

✓ An axle in good condition will have a shiny track worn in its surface where it runs on the balls. If there are any pits in this area, replace the axle.

Fitting new bearings

6 Fill the cup with fresh bearing grease.

7 Either press the cage and balls into the grease or place 11 loose balls in the cup. A clean pen top is ideal for manipulating bearings.

8 Push the balls well into place in the grease, then add more grease over the top of them. Repeat the whole procedure for the other cup.

TIP!

Use a grease injector to store your grease. It will keep the grease clean and uncontaminated and is a lot less messy than a tub.

Installing and adjusting the bottom bracket

The last remaining steps are to fit the overhauled bottom bracket into the frame and then to adjust it.

TOOLS Lockring spanner, fixed cup spanner, spanner to fit adjustable cup.

TIME 20 mins.

DIFFICULTY 🔧🔧🔧🔧

SPARES None.

OBJECTIVE To install the bottom bracket in the frame and correctly adjust the bearings.

Installation

1 Install the fixed (right-hand) cup first. Apply plenty of grease or anti-seize to both the outside of the cups and the threads in the frame. Tighten the fixed cup anticlockwise as hard as possible into the frame.

Longer side in first

2 Switch to the other side of the bike and install the bottom bracket axle and adjustable cup into the frame. One side of the axle will be longer from the bearing shoulder to the end; this side goes in first.

169

Adjustment

3 Screw the adjustable cup into the frame and finish it off with a spanner if necessary. To adjust the bearing, screw in the cup so that the axle will turn freely but cannot be moved up and down in the bottom bracket.

4 Tighten the locknut hard. It may be necessary to hold the cup with a spanner to stop the locknut from tightening it into the frame.

5 Check the adjustment of the bottom bracket by attempting to move the axle. If it can be rattled, loosen the locknut, over-tighten the cup one sixteenth of a turn, then tighten the locknut.

Fitting the cranks

TOOLS Crank puller, spanners to fit puller, copper grease or anti-seize

TIME 10 mins.

DIFFICULTY 🔧🔧🔧🔧🔧

SPARES None.

OBJECTIVE To replace the cranks on the axle.

1 Smear a thin layer of grease or anti-seize on the axle tapers. This will prevent corrosion and ease later removal.

2 Slide the crank on to the axle.

3 Apply grease or anti-seize to the bolt.

4 Tighten the bolt with the 14mm socket in the crank puller.

5 Replace the dustcap. Now repeat the procedure for the other crank, putting it on at 180° to the first.

The pedals

Inside a pedal bearing

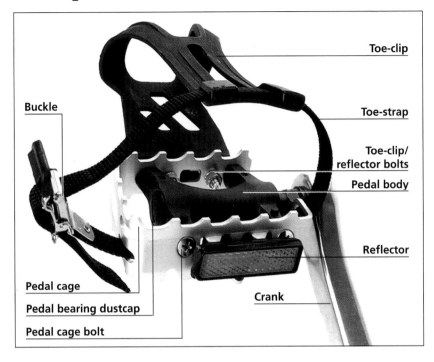

- Toe-clip
- Buckle
- Toe-strap
- Toe-clip/ reflector bolts
- Pedal body
- Reflector
- Pedal cage
- Pedal bearing dustcap
- Pedal cage bolt
- Crank

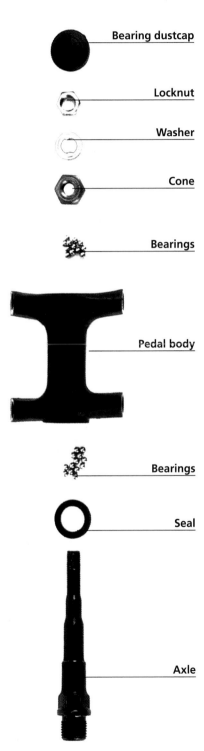

- Bearing dustcap
- Locknut
- Washer
- Cone
- Bearings
- Pedal body
- Bearings
- Seal
- Axle

Routine care and checks

They are the first link in the transmission system, and so it's vital that your pedals work properly. This means that they need to be firmly screwed into the crank arm, the bearings must be adjusted correctly, and accessories like toe-clips and straps need to be properly fitted.

Unfortunately pedals are the closest bearing system to the floor and so they suffer from more frequent exposure to water than any other part of the bike. This means that the bearings need to be well-packed with grease to help keep water out *(see pedal maintenance procedures below)*. It is also important that the thread connecting the pedal to the crank is kept well greased to prevent corrosion and enable easy removal of the pedals.

Loose pedal cages and toe-clips are a major source of mysterious clicking noises; they should be checked as part of the process of diagnosing any odd noise produced while pedalling.

Pedal maintenance

Removing the pedals

It's a pain to try and do any useful work on pedals that are still mounted on the bike. Whether you are fitting clips and straps, adjusting the pedal bearings, or completely overhauling them, the first step is to unscrew the pedals from the bike. *For how to do this, see the special section on 'Removing the pedals' at the beginning of this chapter.*

Varieties of pedals

Pedals vary in their design details. Some have removable metal cages on plastic or aluminium bodies, some have one-piece plastic bodies and cages which don't come apart. In some cases it is almost impossible to get at the bearings, or to adjust them even when you have prised off whatever cap or cover hides them from view. In this case all you can do is replace them.

It is always a good idea to make sure that the bearing is properly greased and for this you need to do a complete overhaul.

Fault Diagnosis

Pedals

SYMPTOM	CAUSE	REMEDY	PROCEDURE
Pedals click under load	Pedal loose in crank	Tighten pedal	Removing and fitting pedals *(see earlier in this chapter)*
	Pedal cage loose	Tighten pedal cage (if separate from pedal body)	Pedal maintenance
	Loose pedal bearings	Adjust pedal bearings (if serviceable; otherwise replace pedal)	Pedal maintenance *(or 'Removing and fitting pedals')*
Clips and straps loose	Loose attachment bolts	Tighten toe-clip bolts	Toe-clips and straps
Pedal broken	Accident/age	Replace pedal	Removing and fitting pedals *(see earlier in this chapter)*
Pedal 'wobbles' on pedal axle	Very loose pedal bearings	Adjust pedal bearings (if serviceable; otherwise replace pedal)	Pedal maintenance *(or 'Removing and fitting pedals')*
Pedal does not spin freely; bearing sticky	Tight pedal bearings	Adjust pedal bearings (if serviceable; otherwise replace pedal)	Pedal maintenance *(or 'Removing and fitting pedals')*
	Water in the pedal bearings; pedal bearings worn	Overhaul and re-grease pedal bearings (if serviceable; otherwise replace pedal)	Pedal maintenance *(or 'Removing and fitting pedals')*

Toe-clips, straps and reflectors

Before any work can be done on the pedal bearing itself, all toe-clips, straps and reflectors must be removed.

TOOLS 8mm spanner, screwdriver (or as needed to fit toe-clip bolts)

TIME 10 mins.

DIFFICULTY

SPARES None.

OBJECTIVE To remove the clips and straps to allow access to the rest of the pedal.

Removing clips and straps

1 Unthread the toe-strap. Pull the strap out of the tidying loop of the buckle, then squeeze the buckle so that it opens and pull the strap out.

2 Take the strap out of the clip and pull it out of the pedal body. Check it for wear. Replace if necessary.

3 If there is a reflector in the toe-clip, pull, push or prise it out as necessary. This reflector needs to be pushed out from the back of the clip body and it's mounting is actually part of the toe-clip.

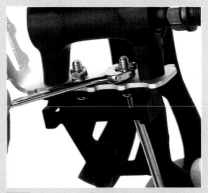

4 Now the reflector is removed, undo the bolts that hold the toe-clip to the pedal cage and take off the toe-clip.

5 If you are proceeding to fully overhaul the pedal, then also remove the rear reflector. If you are just changing clips, then this step is not necessary.

Reflector variant

An alternative to the last two steps might be as shown here. The reflector is glued into its plastic mounting and does not come out. To remove the reflector undo these bolts.

Road bike variant

Many platform pedals on road bikes have clips which attach like this, with three screws on the top of the pedal body.

> ## TIP!
> Toe-clip bolts are notorious for coming loose at really inconvenient times.
> Use Nylok nuts if possible, or Loctite the threads.

Fitting clips & straps

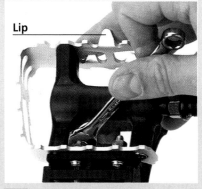

Lip

1 Fitting the clip and reflectors is the exact reverse of removal. Remember to fit the toe-clip to the front of the pedal. You can tell this because the rear of the pedal has a little metal lip.

2 To fit a toe-strap correctly the **first time**, thread the strap through the outside of the cage so that the buckle mechanism faces outwards.

3 Put a twist in the strap as you thread it through the pedal. This helps to stop the strap from slipping through the cage when you pull it tight.

Overhauling the pedal bearing

Dismantling the pedal bearing

To get at the bearings to adjust them, or to overhaul the pedal, you usually need to first take off the pedal cage. You also need to take off all clips, straps and reflectors as shown in the previous procedure.

TOOLS Small flat-blade screwdriver, cross-head screwdriver (or necessary to remove cage bolts),15mm spanner, socket set (spanner size usually 12mm).

TIME 30 mins.

DIFFICULTY 🔧🔧🔧🔧🔧

SPARES New ball bearings if necessary, grease.

OBJECTIVE To dismantle, clean, grease, reassemble and adjust the pedal bearings.

TIP!

Don't disassemble both pedals at once. Doing them one at a time makes it impossible for you to get the axles mixed up.

Variant: Single body and cage

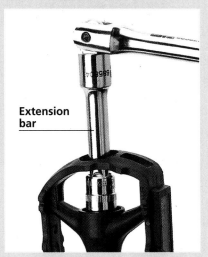

Extension bar

If you cannot remove the cage from a pedal (perhaps because as here, it's a single bit of moulded plastic) you can still adjust the bearings, but you'll have to do everything through the hole in the cage. You'll need an extension bar for your socket set.

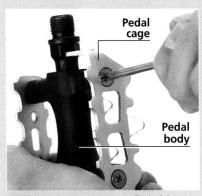

Pedal cage

Pedal body

1 Pedal cages are usually held on with big self-tapping cross-head screws or small Allen key bolts. The former are found in plastic-bodied pedals, the latter in metal-bodied units. Undo them all.

2 Pull the cage off the pedal body.

3 On most pedals the dustcap over the bearings can be prised off. However, sometimes this cap is threaded and needs to be unscrewed. If there are holes for a small tool, try unscrewing it first.

4 Underneath the dustcap is a nut, which cannot be got at with a conventional spanner because it is recessed into the pedal body. This is the bearing locknut, and you'll need a socket to undo it.

5 Undo the locknut with a 12mm socket while holding the axle with a 15mm spanner. Under the locknut, there is usually a washer.

TIP!

If you have a vice, hold the pedal in it to make disassembly and assembly easier. Clamp the thread gently in aluminium 'soft jaws'.

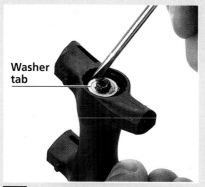

Washer tab

6 To remove the washer, wedge a small screwdriver in against the pedal body to hold the cone (nut) that is under the washer. Turn the axle from below to unscrew the cone and force up the washer.

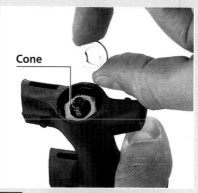

Cone

7 Lift off the washer. Then in the same manner, hold the cone in place with a screwdriver and turn the axle to unscrew the cone from the axle.

8 **Important!** Grab the pedal like this to stop the axle and all those tiny bearings from falling out when you unscrew the cone.

Clean and Inspect

11 Clean and inspect all the parts of the pedal internals. Clean the axle with degreaser. Pour solvent into the cup to clean the balls and replace them if they are pitted or rusty. If any other parts are damaged you will probably have to replace the pedals; spares are almost non-existent except for very expensive pedals.

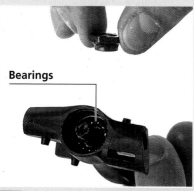

Bearings

9 Lift off the cone; the bearings are underneath it.

10 Turn the pedal over, pull out the axle and allow the bearings to drop into a cup. Collect up all the bearings that remain stuck on the axle or the pedal body.

Assembling the pedal bearing

12 Grease the bearing surfaces inside the pedal.

13 Place the bearings in the cups at both ends of the pedal. The number required varies; there should be just enough to comfortably fill the cup, but don't force in more than this.

Rubber seal

14 Drop the axle back into the pedal. Note the rubber seal at the crank end of the axle; make sure you refit any such parts when you reassemble the axle. Make sure you identify into which end of the pedal body the axle goes.

15 Hold the axle in place and screw the cone all the way down to the bearing. In a similar technique to removal, wedge a screwdriver in beside the cone and pedal body so that you can hold the cone whilst turning the axle. This way you will be able to get the cone all the way in.

Locknut

Washer

16 Replace the washer on the axle, and then the locknut.

17 Screw the nut down on to the cone, **but don't tighten it**. Now proceed to 'Adjusting the pedal bearing'.

Adjusting the pedal bearing

If you are not intending to overhaul the pedal bearing, but simply to adjust it, first remove the pedal cage, prise off the dustcap and then loosen off the locknut, as shown in steps 1–5 of the *'Dismantling a pedal bearing'* procedure.

1 Check the bearing adjustment. The axle should turn smoothly, but should not move sideways in the pedal body.

Cone

Locknut

Washer

2 To adjust the bearing, use a thin screwdriver to push the cone round a small amount. To tighten the bearing, push the cone clockwise, to loosen it, push it anticlockwise.

> # TIP!
>
> *It's usually necessary to adjust the bearing very slightly loose so that when you tighten the locknut the adjustment tightens, leaving the bearing correctly set up.*

Pedal body assembly

3 Tighten the locknut hard and recheck the bearing adjustment. If it is tight, undo the locknut and back the cone off a very small amount, and retighten. If it's loose, undo the nut and screw the cone down very slightly. It may be necessary to do this several times to get it right; it gets easier with practice!

4 Fit the dustcap back into the pedal body.

5 Taking care to get it on the right way round, fit the cage to the body and replace the fixing screws. It's a good idea to hold these screws in place with Loctite.

Saddle and Seat Post

Contents

As long as you keep it greased, and check regularly that it is able to move in all the ways it's supposed to, then there's really not very much that can go wrong with a saddle and seat post. In this chapter we'll show you the types available, and deal with how to adjust the saddle position on these various types and how to look after the area where the seat post and frame join.

Fault Diagnosis
Saddle and Seat Post

SYMPTOM	CAUSE	REMEDY	PROCEDURE
Seat post seized	Lack of grease; corrosion	Generously lube seat post and wait. (Then grease afterwards)	Adjusting saddle height/Routine care
		Horrific strong-arm tactics	Take it to a professional mechanic
Saddle uncomfortable	Saddle position wrong	Adjust saddle position and angle	Adjusting saddle position. (See also Chapter 3 for correct set-up)
	Saddle worn or wrong type (see Chapter 2 for types of saddle)	Replace saddle	Dismantling saddles
	Not wearing cycle shorts (see Chapter 3 for clothing accessories)	Get some shorts	See Chapter 3
Saddle worn or broken	Lot of use or neglect	Replace saddle	Dismantling saddles

Seat post types

A clip-type seat post

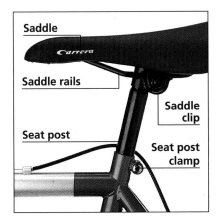

- Saddle
- Saddle rails
- Saddle clip
- Seat post
- Seat post clamp

There are two types of seat post in widespread use:

A 'clip-type' seat post is a plain steel or aluminium tube with a separate clip round the top, thinner section. The clip holds the saddle, and to remove or adjust the clip you undo the nuts on either side. The clip has grooved washers which hold the saddle from slipping and provide adjustment of the saddle angle. The other type is referred to as a 'micro-adjusting' post and uses a single bolt

A micro-adjusting seat post

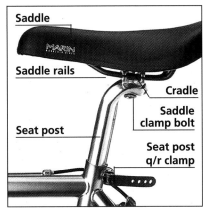

- Saddle
- Saddle rails
- Cradle
- Saddle clamp bolt
- Seat post
- Seat post q/r clamp

under the saddle to hold the seat in a cast alloy cradle. This cradle can pivot on the top of the post – which is specially shaped – and in this way the angle of the saddle can be changed. The name comes from the very fine adjustment possible with these posts, as compared with the coarse angle adjustment provided a clip-type post. In general, better bikes tend to have micro-adjusting seat posts.

Seat post quick release clamp

If your seat post is held in place with a quick release clamp, then it is worth lubing it from time to time to keep it working smoothly.

1 Open the quick release.

2 Lube all the moving parts of the lever.

3 Close the lever firmly, adjusting the nut as necessary.

Routine Care

Neither type of seat post needs any routine maintenance or lubrication as long as it is properly greased on assembly in the first place. Since this sometimes doesn't happen at the factory or bike shop, it's worth doing with any new bike.

If the seat post is difficult to move, or you are installing a new post, or you suspect that the factory or shop has not done an adequate job, then make sure the seat post and the inside of the seat tube are both well greased. This grease is essential to stop the post from sticking in the frame, especially if you have a steel frame and an aluminium seat post.

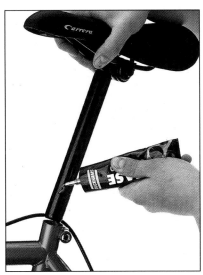

A little bit of lube will save a lot of time and aggravation later.

179

Adjustments

The most common things you will have to do with the saddle and post are to adjust the height of the saddle and the position of the saddle on the post. *See Chapter 3 ('Setting up your bike') for tips on how high the seat post should be and the correct positioning for the saddle.* Here we will simply deal with the mechanics of the adjustment.

Adjusting saddle height

The seat post will be held in the frame by either a bolt (as shown here) or a quick release lever.

TOOLS	5mm Allen Key.
TIME	5 mins.
DIFFICULTY	🔧🔧🔧🔧🔧
SPARES	None.
OBJECTIVE	To raise or lower the saddle as required.

1 Undo the seat post clamp bolt. Usually the bolt will only undo on one side of the frame; the other side has a tab which stops it from turning fully.

2 Grasp the seat post firmly and pull it up or push it down as required.

3 If the seat post is stuck, the first thing to try is to generously lube the joint in penetrating oil and leave it to soak in for a few hours. Then try again. If still no luck, take it to a professional.

4 If the seat post was difficult to move, or if it has not been adequately greased, then grease it now. Grease both the seat post and the inside of the seat tube. This will prevent corrosion and help ensure that the seat post is not stuck in the tube next time you come to adjust it.

Maximum extension mark

5 On all seat posts there is a maximum extension mark. Do not raise your seat post beyond this mark.

6 Finally, when the saddle height is correctly adjusted, tighten the seat post clamp firmly.

Adjusting saddle position – clip-type seat posts

TOOLS 13mm spanner.

TIME 5 mins.

DIFFICULTY 🔧🔧🔧🔧

SPARES None.

OBJECTIVE To change the position of the saddle.

1 Loosen the bolt on the side of the clip under the saddle. You only need to loosen one side; both bolts attach to a stud through the clip. The saddle can then be positioned as follows:

2 **Lateral adjustments:** The saddle all the way back in the clip...

...and all the way forward. Typical saddles allow about 2in of fore – aft adjustment.

3 **Angular adjustments:** Loosening the clip also allows the saddle angle to be adjusted backwards...

...and forwards. Adjustment with a clip is pretty crude, however; you may have to settle on a position which is about right rather than perfect.

4 The saddle can also be rotated on the post when the clip is loose. Make sure, that the saddle is always pointing forward and not at a slight angle.

5 Finally, when all adjustments are done, tighten the saddle clip firmly.

Adjusting saddle position – Micro-adjusting seat posts

TOOLS 6mm Allen Key.

TIME 5 mins.

DIFFICULTY 🔧🔧🔧🔧

SPARES None.

OBJECTIVE To change the position of the saddle.

1 Undo the Allen key bolt under the saddle **until the cradle is slightly loose on the seat post.** Make small adjustments to the saddle and cradle as required, then tighten the Allen key. The saddle can be positioned as follows:

2 Lateral adjustment: Slide the saddle rails through the cradle. This is the backwards limit of the saddle position...

3 Angular adjustment: Move the cradle slightly up or down the curved seat post. This allows the saddle to be tilted back...

...or tilted forward. These pictures are of exaggerated positions; normally only a small amount of forward or backward tilt is needed.

4 To adjust the rotational alignment of the saddle, undo the seat post quick release on the frame and twist the saddle and post. Undoing this quick release also allows height to be adjusted.

5 Finally, once adjustments are complete, make sure both the seat post clamp and the saddle bolt are tightened fully.

Repairs and replacements

You may need to remove the saddle from the seat post either for cleaning it or for replacing it, perhaps because the saddle is uncomfortable. *See Chapter 2 (section on 'Sizing a bike') for a discussion of saddle types, especially women's saddles. See also Chapter 3 (the fault guide entitled 'Riding is uncomfortable') for other suggested remedies to a sore bum.* What follows is the mechanics of how to go about removing (and replacing) a saddle.

Dismantling a clip-type saddle and post

TOOLS 13mm spanner.

TIME 5 mins.

DIFFICULTY 🔧🔧🔧🔧🔧

SPARES None.

OBJECTIVE To remove the saddle and clip from the seat post for cleaning. To remove the saddle from the clip for replacing the saddle.

1 Undo one of the saddle clamp bolts.

2 Lift the saddle off the post.

3 The clip in place on the saddle rails. It's a triple-clamp arrangement with the saddle rails held by a clamp either side of the post.

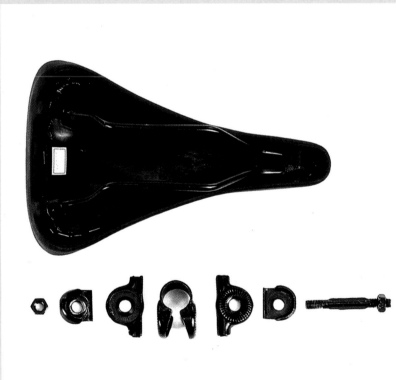

Completely undoing the saddle clip allows it to come free of the saddle rails. This is necessary if you want to replace the saddle.

Dismantling a micro-adjusting seat post

TOOLS 6mm Allen Key.

TIME 5 mins.

DIFFICULTY 🔧🔧🔧🔧🔧

SPARES None.

OBJECTIVE To dismantle the top of the seat post and remove the saddle for cleaning or replacing.

Reassembly

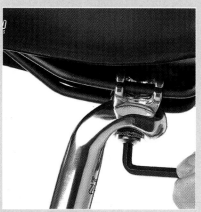

1 Undo the Allen key which holds the seat in place.

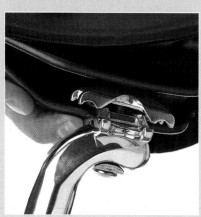

2 Lift the top part of the cradle and turn it 90° so that the saddle can be lifted off.

3 The Allen key bolt needs to be greased, as it is a steel bolt in an aluminium thread and easily damaged by corrosion from salt water thrown up by the rear wheel.

Handlebars

Contents

The handlebars and stem need very little attention, especially if they are assembled properly in the first place. In this chapter we'll look at the assembly of bars and stem, and also, at the very easy mechanics of adjusting them for correct set-up position on the bike.

Fault Diagnosis
Handlebar and Stem

SYMPTOM	CAUSE	REMEDY	PROCEDURE
Bar turns in fork	Stem bolt loose	Tighten stem bolt	Adjusting handlebar height
Bar turns in stem	Bar clamp loose	Tighten handlebar clamp	Adjusting handlebar angle
Stem seized	Corrosion, no grease	Lube stem thoroughly and wait, (grease afterwards)	Adjusting handlebar height
		Professional tactics	Take it to a bike shop
Bars not in right place; (too low, too high, wrong angle)	Poor set-up	Adjust bar and stem. (See also Chapter 3)	Adjusting handlebars
No bar ends	Not included with bike	Fit bar ends	Fitting grips and bar ends
Grips or tape worn	Age/damage	Fit new grips or tape	Fitting grips and bar ends (mountain bikes) Taping handlebars (road bikes)
Bars not centred	Bar clamp loose	Centre bars & tighten clamp	(See within) handlebar and stem disassembly
Bars not symmetrical	Crash damage	Replace handlebars or stem	Handlebar and stem disassembly and assembly

More on handlebar adjustments: *For remedies to problems regarding uncomfortable riding (for example, sore hands, tired arms) refer to the fault diagnosis guide in Chapter 3.*

Adjusting the handlebars

The whole bar and stem assembly can be raised or lowered, depending on your preferences, or the bar can be rotated in the stem to change the way in which it sweeps back to your hands. Make small adjustments; a little difference in position can make a surprising difference to how comfortable you are. *(For advice on the correct handlebar positions for you, consult Chapter 3.)*

TOOLS 6mm Allen Key.	
TIME 5 mins.	
DIFFICULTY 🔧🔧🔧🔧	
SPARES None.	
OBJECTIVE To change the position of the bar and stem.	

Typical bar and stem arrangement

Handlebar

Handlebar clamp

Stem bolt

Handlebar clamp bolt

Stem

Adjusting handlebar height

1 Undo the stem bolt with a 6mm Allen key until it stands proud above the top of the stem.

2 If the stem doesn't come loose in the frame immediately, tap the bolt gently to free it. We've omitted it for clarity, but the bolt should be protected with a piece of wood. Once the stem is loosened, the handlebars can be adjusted up or down as required.

Why tap the bolt?

Wedge

3 The other end of the stem bolt is connected to a wedge (as shown here). When tightened, the wedge forces itself against the stem and tightens it against the headset tube. The purpose of tapping the bolt is to let the wedge drop a bit and so free up the stem.

If the handlebar stem is stuck

4 If the handlebars are stuck, spray the area in WD40 and leave it to penetrate in. Then try again. Try wedging the front wheel between your legs and twisting the handlebars to see if that will free them up. If still no luck, take it to a bike shop.

To make sure the handlebar stem won't be sticky in the future, pull it completely out and grease the wedge and stem with anti-seize. However, not enough cable slack may stop you from pulling out the stem. If that is the case then create some more slack by opening the brake releases and popping the cables out of their stops (if the stops are slotted).

When adjustments are finished

5 When all height adjustments are finished, tighten up the stem bolt. Make sure the stem can't be twisted in the frame. Also make sure that the front brake remains properly adjusted. *(See 'Variant' right.)*

TIP!

*Whatever you do, **don't undo the stem bolt all the way.** This will cause the wedge to drop off the end of the bolt and fall to the bottom of the head tube. Getting it back on the stem bolt is a real pain. At the very least you'll have to take the stem completely out. (See 'Bar and stem disassembly'.)*

Adjusting the angle of the handlebars

To adjust the angle of the bar, undo the clamp bolt and turn the bars in the clamp. Make sure the bolt is fully tightened when adjustment is complete.

Variant: Recessed bolt stems

Some stems have the stem bolt recessed deep in the quill. Here's how to loosen and tighten such a bolt.

1 Remove the top cap from the stem

2 Undo the bolt with the long end of a 6mm Allen key. Use an additional lever to turn the short end. I have a rather nifty bit of tube that does the job.

Adjust the front brake

Roller

3 With some mountain bike stems – those which have a roller (shown here) or stop for the front brake built in – changing handlebar height will now mean the front brake will also have to be adjusted. *(To do this, see Chapter 14.)*

187

Repairs and replacements

Mountain bikes – fitting grips and bar ends

Bar ends are probably the most common upgrade part that people add to their mountain bikes. By providing an extra hand position, bar ends make for easier climbing and more comfortable cruising along on the flat and on gentle down-hills (on steep down-hills your hands will need to be near the brakes, of course).

We've incorporated removing and fitting grips into this procedure because in order to fit bar ends you have to move the grips down the handlebars. Hence you will have to loosen, remove and refit the grips in order to move them. If you are only replacing grips and not fitting bar ends then stop after step 4.

TOOLS Thin screwdriver, degreaser, hammer, 5mm Allen key, Large flat-blade screwdriver, hair spray.

TIME 30 mins.

DIFFICULTY 🔧🔧🔧🔧🔧

SPARES New grips and bar ends as necessary.

OBJECTIVE Remove the grips and replace them or move them in while fitting bar ends.

Removing old grips

1 Slide a thin, long-bladed screwdriver under the grip and spray lube into the gap to lift and loosen the grip from the bar. You may have to run the screwdriver round under the grip to spread the lube and break the seal. Try twisting the grip and repeating the lubing process until the grip starts sliding on the handlebar.

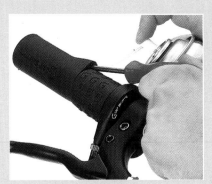

1 **Variant.** If the grip has closed ends, then you will have to lever up the grip and spray lube in from the other end (as shown here).

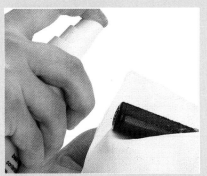

2 Slide the old grip off the handlebar. Clean the handlebar; get off all the lube. Degrease the inside of the grips if you are going to re-use them. If the handlebar has end caps, then remove these if the new grips have closed ends (as is the case in this sequence).

Fitting grips

3 Hair spray is an excellent lubricant (when wet) and adhesive (when dry) for grips; spray plenty on the bar and the inside of the grip. Car spray paint also works well.

4 Slide the grip on. This and the next few steps (5, 6, and 7) must be done fairly swiftly as the hair spray will dry quickly and stick the grip on if you hang about.

Fitting bar ends

5 If the grip has closed ends, tap the end of the grip and bar to cut the centre tidily out of the grip.

6 Pull out the little circle of rubber this cuts.

7 Slide the loosened grip on far enough to make space for the bar end clamp. You may have to move the brake and gear levers down the tube in order to make room. *(See step 10.)*

8 Slide the bar end on to the bar. If the clamp is a little close-fitting, take out the bolt and gently prise it open with a wide-bladed screwdriver.

9 Tighten the bar end clamp hard enough that the bar end cannot be moved by hand. There is no need to tighten bar ends excessively and it is fairly easy to damage a thin handlebar by tightening too hard.

10 When you moved the grips down the tube, the normal reach to the levers and shifters changed. Reposition the brake and gear levers to a position that is comfortable.

Road bike grips

If you're fed up with tape, try fitting foam road bikes grips instead ('Grab-ons' or similar makes). If you're doing this make sure that after removing the old tape, you thoroughly degrease and get all the glue off the handlebars. You will also have to remove the brake levers *(see the next procedure)* and unhook the cable from the lever if the cable and outer is to be routed under the grips.

When fitting the grips use lots of hair spray on the bars and grips and quickly squeeze the new grips up and into position.

Road bikes – taping handlebars

The tape on road bike handlebars eventually gets old and scruffy even if you don't manage to scuff it by parking your bike against a stone wall one time too many. Replacing it is a relatively straightforward job as long as you concentrate on what you are doing, take it steadily and don't attempt to overlap the tape too much.

TOOLS Knife or scissors.

TIME 20 mins.

DIFFICULTY 🔧🔧🔧🔧🔧

SPARES New handlebar tape (polka-dots are optional).

OBJECTIVE To replace old bar tape.

Removing old tape

1 Start by getting the brake lever hoods out of the way by peeling them up the lever enough to reveal all of the tape.

2 Remove the end plugs from the handlebar. These sometimes need a screwdriver to loosen the expanding clamp inside them.

3 Peel off the old handlebar tape. When you've peeled a foot or so, cut it; old, sticky tape is a pain to handle in big lumps.

4 A lot of current road bikes have the brake cable routed under the tape and held in place either with short pieces of electrician's tape, as shown, or with a special plastic cable tunnel. Tape or replace the cable tunnel as necessary.

Putting on new tape

5 Stick a short length of new tape either side of the brake lever so that it will cover the area that the tape will leave behind when it is wound round the bar.

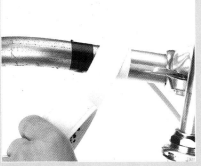

6 Start attaching the new tape from the centre so that the tape can be tucked tidily into the end of the bar. Wind the tape round the bar once, then begin to lay it at an angle so that it begins to wind along the bar.

TIP!

Don't unroll the new tape, hold it in a roll as shown and peel the backing as you need it. That way you won't have to faff around with long lengths of new sticky tape getting twisted.

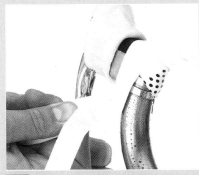

7 When you get to the brake lever go round the underside then pull the tape back up to cover all the metal left exposed. Get this stage right before moving on.

8 Continue to wrap the bar until you get to the end; overlap the end of the bar. If you run out of tape before the end of the bar, you'll just have to unwrap it and start again.

9 Finally, trim the tape so that there is about 3cm at the end, tuck this loose end up inside the bar and fit an end cap to keep everything in place.

190

Handlebar and stem disassembly and assembly

To replace either the bar or the stem it is necessary to dismantle the whole bar and stem assembly. To remove a stem only one set of controls and one grip needs to be removed, while to change the bar you'll need to take off both sets. The main reason you are likely to need to change a bar is to replace it after a crash. Any handlebar which has been bent in a crash should be replaced immediately as it is possible for a bar to be dangerously weakened.

TOOLS Lube, Thin screwdriver, Allen keys to fit shifter and brake lever clamps, 6mm Allen key.

TIME 30 mins.

DIFFICULTY 🔧🔧🔧🔧🔧

SPARES New bar or stem as required.

OBJECTIVE To remove bar or stem and fit new ones.

TIP!

If any clamp is stiff, grease it so that it slides off easily rather than having it scratch along the handlebars.

Mountain bike – straight handlebars
Removing handlebars from stem

1 Remove bar ends if you have them, and remove the grips as in the procedure for fitting bar ends.

2 Undo the clamp bolts for the brake lever and the gear shifter (if separate from the brake lever). Slide both lever and shifter off the bar.

3 Undo the handlebar clamp bolt and...

Removing the stem

4 ...slip the handlebar out of the stem. The handlebar clamp may be tight, don't let it scratch the bar; either grease it, prise it apart a bit, or ideally see the advice below.

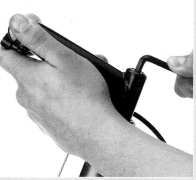

5 Undo the stem bolt.

6 Lift the stem out of the frame. Note the locking wedge at the bottom of the stem.

Handlebar and stem assembly

7 Grease the bolt threads, the underside of the head of the bolt and the inside of the wedge threads.

8 Grease the sides and top of the wedge and the sides of the stem.

9 Fit the stem to the frame and tighten it firmly.

10 Fitting the handlebars is the exact reverse of removal. Make sure that the handlebars are properly centred in the handlebar clamp. *(See below for dealing with tight clamps.)*

Opening tight handlebar clamps

Some handlebar clamps are quite tight and will scratch the handlebar as it goes in. As well as looking unsightly this can actually weaken the bar. You can, of course, gently prise open the clamp with a large screwdriver, but here's a rather more subtle and controlled technique.

1 If it is possible, take out the handlebar clamp bolt and put it in from the wrong direction, that is into the threaded part of the clamp. Put a coin between the end of the bolt and the other side of the clamp.

2 Screwing the bolt in will now push the clamp open so that the bar can be easily threaded through it.

Road bikes – drop handlebars

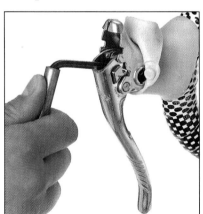

Removing and fitting drop handlebars is almost identical to dealing with straight ones. Handlebar tape will have to be removed instead of grips, and a degree of twisting will be required to pull the bar out through the clamp. The only other difference is the brake lever. The lever clamp is loosened by undoing the bolt inside the brake lever as shown here.

Handlebar stems on a road bike are in principle identical to those on mountain bikes.

Headset

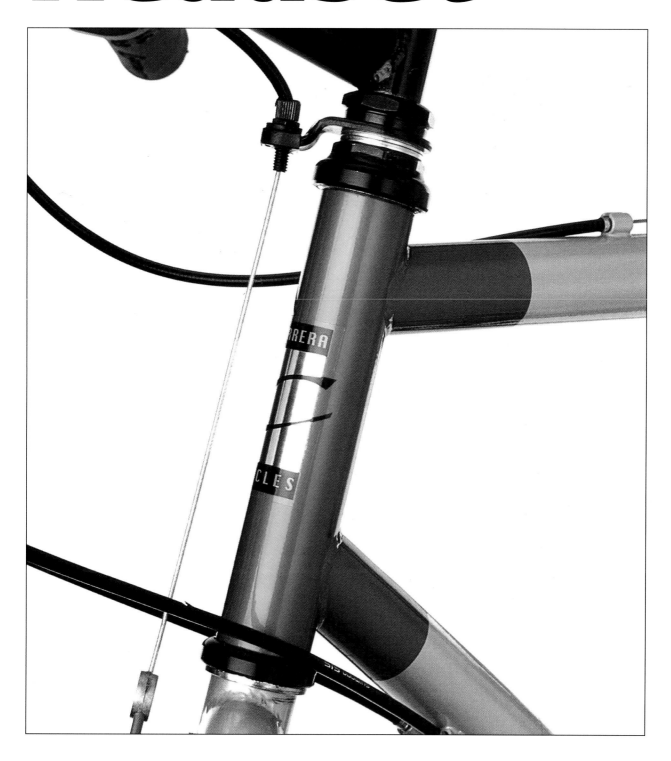

Headset and Forks

Contents

For some unaccountable historic reason, the steering bearing on a bike is called a headset, and it is the most important bearing on the bike from a safety perspective. A badly adjusted headset can produce some quite severe bike handling problems including alarming judder under braking if the headset is loose and peculiar handling traits at both low and high speed if it is too tight. It's therefore essential to look after your headset properly and keep it running smoothly.

In the headset is mounted a fork. A few years ago all bike forks were simple – a couple of tubes attached to the steerer either directly or with a crown, curved to provide offset so the bike steered properly and with dropouts for the front wheel. Then came mountain bikes and first straight forks (which make very little difference to anything but looks) then **suspension forks,** which absorb the bumps and shocks of off road riding, allowing the rider to go faster or be more comfortable, and which improve the handling of the bike by improving front wheel grip.

Normal forks and suspension forks are dealt with briefly at the end of this Chapter.

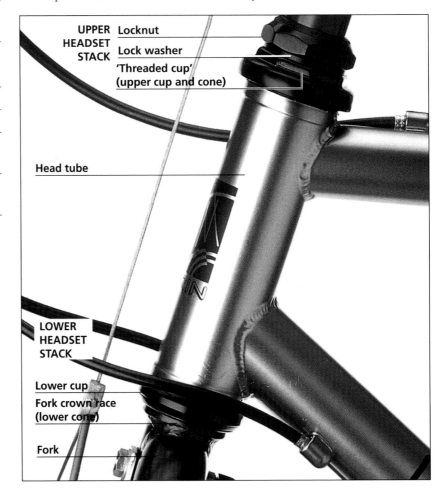

UPPER HEADSET STACK — Locknut
Lock washer
'Threaded cup' (upper cup and cone)
Head tube
LOWER HEADSET STACK
Lower cup
Fork crown race (lower cone)
Fork

The Headset

Note: Inside the head tube is the **steerer tube**; this is the top part of the forks. The bearings ensure the steerer tube swivels easily inside the head tube.

Headset designs

Common headsets

There are two designs of headset in widespread use. The most common (shown and labelled opposite) uses a fork with a threaded steerer tube into which the handlebar stem fits. The headset uses a threaded top cup which is held in place with a locknut.

Aheadsets

Recently threadless designs like the Dia-Compe Aheadset have become popular on bikes from about £350 and up. The steering bearings are a sliding fit on a threadless steerer tube and are held in place by a clamp-on stem. A special fitting in the top of the steerer allows the bearing to be adjusted. *Aheadsets are dealt with briefly later in this Chapter.*

Routine care

The headset is an unusual bearing because it doesn't spin. Instead it takes more or less static loads from the fork, and allows the fork to turn so the bike can be steered. Because the headset moves away from, then returns to the same position, it is possible for the motion of the headset to push grease away from the bearings and for water to

Fault Diagnosis
Headset

SYMPTOM	CAUSE	REMEDY	PROCEDURE
Forks clicks fore and aft when brakes are locked and bike is rocked	Loose headset	Tighten headset adjustment	Adjusting the headset
Fork turns with difficulty	Tight headset	Loosen headset adjustment	Adjusting the headset
Steering is 'indexed' (tight in some places, loose in others)	Damage to headset races	Replace headset	A job for a bike shop – fitting loose balls may be a temporary cure
Adjustment does not produce properly adjusted smooth headset	Ball retainers fitted wrongly	Dismantle and fit correctly	Headset overhaul
	'Pressed-in' headset parts loose in frame or on fork	Dismantle and check	Headset overhaul; bike shop help may be needed
	Corrosion damage	Dismantle and check – replace if necessary	Headset overhaul – bike shop help may be needed
	Fork steerer tube damaged	Dismantle and check – replace fork or steerer tube	Headset overhaul – replacement is a job for a bike shop
Headset will not stay tight	Fork thread damaged	Replace fork or steerer tube	A job for a bike shop
	Inadequate tightening	Tighten it properly with good headset spanners	Adjusting the headset
Forks bent or damaged	Crash	Replace forks	A job for a bike shop
Suspension forks don't work	Not lubed	Lube suspension forks	Routine suspension fork care
	Other reasons	Overhaul suspension forks	A job for a bike shop

then get in, replacing the grease and corroding the bearing surfaces. When this happens the balls rust into place when the bike is stationary, then tear microscopic holes in the bearing surface, which are enlarged by repetition of this process. The problem is made worse by the headset being right in the path of spray from the front wheel.

It is therefore essential to dismantle and lubricate the headset regularly, especially if you ride in the wet a lot. Use good quality waterproof grease such as Pedro's or Finish Line.

Special Tools

Headset spanners

A good set of headset spanners is essential for the proper adjustment of a headset. There are three common sizes: 32mm spanners fit all road bikes and many mountain bikes with 1in headsets; 36mm spanners fit the 'oversize' 1⅛in headsets used on many middle to high-end mountain bikes; 40mm

spanners fit the 'Evolution' 1¼in headsets used on Gary Fisher mountain bikes and a few others such as recent Cannondales.

Headset spanner size

The size of a headset is indicated by the size of the fork steerer tube, which is pretty silly since it is a part of a headset that is impossible to measure without disassembly. The diameter of the handlebar stem is ⅛in less than the diameter of the steerer, so to determine what sized headset you've got you can just measure the stem and add ⅛in. 'Aheadset' type headsets have the stem clamped directly to a threadless steerer and do not require headset spanners.

Adjusting the headset

The most common thing you will have to do to a headset is to adjust it so that it turns smoothly with no play, then to tighten up the locknut so that it stays that way. It is essential to use high quality headset spanners that are a good fit on the spanner flats of the race and locknut (for sizings see

above). The only spanners available are open ones; in a perfect world you'd use a ring spanner to tighten up a nut that needs to be as firmly closed as does a headset locknut, but there's no such thing, so use good headset spanners and take care not to damage the spanner flats.

TOOLS Headset spanners.

TIME 10 mins.

DIFFICULTY 🔧🔧🔧🔧🔧

SPARES None.

OBJECTIVE To adjust the headset so that it turns freely, but with no play or looseness.

Loosen the locknut

1 Put one spanner on the lower of the two sets of spanner flats; this set of flats is the outside of the threaded (adjustable) cup of the upper bearing assembly.

2 Put the other spanner on the locknut. Position the two spanners so they can be squeezed together to undo the locknut by turning the top spanner anticlockwise.

Adjust the bearing

3 With the locknut loose, adjust the bearing. Rock the fork in the frame as you tighten the bearing; correct adjustment is when the headset just ceases to move in any direction other than round.

196

Tighten the locknut

4 Tighten the locknut firmly with one spanner whilst holding the threaded cup stationary with the other.

TIP!

A second pair of hands is useful here to hold the fork, wheel or bars and prevent the headset parts from slipping as you tighten them. Alternatively, hold the front wheel between your knees and tighten.

Check the adjustment

5 To check the adjustment put the bike on the floor, lock the front brake and attempt to rock the bike fore and aft. There should be no rocking movement in the headset. Readjust if necessary.

Headset overhaul

A headset that is very badly crudded up or that does not respond to adjustment may need dismantling, either to figure out what the problem is, or simply to get the parts clean and replace the grease. Be careful to lay out all the parts you remove from a headset in order and the right way up; there are usually sealing rings in there which will not work or which may cause problems if they are replaced the wrong way up. Similarly bearings in cages must be replaced the correct way up or the headset will not adjust properly and will be damaged if used.

While you're taking the headset apart you may as well replace the balls. Loose balls are better than balls in cages because you can get more in, and they are less likely to develop 'indexed steering'. The correct number of bearings is two less than the maximum that will fit.

Sizes of headset bearings

While there is a single common size for most components, headsets (especially specialist ones) can use bearings that are sized anything from ⅛in to ¼in, depending on the intended use and the priorities of the designer (smaller balls are lighter, larger ones much more durable). It's not unusual to find larger size balls in the heavily loaded lower race. It's essential to replace headset balls by comparing new balls with old ones, or even better, measuring the old ones.

197

Disassembling a headset

TOOLS 6mm Allen key, headset spanners.	
TIME 45 mins.	
DIFFICULTY 🔧🔧🔧🔧	
SPARES Replacement bearings.	
OBJECTIVE To dismantle, clean and re-grease the headset, replacing the balls if necessary.	

1 Undo and remove the stem and handlebar assembly. Disconnect all the gear and brake cables, or pop them out of their stops to produce lots of slack, and zip-tie the bar to the frame out of the way somewhere. Drop the front wheel out of the frame.

2 Undo the headset locknut, while holding the threaded cup with the other headset spanner.

Threaded steerer tube

3 Lift off the locknut, exposing the threaded steerer tube underneath it.

4 Lift off the lock-washer; this is a washer with a tab which engages a slot in the steerer and makes adjusting the headset easier.

5 Hold the fork with one hand and unscrew the threaded cup with the other. The fork will begin to drop out of the frame.

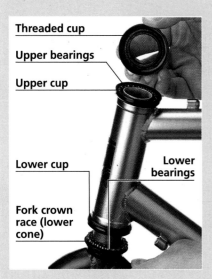

Threaded cup

Upper bearings

Upper cup

Lower cup

Lower bearings

Fork crown race (lower cone)

6 Unscrew the threaded cup all the way and drop the fork out of the frame. The part you have just unscrewed may not look like this; it can be either a cup or a cone. If there is a seal on this threaded part note its orientation.

Lift out the bearings from the upper stack and remove the bearings from the fork crown race (the cone on the fork). There may be a seal on the fork crown race; make a note of its orientation. **7**

Clean and inspect

8 Clean and inspect everything. Check at this stage that there is no sign of damage to the bearing cups and cones, and that the parts which press-fit in place – the fork crown race and the upper and lower cups in the frame – are pressed all the way into their seats and are not loose. **If these parts can be moved by hand, then expert attention is required.**

Re-assembly

9 Put a layer of grease in each bearing cup. (The upper and lower ones in the frame.)

10 Put the bearings into the grease. Note the orientation of the cage; the balls must be able to contact both the cup and the cone. If the cage is the wrong way up it will interfere with one contact, usually with the cone.

11 Add more grease over the bearings. **Make especially sure that there is plenty in the lower stack** as this takes all the loads and all the spray from the wheel.

12 Refit any seals and reassemble the headset (this is the reverse of disassembly). Screw the threaded cup onto the steerer tube, taking care not to cross the threads. If you do cross them the threaded cup will quickly become impossible to turn by hand. Don't use a spanner on the threaded cup; tighten it until it's finger tight only.

13 Put on the locknut, but again don't tighten that just yet.

14 **Adjust the headset** *(see previous procedure),* and then when headset is properly adjusted, tighten the locknut fully. It may be easier to adjust the headset with the front wheel and bars in place.

Aheadset: adjustment and overhaul

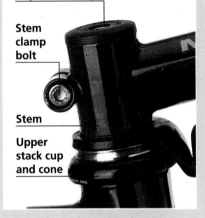

Adjustment cap

Stem clamp bolt

Stem

Upper stack cup and cone

At the end of 1992 Dia-Compe, a Japanese/American bike parts manufacturer, released a new headset design called Aheadset, which has rapidly become popular on mountain bikes from about £350 and up. Actually, like almost everything in cycling the concept was a re-invention rather than a completely new idea; similar designs have popped up now and again for decades.

Aheadset uses a steerer tube with no threads and the bearing is held in place by a special stem which clamps to the steerer. To adjust the bearing, a plastic cap pushes on the stem and this cap is held into the steerer by a bolt which screws into a special washer inside the steerer. If all this is a bit hard to visualise, it will become clear when we take one apart!

Aheadset adjustment

TOOLS 5mm Allen key.

TIME 5 mins.

DIFFICULTY 🔧🔧🔧🔧🔧

SPARES None.

OBJECTIVE To adjust the headset so that it turns freely, but with no play or looseness.

1 Loosen the stem clamp bolt so that the stem turns freely on the steerer. If the stem does not move freely, disassemble the top cap and stem and grease the steerer and the inside of the stem.

2 Adjust the top cap so that it pushes on the stem just enough to take up any slack in the bearing. You're aiming for the headset to turn freely with no play. If in doubt tighten the stem clamp bolt and rock the bike fore and aft with the front brake locked.

3 Tighten the stem clamp bolt firmly and check the adjustment.

Aheadset overhaul

Just as with any other headset, it's necessary to occasionally strip down and re-grease an Aheadset. One of the advantages of this system is that this is relatively easy.

TOOLS 5mm Allen key.

TIME 30 mins.

DIFFICULTY 🔧🔧🔧

SPARES New bearings if required.

OBJECTIVE To clean and re-grease an Aheadset type headset.

Disassembly

1 Undo the bolt in the top cap

2 Lift out the top cap and bolt. If you look down the steerer you will be able to see the special nut which holds everything together.

Special nut

3 Undo the stem clamp bolt. Support the fork with your other hand; at this stage it usually falls out and lands on your foot.

4 Still holding the fork, lift off the stem...

5 ...the brake cable stop and the conical expansion washer.

Conical expansion washer

TIP!

Some Aheadset variants have a circlip between the stem and this washer to keep the fork in place when the stem is removed. However this circlip often causes problems with adjustment because it stops the stem from compressing the bearings. Take it off and don't bother fitting it back.

Clean and inspect

6 Lift off the upper stack cup and pull the fork out of the frame. Clean and re-grease everything, as for a conventional headset.

Reassembly

7 Grease the insides of the bearing cups, expansion washer and stem and the outside of the steerer, then re-assemble the system. Finally adjust the headset as detailed previously.

The forks

Normal forks

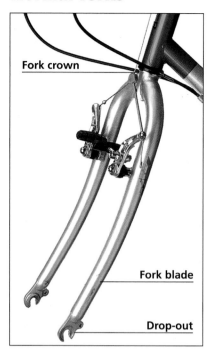

Very little goes wrong with forks except for crash damage. A crash damaged fork is very obvious; it will bend backwards instead of forwards, or will bend forwards substantially less than a fork on a similar bike. The only completely safe cure for a crash-damaged fork is replacement. If the damage is very minor a frame builder may be able to straighten it, but if you are told by a frame builder that the damage is beyond repair, accept this advice and replace the fork. A fork that has been severely bent and straightened could be dangerously weakened.

A rarer form of fork crash-damage is a bent steerer tube. This often shows up as a headset problem; the headset is loose in some positions, tight in others and does not respond to adjustment. A fork with a bent steerer tube must be replaced.

Suspension forks

Most suspension forks which can be serviced cost from £300 for the fork alone; the forks found on cheaper bikes cannot usually be serviced and very few bikes at the less expensive end of the market have suspension forks.

Suspension forks require a set of techniques for their maintenance and adjustment which is really beyond the scope of this book, especially since the leading brands all come with very good manuals, as befits a high-end product. If you think there are problems with your suspension fork beyond the need for a squirt of lube every couple of weeks, you should seek expert advice from a bike shop immediately.

Typical suspension fork

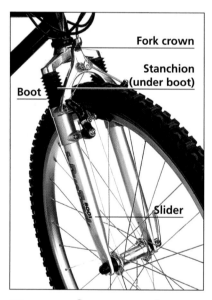

Types of suspension fork

There are two main ways in which a suspension fork works. Some use air springs and hydraulic (oil-based) damping systems. Others have elastomer rubber springs which also provide the damping. (Damping is the motion

control necessary to stop the fork just rebounding off its spring and bouncing you around). Elastomer forks work almost as well as the air/oil type and are much easier to look after. However the more complicated air/oil system ultimately does a better job of suspending the bike.

Routine suspension fork care

All types of suspension fork need to be occasionally lubed. Lift up the boot, if your fork has them, and squirt a little lubricant on to the stanchions at and above the point where they disappear into the sliders. Keep this whole area as clean as possible.

Wheels

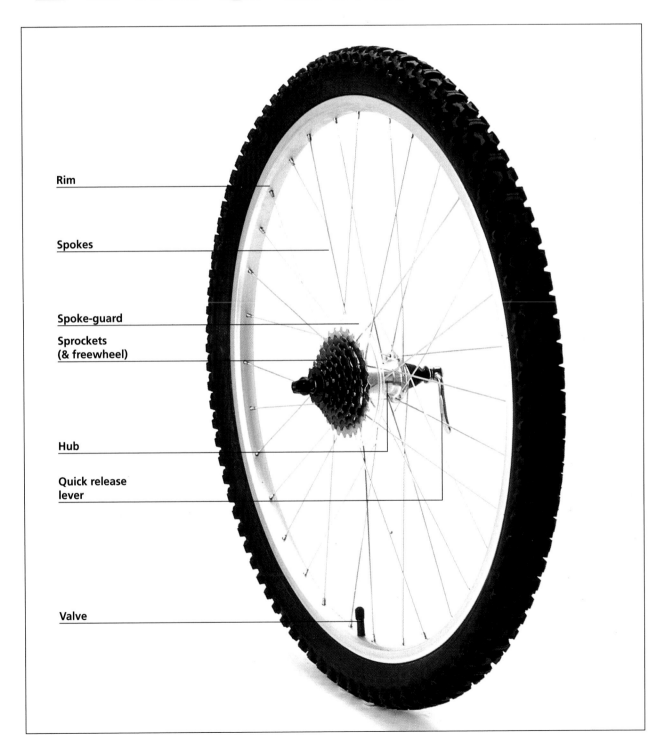

Rim

Spokes

Spoke-guard

Sprockets
(& freewheel)

Hub

Quick release
lever

Valve

203

Contents

The wheels
Freewheels and hubs, rims and spokes

A bike wheel is an exceptionally efficient structure, able to carry up to 500 times its own weight without failing. The secret of the wheel's amazing strength is the way in which it's built. The spokes in a wheel are in tension and when the wheel is loaded, the spokes at the bottom of the wheel carry the load by becoming slightly looser. If the spokes are sufficiently tight the wheel can carry very high loads without buckling.

A full discussion of the engineering of wheels, and the detail of building wheels from scratch, is beyond the scope of this book. We'll look at maintaining and adjusting hubs here, and at truing wheels and replacing spokes, but readers keen to know more about wheels cannot do better than to pick up 'The Bicycle Wheel' by Jobst Brandt, which is without doubt the definitive work on wheels.

Wheel parts

In the centre of the wheel is the hub, which contains the wheel bearings and (on the rear hub) has some method of attachment for a sprocket or set of sprockets to take the drive from the chain. The hub attaches to the bike either by a pair of nuts on the axle, or by a quick release skewer which runs through the hollow axle. Spokes, most commonly 32 or 36 of them, are hooked into holes in the hub flange and attach the rim to the hub. At the rim end, each spoke has a nipple which both anchors the spoke to the rim and allows for the spoke tension to be adjusted.

Sprockets, freewheels and freehubs

Freewheels and freehubs

Under the sprockets is a freewheel mechanism, a ratchet and pawl system which allows the hub to turn freely one way but not the other. The freewheel mechanism is either built into the hub, or it is incorporated into a separate assembly which screws on to the hub shell. The former design was popularised in recent years by Shimano and is called a **freehub**, the latter is referred to simply as a freewheel, though for clarity we will call it a **screw-on freewheel**.

On a freehub, the sprockets are easily removable from the freewheel mechanism. On a screw-on freewheel, the sprocket cluster and the freewheel are a single block and are removed as one from the hub. This will become evident as we dismantle both types.

Alternative names

A Shimano freehub and sprocket cluster is also often referred to as a cassette freewheel. A screw-on freewheel is also known as a freewheel block.

Technical differences

The main functional difference between the two designs lies in the placement of the bearings on the drive side of the hub. A hub designed for a screw-on freewheel has the bearings under the freewheel unit and as a result there is a significant amount of unsupported axle between the drop-out and the bearing. As a result this design is prone to snapping axles. The freehub, on the other hand, puts the hub bearing very close to the drop-out. This significantly reduces the stress on the axle and as a result it is unusual to break an axle on a freehub.

Freehub

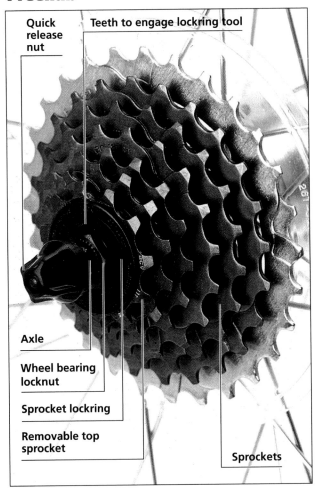

Quick release nut

Teeth to engage lockring tool

Axle

Wheel bearing locknut

Sprocket lockring

Removable top sprocket

Sprockets

Screw on freewheel

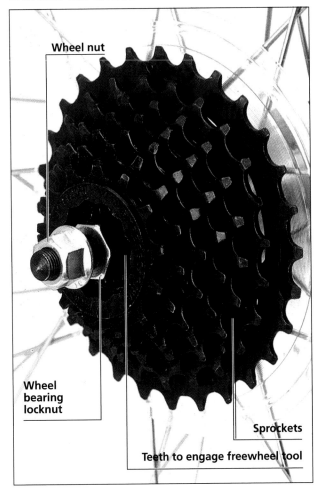

Wheel nut

Wheel bearing locknut

Sprockets

Teeth to engage freewheel tool

Identification of types

Lockring

Identification marks of a Shimano freehub.

Distinguishing between the types isn't easy. To determine whether you have a screw-on freewheel or a freehub and sprockets, look around where a lockring ought to be if it were a freehub. Look especially for lockring, the teeth to engage the lockring tool, and also a small arrow on the smallest sprocket that marks the oversized spline that is on the freehub. *(For more on this see 'Removing and fitting a freehub sprocket set'.)*

Fault Diagnosis
Freewheels and freehubs

SYMPTOM	CAUSE	REMEDY	PROCEDURE
Freewheel sounds 'gritty'	Dirt in freewheel	Flush through with thin lube (first from the front, then remove and lube from the back)	Routine lubrication (+ removing and fitting freewheels/ freehubs in order to lube from the back)
Freewheel spins both ways	Mechanism sticky	Flush through with thin lube (as above)	Routine lubrication (as above)
	Freewheel broken	Replace freewheel or freehub	Removing & fitting freewheels/ freehubs
Freewheel doesn't spin	Mechanism sticky	Flush through with thin lube (as above)	Routine lubrication (as above)
	Freewheel broken	Replace freewheel or freehub	Removing and fitting freewheels/freehubs
Sprockets worn	Age	Replace entire freewheel (if screw-on) or sprocket cluster/individual rings (if freehub)	Removing and fitting freewheels/ a freehub sprocket set

Routine lubrication

It is possible to dismantle a freewheel or freehub mechanism, but it is extremely fiddly and unlikely to be useful; spares are almost impossible to obtain so if the internal bearing races are damaged you will have to replace the freewheel or freehub body anyway. The best routine maintenance you can do is to regularly spray the inside of the freewheel mechanism with light oil.

Freehub

You are aiming to get lube into the gap between the moving external part of the freewheel and the internal stationary part. With freehubs it can be difficult to tell the difference.

Screw-on freewheel

You can usually see a very thin gap between the internal and external parts of a screw-on freewheel; spray oil into it. A more thorough way to lube the freewheel or freehub is to remove it and lube the mechanism from the back. This is detailed in each of the removal procedures.

Repairs and Replacements

Removing and fitting a screw-on freewheel

You will need to remove a freewheel either to be able to give it a good lube or clean if the mechanism is sticky, to replace it, or to provide access to the rear wheel hub; either for overhauling the hub or replacing a broken drive-side spoke.

A freewheel needs replacing if the bearings are damaged, in which case it will spin very roughly and noisily, or if the sprockets are worn from being used with a worn-out chain. Screw-on freewheels require special tools to get them off. These tools are spanner attachments which engage shaped dogs on the inside portion of the freewheel, since any attempt to unscrew the outer part simply rotates the sprockets. The design of the engagement system varies, so it's best to take the wheel with you when you are shopping for a freewheel remover.

Special Tool Freewheel remover

TOOLS Freewheel remover, large adjustable spanner.

TIME 10 mins.

DIFFICULTY 🔧🔧🔧🔧🔧

SPARES New freewheel if required.

OBJECTIVE To remove and replace a screw-on freewheel.

Removal

1 Take off the wheel nut or quick release skewer and fit the freewheel remover to the freewheel. It should be a snug fit into the freewheel removal dogs.

2 Replace the wheel nut (or quick release nut) back on to the axle, over the remover. The nut will keep the remover in place as you unscrew the freewheel.

3 Brace the wheel against the floor and wall and unscrew the freewheel (anticlockwise) with a large adjustable spanner. Stop as soon as you have loosened the freewheel.

4 Remove the axle nut and unscrew the freewheel fully.

Thread
Axle
Freewheel block

5 Lift the freewheel off the hub.

Clean and lube

6 With the freewheel removed it is easy to lube the freewheel from the back, rather than trying to find a gap in the front.

Replacement

7 It is essential to grease the threads thoroughly, especially if you have alloy hubs.

8 No tools are needed to fit a screw-on freewheel; it should screw on easily by hand.

TIP!

Be careful to get the alignment right; this fine thread is easily crossed and damaged.

Pedalling force will screw the freewheel on the rest of the way.

Removing and fitting a freehub sprocket set

Freehubs differ from freewheels in that the sprocket set can be easily removed, leaving the freewheel mechanism in place on the hub. The main symptom of worn sprockets is that a new chain will slip on them, and they will have to be replaced. Sometimes it's useful to take the sprockets off to clean the gaps between them, and, of course, changing the sprocket cluster allows you to change your gear ratios. *(For details on gear ratios, see Chapter 8.)*

The only other reasons for which you will need to take off the sprocket set is to get at the hub to overhaul it, or the drive-side hub flange in order to replace a spoke.

Special tools

Shimano Hyperglide cassette lockring remover

Shimano's TL-HG15 is a simple spanner attachment that is essential for removing the lockring which holds the sprocket set on to a Shimano freehub.

Chain whip

A pair of chain whips is used to dismantle the

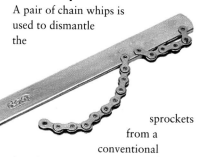

sprockets from a conventional freewheel, a procedure we have not dealt with here because it is now very difficult to get replacement sprockets for cheap screw-on freewheels, and the higher end

Don't mix your sprockets!

Shimano's Hyperglide and Interactive-Glide sprocket systems use shaped teeth and cutaways to speed shifting. Because these systems rely on precise sprocket alignment to provide their excellent shifting it is not advisable to mix sprockets from different clusters. For example, using the top half of a 12-28 cluster and the bottom half of a 13-30 will result in one shift that doesn't work very well.

of the market is dominated by freehubs. However, a single chain whip is needed to remove a freehub sprocket cluster *(as shown below)*.

If you take apart your sprockets and freehub (as we will show you below), you should find yourself with bits akin to these. Note that the number of loose individual sprockets vary; sometimes there is only one, sometimes (as here) there are two. You may also find spacers between these sprockets.

Freehub

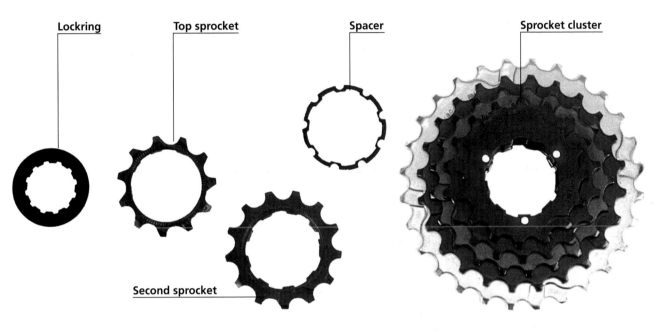

Lockring   **Top sprocket**   **Spacer**   **Sprocket cluster**

Second sprocket

Removal

TOOLS Shimano freehub lockring removal tool (TL-HG15), large adjustable spanner, chain whip.

TIME 5 mins.

DIFFICULTY 🔧🔧🔧🔧🔧

SPARES New sprocket cluster if necessary.

OBJECTIVE To remove and replace freehub sprockets.

1 Take off the spring and nut from the quick release skewer, or remove the axle nut.

2 Fit the lockring removal tool to the lockring and hold it in place with the skewer and nut.

3 Wrap a chain whip round a middle sprocket on the cluster so that it pulls the cluster clockwise.

4 Snug a large adjustable spanner on to the lockring tool and unscrew it, while holding the cluster from moving with the chain whip. The lockring makes loud cracking noises as it comes off; don't worry.

5 Take off the nut from the quick release skewer and the removal tool and lift off the lockring.

6 Now lift off the top sprocket. From here the detail of sprockets and spacers differs slightly between Shimano cassette clusters. Lift the parts off one at a time and lay them out in order so you can reassemble them easily.

The last four or five sprockets will come off in one lump, which will be **7** either rivetted together or held together by long bolts.

Freehub (freewheel mechanism)

Sprocket cassette

Replacement

Large spline gap

8 The freewheel mechanism (also known as a freehub body) has splines for the sprockets. To make sure all the sprockets are aligned properly, one spline gap is bigger than the others.

Alignment arrow

9 There is also an arrow on the sprocket cluster to indicate the correct alignment of the sprockets. When you fit the sprockets back on the freehub, this arrow should be pointing at the largest gap in the spline pattern.

10 Fit back the loose sprockets and screw the lockring in. Fit the removal tool and assemble the quick release skewer and nut (or wheel nut) to hold it in place. Then tighten the lockring down hard. (Note, no chain whip is needed for tightening the lockring). It will make a noise as it goes on.

Freehub body replacement

If the freehub mechanism is very sticky or worn out, then you will have to remove it to replace it. Annoyingly, this requires disassembly of the hub. This is considerably more hassle than the simple job of replacing the freehub body itself. *See the next section, 'Overhauling hubs', for how to get the hub apart in the first place.*

TOOLS 10mm Allen key; (+ suitable cone spanner and locknut spanner for the hubs).

TIME 30 mins (including hub disassembly, reassembly and adjustment).

DIFFICULTY

SPARES New freehub body.

OBJECTIVE To remove the freehub body from the hub and replace it.

Removal

1 Remove the cassette cluster as detailed in the previous procedure.

2 Remove the hub axle. *(See next section on hubs.)* Rear hubs are mechanically identical to front ones; it's simpler to undo the cones on the side opposite the sprockets.

3 Take the bearings out of the cup in the freehub body, then insert a 10mm Allen key into the centre of the hub.

4 Unscrew the freehub body retaining bolt and take it out.

Splined boss

5 Lift the freehub body off the hub shell. As you can see, the body sits on a splined boss on the hub.

Clean and lube

6 If the freehub is sticky, flush it through with lube; you may well be able to get it spinning freely again. When replacing a freehub, take the old one to the shop with you; the exact details of the fit to the hub shell vary.

Replacement

7 Put the freehub body on the hub shell and grease the bolt thoroughly. Screw the bolt in and tighten it fairly hard. Replace the bearings and reassemble the hub *(see next section on hubs).* Finally replace the sprocket cluster as previously shown.

The hubs

The hubs are probably the simplest bearing on a bike, and an excellent place to start if you have never taken a bike bearing system apart, since the tools needed to dismantle them – cone spanners – are easily available and relatively inexpensive.

    The rear hub is functionally identical to the front, but you will have to get off the freewheel or sprockets to properly get at the bearings. *(For how to do this, refer to the previous section.)*

Routine care

Hubs need attention if the bearings become loose, tight or gritty. The best thing to do with any problem hub is always to take it apart, clean everything, install fresh grease and if necessary replace the balls. In a perfect world this is worth doing annually anyway.

Special tools

Cone spanners

Thin spanners with 13mm, 14mm, 15mm and 16mm heads, used for adjusting hub bearings – you need two. If you're going to get into adjusting bearings, this is a good place to start as the tools are

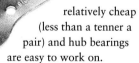

relatively cheap (less than a tenner a pair) and hub bearings are easy to work on.

Typical hub

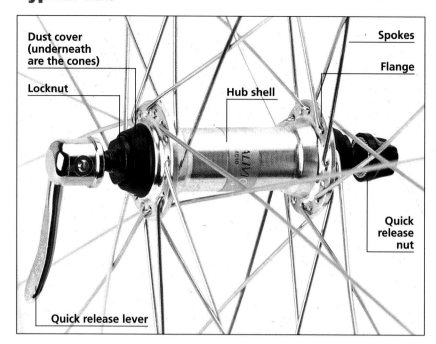

Dust cover (underneath are the cones)

Locknut

Spokes

Flange

Hub shell

Quick release nut

Quick release lever

Fault Diagnosis

Hubs

SYMPTOM	CAUSE	REMEDY	PROCEDURE
Axles turn with difficulty	Hub bearing tight	Loosen bearings	Adjusting your hubs
Axles loose in hub or wheel rattles sideways in frame	Hub bearing loose Broken axle	Tighten bearing Replace axle	Adjusting your hubs Overhauling your hubs
Hubs dirty, sticky, sounding 'gritty'	Age	Re-grease hubs	Overhauling your hubs
'Creaky hubs'	Water in the hubs	Re-grease hubs	Overhauling your hubs

Adjusting your hubs

If when you turn the axle you feel resistance (hub is too tight), or if you can rattle the axle in the hub (too loose), then the hub needs adjusting. If the bike has been ridden a lot with the hub out of adjustment then it is very likely that the bearings inside will require an overhaul and a re-grease. Hence, unless you have done that recently, don't only adjust your hubs but overhaul them now as well.

Note To adjust the bearing, you will only have to adjust the cones on one side of the hub. If you are adjusting the rear wheel, then adjust the cones on the left (non-drive) side.

TOOLS Set of cone spanners (13 mm–16 mm); conventional spanner to fit locknut (usually 17 mm).

TIME 10 mins.

DIFFICULTY

SPARES None.

OBJECTIVE To adjust the hubs so that they spin freely, but with no play or looseness.

1 Take the wheel off the bike, undo the quick release nut, and remove the quick release skewer. Although it's not strictly necessary, if the wheel has wheel nuts, remove them so that they're out of the way.

2 If your hub has them, peel off the dust covers.

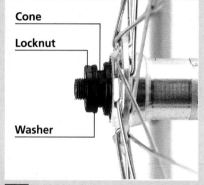

Cone
Locknut
Washer

3 With the dust covers removed the ends of the axle will look something like this: a locknut, washer and the cone all screwed on to the axle.

4 Hold the cone with a cone spanner and loosen the locknut.

5 Use a cone spanner to adjust the bearing. If the bearing is too loose (it rattles in the hub), turn the cone clockwise to tighten it. If it is too tight and the axle won't spin freely, turn the cone anticlockwise to loosen it.

TIPS!

• If the hub has a solid axle (wheel nuts), the axle should turn smoothly and not rattle in the hub at all.
• For a quick release axle the bearing should have a tiny amount of play; the clamping force of the skewer will remove this play.

213

6 When the hub is properly adjusted, tighten the locknut hard while holding the cone.

7 Tightening the locknut may upset the bearing, so check the adjustment once more by turning the axle and attempting to rattle it. If it is tight or loose, repeat the adjustment, moving the cone as necessary to correct the problem.

8 Finally refit the dust cover (if it has one) and then replace the quick release skewer (or wheel nuts). Put the wheel back on the bike. *(See Chapter 13 for important tips on the correct uses of quick releases.)*

TIP!

It may be necessary to adjust the bearing very slightly loose so that when you tighten the locknut the adjustment tightens, leaving the bearing correctly set up.

Overhauling your hubs

It is always a good idea to make sure that your hub bearings are properly greased. Overhauling them is a simple procedure. Here's how:

TOOLS Set of cone spanners (13 mm–16 mm); conventional spanner to fit locknut (usually 17 mm).

TIME 25 mins.

DIFFICULTY 🔧🔧🔧🔧🔧

SPARES Replacement ball bearings as necessary.

OBJECTIVE To disassemble, overhaul and rebuild the hub bearings.

Disassembly

1 Take the wheel off the bike, remove the quick release skewer (or wheel nuts), and the dust covers (if it has them). Then, hold the cone with a cone spanner and unscrew the locknut.

2 Remove the locknut completely.

3 Then remove the washer under the locknut (if there is one).

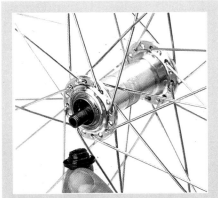

4 Remove the cone from the axle. This one has a built-in seal which forms a labyrinth seal with the matching part of the hub; many cones are simply plain.

5 From the other end of the hub, pull out the axle. See that the second set of locknut, washer and cone is still attached. Unless you have to replace these parts, leave them on and clean and inspect them in situ. *(See tip below on 'Protruding axles').*

6 Fish the bearings out of the hub and put them in a handy container.

Clean and inspect

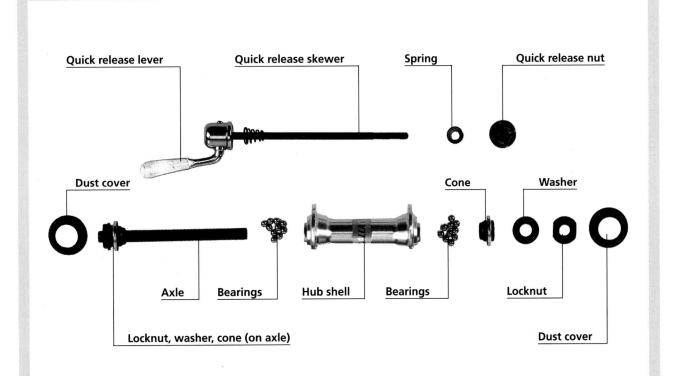

Quick release lever — Quick release skewer — Spring — Quick release nut

Dust cover — Cone — Washer

Axle — Bearings — Hub shell — Bearings — Locknut

Locknut, washer, cone (on axle) — Dust cover

7 With degreaser, clean all the parts; the cups within the hub, the cones, the axle and the bearings. Inspect them for corrosion and pitting in the surfaces. Get replacements for any damaged or pitted parts; take the old ones with you when you go shopping for new bits. If the hub itself is damaged – that's bad news. You're probably looking at a replacement wheel.

215

Re-greasing and reassembly

8 Fill the cups with grease; do both sides.

9 Put the bearings in the grease; again do both sides. A pen top with a dab of grease on the end is very handy for putting in ball bearings.

10 Fit the axle into the hub. Then from the other side replace the cone and washer.

11 Finally screw the locknut down the axle until it stops against the bearings. Now adjust the bearings. *(Move to previous procedure, begin at step 5.)*

12 Finally, when adjustment is complete don't forget to tighten the locknut down hard (and recheck the adjustment again). Then replace the dust covers and quick release skewer (or wheel nuts) and fit the wheel back on the bike.

TIP!

Front hub bearings are usually ³⁄₁₆in and there are usually ten per side. Rear hub balls are usually ¼in and nine per side.

TIP!

Protruding axles

The ends of the axle of a quick release must protrude enough to engage the drop-outs, but not so much that they extend beyond the ends of the drop-outs as this will stop the quick release from closing properly. If you have to remove both cones to replace them, first measure the distance from the end of the axle to the locknut and reset to this distance when you assemble the hub.

The wheels: Rims and spokes

The hub is a pretty straightforward bearing. The parts of the wheel which really give people problems are the structural components; the spokes and rim. A wheel is a tensioned structure, and it is crucial that the spokes are evenly tensioned and tight for a wheel to be strong and durable. However, if they are too tight the wheel will fail; the crucial aspect of any work on wheels is learning where the balance point is between tensioning a spoke enough and tensioning it too much. Professional and would-be professional wheel builders use experience and tensiometers to determine this; the amateur mechanic has to rely on caution and intuition. The subject of wheels, and especially wheel building, is large enough for a whole book of its own, (as mentioned at the beginning of the chapter). The following discussion is restricted to the most common and easiest wheel repair problems; truing a slightly out-of-line rim and replacing a broken spoke. First, let's look at some general points you need to know about wheels.

General points on wheels and spokes
Spokes

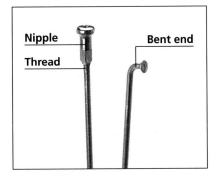

The spoke consists of a steel wire with a thread at one end and a flattened, bent head at the other where it fits in the hub, and a nipple which is basically a four-sided nut which holds the spoke into the rim and allows the tension in the spoke to be adjusted.

The nipple and spoke have right-hand threads, so tightening and loosening them is done in the normal way, though the perspective from which you view a wheel may make you confused about which way to turn a nipple.

If in doubt rotate the wheel so that the spoke is at the bottom of the wheel and you are above it. The spoke nipple tightens the spoke if turned anti-clockwise from this point of view.

Spokes can either be 'left-side' or 'right-side'. This depends on whether they are connected to the left or right flange of the hub. Tightening a spoke that is connected to the left flange will pull that part of the rim to which the spoke is connected to the left, and vice versa for tightening a right-side spoke.

Wheel dish

The spokes of a front wheel are evenly tensioned on either side of the hub, but those on a back wheel are not. This is to provide 'wheel dish' which is basically the amount by which the rim is offset between the hub flanges to make room for the sprockets. On a rear wheel this means that the drive side spokes are as much as twice as tight as the non-drive side, and so any changes to the spoke tension you make on the drive side will have twice the effect on the vertical position of the rim as adjustments to the non-drive side. If this sounds complicated try tightening a drive side spoke a full turn, see what happens to the position of the rim, then tighten a non-drive side spoke a turn and observe the effect. Don't forget to return each spoke to its proper tension afterwards.

Wheel dish is only a major problem for wheel builders. You can easily tell if your wheel is out of dish by turning it round in the frame and checking the position of the rim against the brake blocks in both orientations.

Adjustments

The golden rule is make small adjustments. It's easy to produce true wheels if you make all your adjustments very small, and work carefully and methodically. When you have more experience you will know when you can add a full turn of tension to a spoke, but start by working in quarter-turns and half-turns.

Lacing

You'll sometimes hear people use phrases like 'three-cross' 'two-cross' and 'radial' when talking about wheels. These terms refer to different ways of assembling the spokes in the wheel, and indicate the number of times a spoke is crossed by other spokes between the hub and the rim; a wheel with no spoke crossings at all is called radial because the spokes follow the radius of the wheel. Bike bores have hours of fun debating the merits and demerits of different spoking patterns. Those of us who prefer to ride have three-cross wheels because that is the industry standard for a host of very sound engineering reasons. My only contribution to the debate is to warn you away from radial wheels, which put stresses on the hub flanges in ways they are not designed to take and can crack them, causing catastrophic wheel failure. The other important aspect of lacing is that the spokes should be interlaced so that they touch at the last spoke crossing before the hub.

Fault Diagnosis
Wheels & spokes

SYMPTOM	CAUSE	REMEDY	PROCEDURE
Rim not true; rim rubs against brake blocks	Accident or poor original building	True wheel	Truing a wheel
Spoke broken	Accident, age or poor building	Replace spoke	Replacing a spoke

Speaking about spokes

Hub flange

In a typical wheel the spokes alternately thread through the flanges from each side, then cross.

In a properly laced wheel, a spoke comes out of the flange, threads over two spokes, then goes under the third, which it therefore touches.

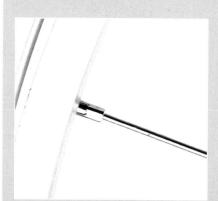

The rim, a spoke and one of the nipples which hold everything together. The flat surfaces on the nipple allow you to grip them with a spoke key.

The spokes in the rim well. The screwdriver slots in the nipples allow wheel builders to quickly bring a wheel up to tension.

TIPS!
Seized nipples
- If the nipples are tight or feel seized, put a drop of penetrating oil on the spoke above each nipple and spin the wheel hard to drive it into the threads.

- If a nipple is irretrievably seized, use a screwdriver on the nipple, or a Mole grip, to loosen it completely, then cut it and replace it.

- NEVER cut spokes while they are in tension. Use side-cutters or pliers with good cutting jaws, NOT cable cutters.

218

Truing wheels

This is the most difficult job tackled in this book. If you are not confident of your general mechanical skill, then wheel adjustments should be approached with caution. If you appear to be making things worse instead of better, **stop and seek expert advice** – take the wheel to a wheel builder and have them sort it out.

That said, a wheel with only a small deflection from straight or round (less than half a centimetre) should be well within your capabilities. You need to recognise that some wheel problems cannot be fixed without advanced techniques, however. Rims which have visible dents from impacts with rocks; wheels which are more than 1cm off straight; wheels which have assumed the shape of a crisp after a crash; and wheels where the spokes in the outside of a sideways bend are still very tight (a sure sign of a laterally dented rim) are only partially curable by brute force techniques which are beyond the scope of this book. The best thing to do with such a wheel is to get it rebuilt, or to buy the necessary tackle and teach yourself wheel building.

I have assumed here that you are dealing with a ready-built wheel which is properly tensioned; wheel truing techniques do not work on very loose wheels. If your spokes seem to be loose compared to other people's or wheels on new bikes in shops, get them tightened. Tight spokes make for durable wheels.

It should be clear that the techniques which follow are intended only as an introduction to wheel maintenance and repair; enough to get a damaged wheel usable again, and perhaps get you home, but not the full set of skills which a wheel builder needs. If you want to know more (lots more!) then you need a copy of 'The Bicycle Wheel' as mentioned previously.

TOOLS Spoke key.

TIME 10 mins to 1hr+.

DIFFICULTY 🔧🔧🔧🔧🔧

SPARES None.

OBJECTIVE To adjust spokes so that the wheel runs straight and round.

Warning

In the process of truing a wheel it is possible for a spoke to snap without warning and for the rim end to fly thought the wheel at considerable speed. The hazard to eyes is obvious. NEVER look along the length of a spoke that you are tightening.

Special Tools

Spoke key

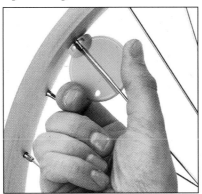

Vital for adjusting wheel shape, but also the tool which offers most potential for foul-ups. Spoke keys come in a number of sizes because the different thicknesses of spoke have different nipple sizes. Almost all spokes on production bikes use 14g nipples, but European 14g nipples are slightly different from Far Eastern ones; get the snuggest fit you can.

Wheel jig

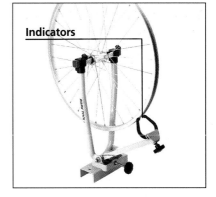

Indicators

A wheel jig is not essential, but it helps, by providing a firm mounting for the wheel and adjustable indicators so that you can determine the areas of the wheel which need attention. We've used one here because it makes for clear illustrations, but you can get good results by holding the wheel in the bike frame, and I know several amateur mechanics whose first wheel jig was a home-made contraption rigged up from an old fork.

If you are using a bike, and therefore using the brakes as indicators, you should loosen the brakes off as much as possible, so that the wheel spins through the blocks, then use the cable adjusters to move the blocks in until one just touches a spinning wheel.

219

Before you start

If you're using a wheel jig it's essential, and even if you're not it's strongly advisable to remove the tyre, tube and rim tape from the wheel. This way you can properly look at errors in the rim.

Basic techniques
Spoke tightening

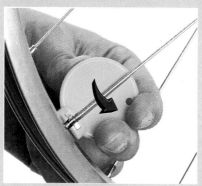

Tighten the spoke by turning the spoke key anticlockwise as seen from the hub, so that it screws the nipple up the spoke and pulls the rim in the direction of the spoke. Unless you are dealing with a high quality, hand-built wheel, most of the truing you do will be done by tightening spokes, since factory built wheels are always at the low end of the acceptable range for spoke tension.

Spoke loosening

Loosen the spoke by turning the spoke key clockwise as seen from the hub, so that it screws the nipple down the spoke and allows the other spokes to pull the rim away from the spoke you are loosening. You may need to loosen spokes to true a wheel which is very tight. Over-tightening a wheel can cause it to fail, or damage the rim at the spoke holes.

Stress-relieving the spokes

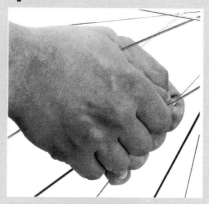

After any amount of work on a wheel it should be stress-relieved. Spokes usually wind up slightly in the rim because the nipple can move an eighth of a turn or so before it starts turning on the spoke. This stress will relieve itself when the wheel is ridden, but this can cause the wheel to go out of true. To get rid of it, **grab groups of four parallel spokes** as shown and squeeze very hard (it should hurt). Do this all the way round the wheel, then correct any problems with the wheel alignment which result.

Methods of truing
Sideways errors

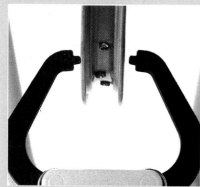

1 Start by correcting sideways misalignment. Spin the wheel. Move the blocks or indicators in until one side just touches part of the wheel. This is the largest sideways error and needs to be corrected first.

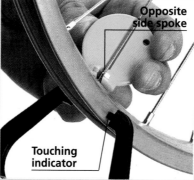

Opposite side spoke

Touching indicator

2 Find the spoke nearest the error on the opposite side of the rim and tighten it a quarter to half a turn. Repeat these steps until the sideways error is acceptable. With practice you should be able to get it down to less than half a millimetre.

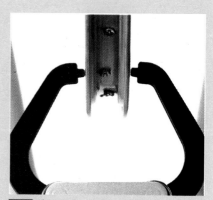

3 This is the objective: a wheel which is evenly spaced between the indicators or brake blocks, with just a very small gap either side of the rim. When you spin the wheel, the indicators should not rub on any part.

Up and down errors

Tighten both spokes

4 Next, deal with up and down errors. Move the jig indicators under the rim, spin the wheel and move the indicators up until the rim touches. If you're using a frame, use an Allen key attached with a large lump of Blu-tack as an indicator and push it towards the rim as it spins.

5 Stop the rim at the point where it touches and find the two spokes nearest the contact point.

6 Tighten the two spokes at the contact point a quarter or half turn each. Tightening spokes in pairs corrects up and down errors while having little effect on the sideways position of the rim. Repeat these steps until the up and down errors are acceptable.

7 Finally, after all truing adjustments have been made, Stress-relieve the wheel.

Replacing a spoke

One of the most common problems is of broken spokes, especially on the highly stressed drive side rear wheel spokes. It is sometimes worth replacing a spoke, but at other times spoke replacement should be viewed as a strictly temporary measure. To understand why you need to know why spokes fail in the first place.

One cause of spoke failure is accidents. If the chain derails into the spokes and gouges big chunks out of some of them, then they will need replacing, and similarly a kamikaze tree branch can wreak havoc with mountain bike spokes. Barring accidents, however, spokes usually fail because of metal fatigue caused by the repeated loading and unloading that happens to a wheel. This means that if one spoke in an

elderly wheel fails, it is likely that others will follow pretty closely.

This is especially true of wheels with dull-looking 'rustless' spokes which are zinc-galvanised, and wheels which are factory built by machine, rather than hand-built by a skilled wheel builder. The best spokes are made of stainless steel, which can take higher loads without failing because of fatigue. Loose spokes also fail sooner than properly tensioned spokes, which is why good wheels are tight. The practical upshot of all this is that if spokes start failing in a loosely spoked, factory built wheel with dull spokes, it is almost certainly not worth replacing them; better to get the whole wheel rebuilt with stainless spokes by an expert wheel builder.

Getting replacements

If you break a spoke you'll need a replacement. Spoke lengths vary enormously between wheels and a description of the bike will not help the shop find you a replacement spoke. However, if you tell them the make and model of hub and rim, the number of spokes in the wheel, the wheel size and the lacing pattern (three-cross, or whatever) then a good shop should be able to help. Alternatively, take the wheel into the shop with you, thus removing all uncertainty.

221

Replacement procedure

TOOLS Spoke key.

TIME 15 mins.

DIFFICULTY 🔧🔧🔧🔧

SPARES Replacement spoke.

OBJECTIVE To replace a spoke and re-true the wheel.

1 Take off the tyre, tube and rim tape. If the spoke is on the drive side of the wheel, take off the freewheel or the sprocket cluster and the plastic spoke-guard so that you can get at the flange underneath it *(see the section on freewheels in this chapter)*. Then, pull the broken spoke out of the wheel.

2 Thread the new spoke into the hub from the opposite direction to the two either side of the gap. That is, if the spokes either side of the hole come from the inside of the flange to the outside, then the new one goes in from the outside. Point the spoke into a gap on the other side of the wheel, as shown, so it does not get tangled up with the other spokes in the wheel.

3 Lace the spoke so that it goes under the first two spokes it crosses and under the last one, or the other way round. (This depends on the direction of the spoke.)

4 Pull the spoke to the hole in the rim and fit a nipple.

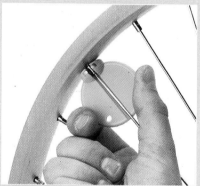

5 Tighten the spoke to the same tension as the other spokes in similar positions on that side of the wheel, or until the sideways wobble produced by having a missing spoke is gone. It should be possible to get the wheel pretty much true by just tightening the one spoke.

The frame

Contents

Problems with frames are almost always the result of a crash or other mishap, like getting a twig caught in the transmission, which then bends or breaks the gear hanger. In this chapter we'll look at the most common problems with frames and how to deal with them.

Rust prevention

Most frames that I have seen damaged by rust have been eaten away from the inside out. It's relatively easy for water to get inside a bike frame, especially in heavy rain, or if you ride off-road through streams, but it's also relatively hard for it to get out. As a result water pools inside the frame, especially in areas like the bottom bracket shell. It makes sense to drill a hole in the bottom bracket shell to allow water to drain out, and to fit a plastic shell between the cups to keep water out of the bearings of a cup and cone bottom bracket.

It also makes sense to spray the inside of your frame tubes with a spray grease or other rust blocker; even WD40 will do. Squirt generous amounts of lube through the holes near the ends of the frame tubes.

It is not a good idea to try and seal these holes. It's highly unlikely that you will succeed in perfectly sealing the frame, but you will make it even harder for water that does get in to evaporate or escape by draining out. A 'sealed' frame will therefore be more likely to rust than one which is left open to the elements.

Paint damage

Paint is essential to protect the frame from rust; that's why it's there. Damage to paint happens as a result of everyday dings and dents and because of minor crashes. Bike paint has improved markedly in the last few years with big companies like Dawes and Raleigh working hard to develop tougher paint finishes, but on older bikes, and especially bikes painted with traditional stove enamel paint (which is baked in an oven to harden it) paint damage is a fact of life.

The simplest way to protect your frame if the paint gets scratched is to cover the scratched area with clear nail varnish (or bike lacquer) as soon as possible after the scratch happens.

To do a better job is tricky, not because there's anything very difficult about touching up the paint on your frame, but because you will find it anywhere between difficult and impossible to find exactly the right shade of paint to match your frame. Some people say this is a good reason to have a black bike! If you are very bothered about the appearance of your bike, then the best thing to do is to have the frame completely repainted every year or two, and any good bike shop will be able to arrange this for you.

223

Frame damage

Dings and dents

There's not much you can do about minor dents to the frame tubes. As long as a dent is not more than a couple of centimetres deep and does not have any sign of a crease in the bottom it is almost certainly not going to present problems as far as the structural integrity of the frame is concerned. If you are concerned about the effect of a particular dent, have a good mechanic or frame builder look at it.

Major damage

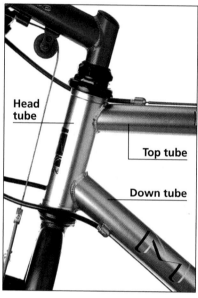

Head tube

Top tube

Down tube

Crashes are the source of most major damage to frames and the most common form of damage is for the frame to be bent at the top and down tube, just behind the head tube. The head tube is pushed back toward the bottom bracket by some sort of front-end collision, and there is usually, but not always, damage to the fork as well.

After any sort of front-end collision you should inspect the area behind the head tube for rippling of the frame or cracking of the paint. Any sign of damage indicates that the frame should not be ridden and should be inspected by a mechanic as soon as possible.

Aluminium frames in particular should be frequently inspected for tiny cracks behind the head tube, at the joints with the top and down tube and especially under the junction with the down tube. It's not that aluminium frames are particularly liable to fail, more that if they do, they will do so suddenly and with very little warning. The consequences of the head tube of a frame falling off while you are riding along are pretty unpleasant.

Steel frames, fortunately, are far more likely to bend than to break, because of the way in which steel behaves. However, a crash-bent steel tube will break eventually, which is why it should not be ridden.

Alignment damage

If your bike seems to be handling oddly after a crash, then it is likely that you have knocked it out of alignment. Symptoms include the steering pulling to the left or right, a sure sign that frame or fork are out of track, or the bike suddenly becoming unrideable when you lift your hands off the handlebar. (As an aside here I should mention that attempting to ride 'no-hands' for a moment on a quiet street is a sensible test for frame alignment, since a straight frame will keep going in a straight line with no steering input from the rider, but it is generally a very silly thing to do, and while hammering round Hyde Park Corner in the rush hour is not a sensible time to check your frame alignment.)

A simple check for frame alignment is to run a piece of string from the rear dropouts to the head tube; it should be the same distance either side of the seat tube.

This method isn't perfect; it can make a misaligned frame appear to be OK, and you should therefore have a good shop or frame builder check your frame if you are at all uncertain about it.

Realigning a frame requires a fair degree of skill and experience and is best left to frame builders.

Gear hanger damage

The tab which carries the rear mech is one of the most vulnerable parts of the bike, because it is easily damaged if something drags the rear mech backwards or sideways from the frame. Fortunately it is fairly easy to repair the most common form of hanger damage, as long as it happens to a steel frame. Aluminium frames usually have removable hangers so they can be replaced if they get bent or broken; a bent aluminium hanger should not be straightened as the attempt will almost certainly severely weaken or break it.

Indexed derailleur systems rely on accurate hanger alignment to work properly; if the hanger is bent they will almost certainly not work well. The following method usually gets hangers straight enough for the gears to work, but you may need to have a bike shop look at the problem; they have highly accurate special tools for aligning gear hangers.

Straightening a gear hanger

TOOLS 2 adjustable spanners.

TIME 10 mins.

DIFFICULTY 🔧🔧🔧🔧

SPARES None.

OBJECTIVE To straighten a bent hanger.

1 Clamp one spanner on the faces of the dropout and the other on the hanger, so that the hanger spanner is perpendicular to the bend.

2 Bend the hanger carefully back into place. Fine adjustments can be made by repositioning the spanners and using the spanner on the dropout as a gauge; when the spanner on the hanger is parallel to the spanner on the dropout, the dropout is straight.

Frames and frame tubing

Almost all frames are built from some sort of steel tubing. There is a wide variety of tubing available, from the basic high tensile steel used for budget bikes to the high-strength, heat-treated alloy steels used in the very best racing and mountain bikes. The main difference between different steels is their strengths; in order to make a frame that is strong enough, much less is needed of a very strong steel than of a weaker one, and so frames made from expensive, high strength steels such as Reynolds 753 and Tange Prestige are lighter.

These increases in strength which allow lighter frames are achieved in three ways. The simplest is to add alloying elements to the steel. Chromium, manganese and molybdenum are the most common substances added to steel. Reynolds 531 has manganese and molybdenum, for example, while most common steels used for mountain bikes have chromium and molybdenum added to them, and are referred to as chromoloy steels for this reason.

Almost all steel tubing is 'work hardened' to increase its strength. This simply means that in the manufacturing process the tube is manipulated under pressure by rollers, which affects the microscopic structure of the metal in such a way that it gets stronger.

The final process is heat treatment. At high temperatures some steel alloys re-arrange themselves internally into a very strong form. If the metal is then cooled quickly, that structure can be 'frozen', which is a very useful way of producing very high strength steels.

Alternatives to steel

In the last few years other materials have been used for bike frames. The most common of these is aluminium. Aluminium is used because the low density of the material offers the possibility of very light frames, and the lightest aluminium frames are almost 20 per cent lighter than the best steel frames. However, the strength to weight ratios of the best steel and aluminium alloys are actually quite similar; the reason for the light weight of some aluminium frames is to do with the fact that aluminium can be made into lighter tubes that are strong by dint of being large. This is impossible with steel because very large steel tubes would have to be so thin they couldn't be welded into frames and could be crushed with your bare hands.

The biggest buzz-word in cycling in the last few years has been titanium. This expensive-to-extract material seems to have the best compromise of strength, density, resistance to fatigue and corrosion and ride-feel of any metal. Unfortunately it is expensive because of the difficulty of extracting the metal from its ore, and of working with it subsequently. If you ever get a chance to ride a bike made from this wonder metal, though, do so.

Accessories

Contents

Most of the mechanical repair and maintenance stuff that you need to know concerns the bike itself, but some accessories like pumps, lights and your helmet, need at least occasional inspection and in some cases a bit of regular care.

This chapter will deal with how to keep your accessories in good working order. *For more discussion on accessories, especially which ones to have, refer to Chapter 3.*

Pump

Because your pump has a plunger that slides in and out of an external sleeve it needs similar attention to a bearing. However, you do have to be a little careful about what you lubricate it with; many spray lubricants contain solvents that will damage the plunger, or the inside of your tubes if they get into them.

Greasing a pump

1 Pull out the handle and unscrew the threaded collar which holds the pump together.

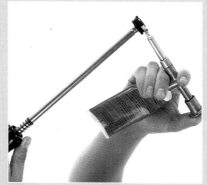

2 Take out the plunger and smear a little grease on it.

3 Grease the inside of the pump as well, then put it back together.

Lights

Routine care

The most important thing to do with lights is to keep them as dry as possible. After a wet ride, open the battery case, take off the lens and leave the light somewhere warm and well-ventilated to dry out.

Almost all the problems that develop with lights do so because the switches get corroded by moisture getting into the body of the light. An occasional squirt of WD40 and, if necessary, gently sanding the contact clean, will keep the light working.

TOOLS Emery cloth; WD40.

TIME 5 mins.

DIFFICULTY 🔧

SPARES None.

OBJECTIVE To clean and protect battery connections.

1 Remove the lens to reveal the back of the bulb and the switch.

2 Sand clean the bulb and the switch contact.

3 Open the bottom of the battery case and drop out the batteries.

4 Sand clean the top set of battery contacts.

5 Sand clean the bottom set of battery contacts.

6 Spray WD40 at all the contacts.

Computers

Small electronic speedometers are popular accessories and are as useful to recreational cyclists who simply want to know how far they have ridden as they are to 'serious' cyclists who need to know average speed, time and even their heart rate.

Installation of computers is slightly different for each model, and will be covered in the manufacturer's literature. Problems with computers usually boil down to damaged wiring, which will have to be replaced; flat batteries (they last 1-2 years); and misplaced sensors and magnets.

Computer care

The magnet should be pretty much as close as possible to the sensor; if the computer suddenly stops working check that the sensor or magnet haven't moved, and that the magnet is within 2mm of the sensor.

Occasionally the computer will throw up problems because there is water in the contacts; to prevent this, take off the computer and spray the mounting and contacts with WD40.

227

Helmet

Inspect your helmet frequently for dings and dents. A badly dented helmet should be replaced immediately, as should one which has been crashed. Helmets should also be replaced about every two years even if they have not been crashed; the materials used can degrade as a result of the effect of ultra-violet light and exposure to everyday lubes and solvents that are likely to be around bikes.

Mudguards

Mudguards of some sort are essential for commuting in Britain; it rains, you'll get wet, so it's better to have some protection from it than to get completely drenched. If you ride with others then full-length mudguards with mud flaps will stop spray from your wheels from soaking anyone who is following you.

Mudguards have a habit of getting bent and of rattling loose. They can be straightened by gently bending the stays to bring the guard over the centre of the tyre. The bolts at the tops of the stays should be checked frequently to make sure they are tight.

Few mudguards are supplied with the necessary bolts to attach them to the frame. Usually you need M5 bolts to fit the threaded eyes in the frame; ones with 4mm Allen key heads are good.

If possible, use Nylok nuts as lock nuts where the mudguards attach to the frame. These nuts have nylon inserts which prevent them from rattling loose.

Racks

A rear rack and panniers is the most comfortable way of carrying loads. Get one which attaches to the frame at four points for maximum rigidity. Premium brands include Blackburn and Cannondale, which are very good, though there are lots of far eastern copies of these designs around, most of which are very serviceable.

Like mudguards, racks need fairly frequent checking to ensure that the bolts are tight. If you are fitting mudguards and a rack, and have only one set of eyes on your frame, you will need to use longer bolts. Put the mudguard stays on the outside of the rack so that the more heavily loaded rack is close to the frame and therefore loads the bolts less.

Locks

Your lock hardly needs any maintenance, but a regular squirt of lube into the lock mechanism will ensure that it doesn't become sticky or, heaven forbid, seize.

Part Four
Appendices

Roadside repair

When you're out riding, things go wrong, and often you have to improvise or make do to get home. Being able to bodge your way out of trouble is especially important for mountain bikers, who are likely to be faced with a long hike home carrying a bike if they cannot sort out a problem. This sort of thing even happens to hacks who should really know better; I was cured forever of occasionally forgetting my chain tool by a five mile cross-country walk to the nearest road, where I was lucky enough to meet a group of road cyclists, one of whom had a chain tool. As he remarked, "It's the one tool which you're completely stuffed if you need it and don't have it."

Of course, the sensible thing to do is to carry a tool kit and know how to use it. As I say in Chapter 12, I now carry a minimum of a Cool Tool, tyre levers, spare tube, pump and puncture repair kit, so I can deal with most minor problems that arise. This kit doesn't weigh much and it's a small price to pay for peace of mind.

Looking after your bike properly also helps to minimise the risk of things going wrong; bike parts don't spontaneously fail, they go wrong because developing problems have been ignored or overlooked. Being familiar with your bike, and with how it should work, and fixing problems before they become serious, is the key to trouble-free riding.

If things do go wrong and you have no spares or tools, it's worth having a quick look around you for bits of wire and wood that you can use to bodge a repair; you can sometimes use a piece of wire to hold the bottom run of the chain together well enough to get you home, for example. You'll have to 'ratchet' the pedals, but it's better than walking. I have seen it suggested that you should carry tape, a bungee cord, bits of wire and zip-ties so you can bodge your way out of almost anything. This is silly; if you're going to remember to carry that lot, you might as well remember to carry a couple of spare cables, a short bit of

chain, a few spare bolts and a proper tool kit so you can fix things correctly.

Puncture

Filling your tyres with grass and other vegetation is an old cyclist's bodge that works just about well enough to get you home, and will do if it's the only alternative to walking.

However, if you have a pump, but no spare or tube or repair kit, a better solution is to find the hole and tie a knot in the tube so that the hole is sealed from the rest of the tube. The tube will now work more or less as normal, though it might have a bump every revolution.

Tyre gash

Put something – a bit of cloth, some tape, whatever – behind the gash to prevent the tube poking out. Americans can use dollar bills, but British currency is too flimsy.

Snapped chain

Fix it using your chain tool. Oh, it's at home? Use a piece of wire to bind the chain together. You may find you have to stay in the big sprocket so that the wire doesn't catch on the other sprockets.

Trashed rear mech

A stray branch can wreak havoc with your rear mech, bending the hanger and derailleur. Shorten the chain (you'll need a chain tool for this) and run the bike as a one speed, bypassing the mech.

Crisped wheel

You can usually get a crash-damaged wheel straight enough to pass through the frame by pushing it back into shape with all your weight, or by whacking one of the four points of the shape hard on the ground.

Rattled out bolts

The bolts that hold your rack and mudguards on are the same thread as

your water bottle cage bolts; cannibalise them and stuff your bottle in your pocket if your rack bolts get loose. Look for similar places where a less essential bolt can substitute for a crucial one.

Broken handlebar

After you've made sure nothing's broken on you – a snapped bar usually causes a big crash, or is caused by one – see if you can find a lump of wood that fits inside the bar well enough to hold the pieces together and bang each end on to it.

Damaged cable

Just occasionally Shimano outer gear cable splits from wear and your gears stop working. A zip-tie or two round the casing will hold it together long enough to get you home.

Bent chainrings

Bent chainrings can be straightened enough to get you going again by simple application of brute force from a small adjustable spanner.

Jammed transmission

If your chain is too short it is possible to jam the transmission by shifting into the big ring and big sprocket at the same time. It is impossible to shift out of this situation. The technique which usually works is to loosen the rear brake, pull the rear mech back out of the way and hit the wheel so it comes out of the dropouts. This can require a considerable blow.

If the wheel won't move, try splitting the chain. Be very careful; it's under a lot of tension and may flail around as it comes apart. Keep your face well clear. Alternatively, if you happen to be carrying the right tools, take off the right-hand crank. Special crank bolts – Allen key release bolts – which enable this are available from bike shops.

Fault finding

In each repair chapter there is a fault diagnosis table relating to that particular component. Hence, for instance, if you know that you have a problem with your brakes, turn to Chapter 14 and consult the fault diagnosis there.

This guide is intended to point you in the direction of a repair chapter if you have one of those 'general problems', and it is not immediately obvious which part of the bike is to blame.

General problems whilst riding

SYMPTOM	CAUSE	REMEDY	SEE CHAPTER
Bike is uncomfortable to ride	Bike set-up wrong	Set bike up correctly	3 Setting up
	Saddle tilt wrong	Adjust saddle tilt	3 Setting up 17 Saddle
	Bar reach, shape or position wrong	Correct problem	3 Setting up 18 Handlebars
	Duff saddle	Buy and fit a better one	3 Setting up 17 Saddle
Bike is tiring to ride	Transmission, especially chain, corroded	Lube it	15 Transmission
	Wheel rubbing on brakes	Adjust brakes	14 Brakes
		True wheel	20 Wheels
	You're unfit	Ride more!	5 On the road 6 Off the road
Noticeable resistance while freewheeling	Wheel rubbing on brakes	Adjust brakes	14 Brakes
Noticeable resistance while pedalling	Wheel rubbing on brakes	Adjust brakes	14 Brakes
	Bottom bracket bearing badly seized or corroded	Replace or overhaul	16 Chainset
Bike pulls to one side, especially when ridden no-hands	Frame or fork are bent or misaligned	Probably a job for a bike shop	21 Frame

SYMPTOM	CAUSE	REMEDY	SEE CHAPTER
Bike wobbles and feels unsafe	Loose headset	Adjust or replace	19 Headset
	Loose hubs	Adjust or replace	20 Wheels
	Loose bottom bracket	Adjust or replace	16 Chainset
	Wheels out of true	True wheels	20 Wheels
Bike vibrates at speed	Misadjusted headset	Adjust or replace	19 Headset
	Wheels out of round or true	True wheels	20 Wheels
Bike vibrates when braking	Rim dented	Replace rim: a job for a bike shop	20 Wheels
	Brakes badly adjusted	Adjust brakes	14 Brakes
	Headset loose	Tighten headset	19 Headset
The ride is too bumpy	Tyres under-inflated	Pump up tyres	13 Tyres and tubes
Brakes don't work	Blocks worn	Replace blocks	14 Brakes
	Cables stretched	Adjust cables	14 Brakes
	Brakes corroded	Overhaul brakes	14 Brakes
	Cables sticky or frayed	Lube or replace	14 Brakes
Gears don't work	Indexing misadjusted	Adjust gears	15 Transmission
	Cables sticky	Lube or replace	15 Transmission
	Gear mechanisms corroded or dirty	Overhaul	15 Transmission
Chain falls off repeatedly	Stop screws of one or both mechs are maladjusted	Adjust correctly	15 Transmission
Frequent punctures	Tyres worn out	Replace	13 Tyres and tubes
	Object embedded	Inspect tyre closely and remove problem	13 Tyres and tubes
	Local farmers fond of trimming hedges	Complain to local highways authority; under Litter Act and Highways Act farmers have a responsibility to clear up hedge trimmings	
		Fit tyre sealant	13 Tyres and tubes

Chapter 24 FAULT FINDING

Noises

SYMPTOM	CAUSE	REMEDY	SEE CHAPTER
Clicking noise, apparently from bottom bracket area, once per pedal revolution (known in the trade as 'mysterious clicking noises', these are the hardest faults to diagnose. The list is as exhaustive as possible, but may not be complete!)	Loose pedal cage screws	Tighten	16 Chainset
	Loose toe-clip bolts	Tighten	16 Chainset
	Pedal loose in crank	Grease and tighten	16 Chainset
	Crank loose on axle	Fit properly	16 Chainset
	Chainring bolts loose	Tighten	16 Chainset
	Bottom bracket cup loose in frame	Tighten and adjust	16 Chainset
	Bottom bracket bearing misadjusted, damaged or worn	Dismantle and adjust	16 Chainset
	Bottom bracket shell parting company from frame (I have seen this happen!)	Inspect frame. Expect warranty replacement unless frame has been crashed	
	Spokes in rear wheel extremely loose	Tighten spoke or rebuild wheel	20 Wheels
Clicking noise twice per pedal revolution	Bottom bracket misadjusted (loose)	Adjust	16 Chainset
Clicking noise once per chain revolution	Stiff link in chain	Loosen link	15 Transmission
Constant rattling noise	Something somewhere is loose, usually a bolt-on accessory	Check mudguard, rack and bottle cage screws and tighten	
Clicking or scrubbing noise from wheel	Out of true wheel hitting brake block	True wheel	20 Wheels
Irregular rattling noise (e.g., when you ride over a bump)	Something somewhere is slightly loose, usually a bolt-on accessory	Check mudguard, rack and bottle cage screws and tighten	

Jargon

Fed up with not knowing what a certain bike-word or phrase means? Look no further than here.

Aheadset: Brand name of a design of headset which uses a threadless steerer tube.

Alloy rims: Wheel rims made from lightweight aluminium alloy rather than steel.

Anti-seize: Special grease containing very fine metal particles, used to stop threaded parts from corroding together.

Bar ends: Bolt-on handles which fit on the ends of a flat handlebar and give extra hand positions.

Barrier cream: Special cream which blocks oils and solvents from being absorbed into your skin.

Bead seat diameter: Diameter of the tyre bead.

Bearing adjustments: Adjustments performed on the bearings so that they run smoothly but don't rattle.

Bearings: Low-friction mechanism, usually using steel balls, which allows parts to turn.

Bimetallic corrosion: Aka galvanic corrosion; this is corrosion damage caused by a chemical reaction between two dissimilar metal surfaces and salt water. The most common example is aluminium seat posts corroding in place in steel frames because of the constant washing in salt water this area gets in a British winter.

Blackburn: American manufacturer of high quality pannier racks and other parts.

Bolt circle diameter: Diameter across the chainring bolts. Determines the degree of inter-changeability of chainrings on the particular chainset.

Bondhus: Brand name of manufacturer of ball end Allen keys.

Bottom bracket: The bearing that the cranks turn on.

Brake reach: The distance from the handlebar to the brake lever.

Cable end cap: Metal cover used to prevent the end of a cable from fraying.

Cable stop: Receptacles on the frame for the ends of cable outers. Determine the cable routeing on a bike.

Cadence: Pedalling rate.

Cantilever brakes: Brakes which attach to the frame tubes either side of the rim and have two separate pivots; used on mountain bikes and hybrids.

Cartridge bottom bracket: A crank bearing assembly in a single unit which cannot be serviced.

Centring: Aligning the brake so that the blocks are equal distances from the rim, or the rim is centred between the blocks.

Chain stays: The two thin frame-tubes that run out from the bottom bracket to the rear wheel.

Chainguard: A protective cover around the chain.

Chainrings: The cogs on the cranks, driven directly by the pedals.

Chainset: The cranks, chainrings and bottom bracket.

Chromoloy: Very widely used class of steel alloys containing chromium and molybdenum to improve the steel's strength.

Cleats: Shoe mounted clips that fit into special pedals.

Cogs: Any toothed wheel.

Combination pliers: Pliers with multiple jaws: flat for gripping, rounded for gripping and a cutting jaw.

Combination spanner: Spanner with a ring fitting at one end and an open fitting at the other.

Cool Tool: All in one tool which contains Allen keys, adjustable spanner chain tool and so on, in one easily carried unit.

Cradle: Top section of seat post.

Cranks: The levers which connect the pedals and the chainrings.

Credit card touring: Luxury touring using a back up vehicle.

Crossed threads: Screw threads which are not properly aligned, that is, the threads are 'crossed' rather than meshing smoothly. To be avoided as it always causes thread damage.

Cup and cone bottom bracket: Traditional bottom bracket with a service-able cup and cone bearing assembly.

Cup and cone: Inner and outer parts of a bearing assembly.

Cutaways: Shaped parts of Hyperglide sprockets which provide their excellent gear shifting.

Cylinder key: Round, rather than flat, key. Widely used in bike locks.

Damping systems: Ways of controlling the movement of a suspension fork.

Degreaser: Solvent which removes grease.

Derailleur gears: Gear systems which move the chain across a number of sprockets and chainrings.

Diamond frame: Frame with a high top tube; 'man's frame'

Dogs: Teeth in a tool which engage some part of the component to be fitted or removed.

Double butted tubing: Tubing which has thicker walls at both ends than in the middle.

Double butted spokes: Spokes with thicker ends than middle.

Down tube: The lower frame-tube that runs from the headset to the bottom bracket.

Drive side: The right-hand side of the bike, where the chain and gears are.

Drive ratios: Same thing as a gear ratio – *see Chapter 8.*

Elastomer forks: Suspension forks which use elastomers – special synthetic rubbers – to produce both springs and damping.

Evolution headset: Oversize headset using 1¼in diameter steerer tube.

Fat tyre bikes: Any bike with wide tyres; mountain bikes and budget, mountain bike-style bikes.

Ferrules: Cylindrical metal 'end-cap' for a cable outer, with a hole for the inner to pass through.

Fine pitch: High threads per inch count; can be fragile.

Finish line: Specialist bike lubricants manufacturer.

First gear The lowest (easiest) gear.

Flange: The part of the hub shell into which the spokes fit.

Fork crown race: The part of the headset which fits on to the fork just above the blades.

Forks: The two frame-tubes that hold the front wheel.

Frame size: The size of the frame, measured from the bottom bracket to the insertion of the seat post; determines what size of person the frame will fit.

Freehub: Rear hub which includes the freewheel mechanism in its structure.

Freewheel mechanism: Ratchet and pawl mechanism which allows the sprockets to spin freely in one direction and drive the hub in the other.

Front mech: The gear mechanism or derailleur which moves the chain across the chainrings.

Gear range: The difference between the highest and lowest gears on a bike.

Gear ratio: A measurement of a gearing.

Gear hanger: The part of the frame that hangs down from the rear drop-out and to which is attached the rear mech.

Gear range: The difference between highest and lowest gears.

Gerber hiking multi-tool: Hiking/camping tool which incorporates pliers, blades, screwdrivers, bottle opener and so on.

Gore-Tex: Expensive waterproof fabric which 'breathes', that is, lets out water vapour from sweat.

Half-clips: Effectively, toe-clips without the straps.

Head tube: The short frame-tube that runs from forks to the handlebar stem.

Headset: The steering bearing assembly.

High gear Big chainring/small sprocket; hard to push, bad on hills.

Higher/lower gear range: Road bikes tend to have higher gears overall, hence they are referred to as having a high gear range, while the lower top and bottom gears of a mountain bike mean that it has a lower gear range.

Hook up one's rear tyre: Slang for a tyre gripping a surface.

Hub gears: Gear system in which the mechanism is completely enclosed in the rear hub.

Hub shell: The outer part of the hub.

Hub: The central part of the wheel to which the spokes are attached and which contains the bearings that the wheel turns on.

Hybrid: Bike with mountain bike gears and controls and road bike size wheels.

Indexed gears: Gears you can 'click into' rather than have to find by feel.

Indexed steering: Steering which has distinct 'stops' because of a damaged headset.

Jockey wheels: The two small plastic wheels in the rear derailleur.

Knobblies: Deep-treaded tyres for riding off road.

Labyrinth seal: Seal made up of close-fitting steel collars which, filled with oil or grease, create a labyrinth which is difficult for dirt to penetrate.

Lacing: The initial stage of wheel building. Also, the way in which spokes are arranged so that they go under and over each other.

Link wire cantilever brake: Cantilever brake which uses a connecting wire between the main cable and one cantilever arm. The main cable goes to the other arm.

Locking compound: Liquid used to 'lock' threads together. Loctite is the most common, comes in various grades.

Lockring: Special nut used to hold a threaded part in place.

Low gear Small chainring/big sprocket; easy to push; good on hills.

Low riders: Front pannier racks which holds the panniers low, next to the front wheel hub.

Lube: General term for any lubricant such as oil or grease.

Lycra: Stretch nylon used for cycling and other sports clothing.

M5: Designating a thread with 5mm shaft.

Mating surfaces: Any surfaces which touch: the inside and outside of a thread for example.

Micro-adjusting seat post: Saddle mounting which allows fine adjustment of saddle angle.

Mineral-based: Oil made from petroleum.

Mole grip: Gripping tool which has a lever mechanism to lock it very tightly on the part.

Neoprene: Synthetic rubber used for wetsuits; waterproof and insulating.

Non-drive side: The left-hand side of the bike, away from the chain and gears.

Nylok: Nuts with nylon inserts to prevent them from shaking loose.

Open frame: Frame with dropped top tube, often referred to as a woman's frame.

Oversize headset: Any headset which uses a steerer tube larger than the original 1in diameter standard, usually a 1⅛in diameter tube.

Park: American manufacturer of bike tools.

Pedro's: Specialist bike lubricants manufacturer.

Peened: To have wedge-shaped ends – as in the pins of a Hyperglide chain.

Pertex: Very fine weave nylon which resists water penetration and breathes. Waterproof versions are available. Cheaper than Gore-Tex.

Phillips screwdriver: Screwdriver with cross-shaped head.

Pitch: The size of a thread, measured in threads per inch.

Pressed on: Parts that are 'machine-forced' together at manufacture. (e.g. The fork crown race is a very tight fit – called an 'interference fit'– on the fork and therefore needs force to fit it.)

Presta: Thinner valve usually found on road bikes and higher-end MTBs.

Quick release: A mechanism in the hub which allows the wheel to be easily removed and fitted without tools.

Rapidfire shifters: Gear shifters with two levers, one for shifting up, the other for shifting down.

Rear mech: The gear mechanism or derailleur which moves the chain across the sprockets on the rear hub.

Reynolds 531: British-made alloy steel bike tubing.

Rim well: The recess inside a rim where the spokes fit.

Rim: The outside of the wheel, on which the tyre is mounted.

Roadster: The classic English 3-speed.

Schrader: The type of valve usually found in cars.

Screw-on freewheel: Separate freewheel mechanism; not part of the hub structure it screws on to the hub body.

Seal: Any part intended to protect a bearing or other fragile part from the ingress of water or dirt.

Seat stays: The two thin frame-tubes that run down from the seat-post to the rear wheel.

Seat post: The pillar on which the seat is attached.

Seat tube: The vertical frame-tube that runs from seat post to bottom bracket.

Shackle lock/U-lock: Basically an enlarged padlock with a locking mechanism in a hollow cylinder that engages the ends of a solid U-shaped bar.

Shifters: The levers or other mechanism which activates the derailleurs.

Shifting: Changing gear.

Shimano Hyperglide chain: Special type of chain made by Shimano. Found on most medium-priced new bikes. Splitting of these chains is not recommended.

Shimano: Japanese bicycle component manufacturer which makes something like 80% of all bike parts.

Side-pull brakes: Brakes which attach to the frame above the tyre and have one pivot on the attachment bolt; used on road bikes and 3-speeds.

Sidewall: The sides of a tyre.

Slick/semi slick tyres: Tyres with completely or partially smooth tread for road riding.

Slop: Movement in a bearing or fit of pressed or screwed parts. Indicates mis-adjustment or poor fit.

Spin: Fluid high speed pedalling.

Spoke nipple: The special nut which holds the spoke into the rim.

Spoking pattern: The arrangement of the spokes within the wheel, usually referred to by the number of times a spoke is crossed by other spokes.

Sprockets: Cogs on the back wheel.

Steerer tube: The top tube of the fork. The stem goes inside it and the headset goes around it.

Stem: The part which joins the handlebar to the frame, as in handlebar stem.

Straddle cable cantilever brake: Cantilever brake which uses a cable linking the two arms, which is then pulled by the main brake cable.

Stress-relieving: A stage in wheel building or truing which ensures the spokes are not wound up.

Swarf: Metal flakes left over from a cutting process.

Sympatex: Another type of waterproof fabric which allows water vapour out so you can sweat through it.

Teflon: Very slippery polymer, used for non-stick pans and in some bike lubes.

Threads: The helical grooves in a screw or hole that a screw fits into.

Tinning: Coating the end of the cable with solder to keep the strands of the wire from fraying.

Titanium: High strength to weight ratio metal used for bike frames and parts. Exceedingly expensive!

Toeing in: Adjusting the brake blocks so that the front edge hits the rim before the back edge, to prevent brake squeal.

Top tube: The horizontal frame-tube that runs from handlebar stem to seat post.

Track pump: Floor-standing tyre pump.

Transmission: The complete gear system; chainset, derailleurs, sprockets and chain.

Tyre bead: The steel wire round the inside of a tyre, which holds it together.

Tyre seat: The part of the rim where the tyre bead sits. A properly fitted tyre is therefore correctly 'seated'.

Universal cable: An inner cable with a nipple at each end.

Vegetable based: Oil made from plant oils.

Water dispersing grooves: Slots in the face of the brake block to allow water to clear from the block.

Wheel dish: The offset from the hub flanges necessary to centre the rim in the frame.

12-28 Sprocket cluster: A sprocket cluster with a largest sprocket of 28 teeth and smallest of 12 teeth.

24/36/46 Chainrings: A three-chainring set of 24, 36 and 46 teethed rings.

Index

Credits

Words by John Stevenson

John Stevenson has established himself as *the* expert name in cycle repair and maintenance in the 90's through his work on *Mountain Biking UK*. He got into bikes in his late teens, and soon got hooked on riding the roads and trails of his native Yorkshire. After dropping out of a couple of universities he went to work in a bike shop in Leeds; ran a successful mountain racing team; raced himself with a spectacular lack of success and founded the Yorkshire Mountain Bike Club, the UK's first local MTB group. In 1988 he began writing for *Mountain Biking UK*. He is currently self–employed and was last seen pedalling towards the Alps...

Pictures by Steve Behr

Steve Behr is one of the top cycling photographers in the UK today and his pictures readily adorn the pages of such magazines as *MBUK* and *MTB Pro*. Born in Cape Town, he has been at times a surf bum, a solicitor, a globetrotter in search of the perfect wave. Always an accomplished amateur photographer, he discovered his perfect career when he combined his skill at photography with his passion for biking. He now owns a large cycling photo–library (Stockfile) and travels on various photography assignments to locations as diverse as South Mimms and California. When not taking pictures of bikes, his favourite pastime is riding them.

A Book by Haynes Publishing

In 1956, whilst still at school, John Haynes bought a 750cc Austin Seven for £15 with money loaned to him by his father. He converted the Austin into a sports car, and then thought it might be a good idea if he wrote a book about it, basing it on his practical experience. The 48 page booklet sold for 5 shillings and he ran off 250 copies on a hand driven stencil machine. He sold them all in 10 days.

Since then over 1,000 different Haynes manuals have been published in over a dozen languages and have sold so many around the world that everyone has lost count. Today, Haynes are the world leading publishers of practical books. This is the first Haynes book about bicycles.

The makers of The Bike Book would like to thank the following people and organisations:

Authors acknowledgements:
Big shout to all the following people, who all contributed, either actively or through their writing, toward the inspiration, perspiration, information and enthusiasm that went into this book:
Lesleigh Russell, Patrick Barker at Madison Cycles, Lloyd Townsend at ID Sports, Tim Flooks at Caratti Sport, Brant Richards, Paul Smith, Dave Yates, Keith Bontrager, John Forester, Dorre Robinson, Jobst Brandt, Tym Manley, Pete Woodcock, Richard Ballantine and the Netizens of the rec.bicycles Usenet groups.

Props supplied by:
Halfords plc – Carrera Cycles
Madison Cycles plc – Rhode Gear helmets, Bellweather clothing, Shimano components, Citadel locks, Sigma bicycle computers, Madison sunglasses, Blackburn racks and Finish Line lube products.
Carratti Sport – Kryptonite locks and Pedro's lube products

Centurion safety products – Centurion helmets
Freestyle clothing – Waterproofs
Sensible products – Crud Catchers
RJ Chicken & Sons – Trelock locks

Also: Jill Behr, Dave Curl, David Duffield, Martin Hamblin Research and the everyday cyclists of Nailsea, Derek Jones, Paul Lyons, Pizza Express (Bath), RoSPA, and especially Richard White and everyone at the Yeovil Cycle Centre.

Finally a special thanks to those employees of Haynes without whose advice, tolerance, and hard work, this book would not have been possible.

Product testers and general guinea pigs:
Tami Parker, Jeremy Churchill, Jeremy Maynard, Claire Ellard.

Plus: John Austin, Alan Bishop, Paul Buckland, Phillip Cox, Sarah Furness, Bernie Goldrick, Kevin Heals, Tony Kemp, Dave Rankin, Darryl Reach, Pete Shoemark, Liz Singer, Alan Sperring, Nigel Tate, Pete Vallis, John Warry, Andy Youngs and all the members of the internal focus panels.

Picture Credits
All pictures by Steve Behr except:
Key: *t* top, *m* middle, *b* bottom, *l* left, *c* centre, *r* right, (*s/f* stockfile).
Han Balk (*s/f*): p. 5 *tr*
Sue Darlow (*s/f*): pp. 5 *tl*, 9 *r*, 15 *tc*, 15 *tr*, 37 *r*, 39 *c*
Bob Smith (*s/f*): pp. 5 *b*, 34, 35, 53 *c*
Robert Reichenfield (*s/f*): pp. 4 *c*, 8 *c*, 38 *tr*
Mark Gallup (*s/f*): pp. 4 *mr*, 40
Jim McRoy (*s/f*): p. 9 *bl*
Allsport: pp. 5 *ml*, 9 *tl*, 39 *br*

Front cover:
Main picture by Rick Rusing.
Other pictures by Steve Behr, Sue Darlow, Mark Gallup, Jim McRoy, Bob Smith.

All repair sequences have been photographed in the Haynes Project Workshop, Sparkford, Somerset.